Detail in
Contemporary
Landscape
Architecture

LAURENCE KING

Published in 2008 by
Laurence King Publishing Ltd
4th Floor
361–373 City Road
London
EC1V 1LR
United Kingdom
e-mail: enquiries@laurenceking.com
www.laurenceking.com
Tel: +44 (0)207 841 6900

A catalogue record for this book is
available from the British Library.

ISBN 978 1 78067 023 2

Designed by Hamish Muir
Picture Research by Sophia Gibb
Printed in the UK

Laurence King Publishing is
committed to ethical and sustainable
production. We are proud participants
in The Book Chain Project
bookchainproject.com

**BOOK
CHAIN
PROJECT**

Detail in Contemporary Landscape Architecture

Virginia McLeod

Laurence King Publishing

Contents

As a companion volume to *Detail in Contemporary Residential Architecture*, this book seeks to reveal the details of contemporary landscape design. The key to the choice of projects in this volume is in the title – all of the projects presented here, while often falling within traditional landscape categories of parks and gardens, nonetheless have an architectural component that separates them from being predominantly plant-based. It is impossible to deny, even in the most densely urban of contexts, that landscape underscores all of our daily interactions with the built environment. All too often, however, strategies for creating meaningful landscapes in urban environments are at best an afterthought and at worst leave the spaces between and around buildings as blighted, even dangerous places to be. It has become all too clear that landscape architects, planners and even those who commission buildings and landscaped spaces ignore the problems of unchecked urban growth and the potential for landscape as a redeeming urban quality at their peril.

The projects here, by comparison, are examples of how landscaped spaces can, and should, be. Almost all of the designs featured here exist in urban environments – from the densest city contexts, for example Edouard François' Flower Tower in Paris, which utilizes the building itself as a site for the application of a vertical landscape, to PWP Landscape Architecture and Partners Nasher Sculpture Center which responds to the towering skyscrapers which surround it in downtown Dallas. Other projects, while perhaps in more traditional open settings nonetheless utilize elements of architecture to create environments of great impact and usability.

As such, this book focuses on the details that make up the architectural components of all of these disparate projects, including stairs, paving, water features, and of course the way these elements interact with all types of planting. Construction details are as vital a part of landscape architecture as its external form and layout. Whether so subtle as to be invisible, or revealed as extraordinarily complex, details determine the quality and character of a landscape. Good detailing entails exercizing the utmost care and attention at the junctions between materials, between the different elements of a landscaped space, and where a material changes direction. Through details, the myriad parts that make up a landscape come together to form a whole – joints, connections, seams, openings and surfaces are transformed via a combination of technology and invention into a meaningful landscape.

We are accustomed to being presented with photographic representations of landscape architecture in books, magazines and online, with the inspiring image continuing to be the focus of the two-dimensional representation of landscape. Increasingly these images are now often accompanied by site plans to provide a better understanding of the way a landscape works. The availability of site plans is, of course, of enormous assistance in helping us to understand the spatial sequences, the extent and scale of a space, however it is not inherent in the purpose of a plan or a photograph, even if accompanied by a section, to reveal the individual elements that go together to make up a section of paving, an arbour, a pool, a planting bed and so on. Construction details, however, do just this, and this book unites the photograph, the site plan and section, as well as the details to bring to the reader a comprehensive insight into the true workings of the landscape.

Landscape architects draw details specifically to reveal the inner workings of a landscape – primarily, of course, they are used by the builder in order to put the elements together. Readers of architectural publications, however, are all too rarely given the opportunity to examine the details – the 'real' representation of how a landscape is put together. This book aims to remedy that situation and provides a guide to the inner workings of 40 of the most inspiring examples of contemporary landscape architecture. This book brings to the reader what has previously remained invisible. These details reveal not only an 'x-ray' of the landscape presented, but an insight into the cognitive processes of the architects and artists who brought the landscapes into being.

Details make up to 95 per cent of the sometimes hundreds of drawings produced to describe the way a landscape is put together. They act as the means by which landscape architects communicate their intent to builders, engineers and other participants in the building process. They also act as one of the most challenging intellectual and technical exercises for any landscape architect, producing, as they must, a series of what are essentially graphic representations of every single junction and connection in the built space. Because these details are made up almost exclusively of two-dimensional representations (plan and sectional drawings), the challenge resides in the architect's ability to imagine the most complex of junctions, assemblies and components in three dimensions – as they will actually be built on site – and translate them onto paper or on screen into two dimensions, into the conventional drawn representations that have been used in the construction industry for decades, even centuries.

While the selection of details presented for each of the landscapes in this book is necessarily limited by space, they nonetheless go a long way towards deconstructing the image of the finished landscape. As a result, they not only inspire, they also help us to understand the thought that went into the making of the building, and perhaps the technical problems that were solved along the way. Details also reveal the preoccupations and specialties of an individual landscape architect. Each of the landscape architects in this book were asked to provide their personal selection of the details that they felt best represented the garden or park in question. As a result, a focus on the way paving is put together with the trees that are planted within it may be revealed in some projects, while the sculptural qualities of a balustrade or a water feature may come into focus through the details in others.

In many cases, details also reveal cultural differences as well as commonalities. The scope of this book covers four continents – Europe, North America, Asia and Australia. Many of the landscapes appear to have aesthetic qualities in common, perhaps revealing similarities in the way landscape architecture is taught at universities around the world, as well as the contemporary cultural influences that cross geographical boundaries. However, many differences are revealed in the details. The climate or economics in one country or region may make concrete inappropriate or too expensive. Timber or stone may, instead, be the most available, affordable material.

Similarly, culture is inextricably linked to place, and therefore unites landscape and architecture. For example, Mosbach Paysagistes' elegant landscape for the Bordeaux Botanical Gardens in France embraces the challenge to illustrate thousands of years of both natural and man-made landscapes in the River Garonne area. The vibrant and exuberant landscape created by Room 4.1.3. by contrast, bravely tackles the complicated and often emotional subject of Australia's past, embracing the prickly issue of the history of native Australians. In a similar vein, Turenscape have created a place for contemplating China's Cultural Revolution, bravely acknowledging one of the most troubling periods in that country's recent past through a landscape that is available to all.

A continuing preoccupation of landscape design is the regeneration of industrial sites, typically created in the nineteenth century as, for example, shipyards or power stations that ended their lives in the wake of improving or changing technologies in the late twentieth century. Often located in inner-city locations, the transformation of these vast sites into meaningful public spaces has, more often than not, had an enormous impact on the economic and social well-being of the city in question. This is a global phenomenon that is reflected in several projects presented here, including the Tide Point Urban Waterfront in Baltimore, Maryland, USA, by W Architecture – the transformation of a soap production plant into a popular harbour-side recreation facility. Similarly, Camlin Lonsdale has successfully regenerated Belfast's Donegal Quay to reflect both its aspiration as a vibrant global city, as well as its history as a city of trade. The Eden Project in Cornwall, England, takes the most unpromising of sites – a defunct clay pit – and transforms it into one of the most celebrated landscapes of recent years.

The design of relevant, meaningful landscapes, such as those illustrated in this volume, involves the integration of ecological, technological and cultural forces through sensitive responses to place and people, and requires the concerted efforts of informed, sensitive designers. The projects collected here offer many interpretations and possibilities for the relationship between architecture and landscape. What they have in common is that this relationship has been considered at every stage in the design process, at every negotiation in the procurement process, and show that culture and place can be incorporated with understanding and intelligence. This collection is based on the fact that the architecture–landscape symbiosis is at the centre of inspired design.

Virginia McLeod

Notes

Imperial and Metric Measurements
Dimensions have been provided by the architects in metric and converted to imperial, except in case of projects in the USA in which imperial dimensions have been converted to metric.

Terminology
An attempt has been made to standardize terminology to aid understanding across readerships, for example 'wood' is generally referred to as 'timber' and 'aluminum' as 'aluminium'. However materials or processes that are peculiar to a country, region or architectural practice that have no direct correspondence are presented in the original.

Floor Plans
Throughout the book, the following convention of hierarchy has been used – ground floor, first floor, second floor, and so on. In certain contexts, terms such as basement level or upper level have been used for clarity.

Scale
All floor plans, sections and elevations are presented at conventional architectural metric scales, typically 1:50, 1:100 or 1:200 as appropriate. An accurate graphic scale is included on the second page near the floor plans of every project to aid in the understanding of scale. Details are also presented at conventional architectural scales, typically 1:1, 1:5 and 1:10.

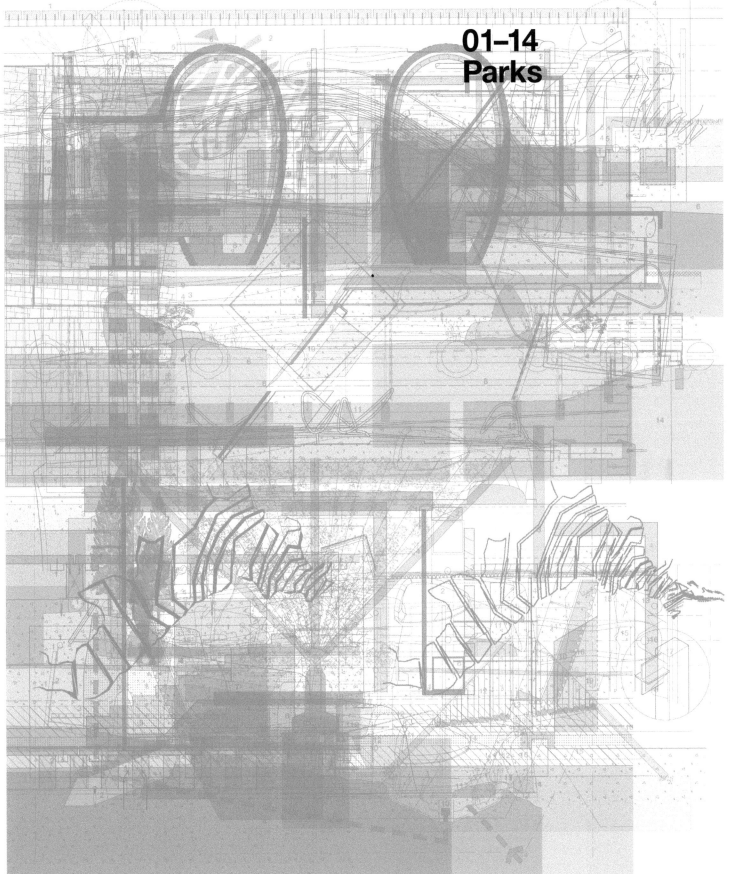

01–14
Parks

Anton James Design

**Mount Penang Gardens
Mount Penang, New South Wales,
Australia**

Client
NSW State Government Festival
Development Corporation

Area
6 hectares (14.8 acres)

Project Team
Anton James, Geoffrey Britton, Matt
O'Connor, David Duncan, Diana
Pringle, Romilly Davis, Jenny Clarsen

Structural Engineer
Structural Mechanics and Dynamics

The Mount Penang Gardens are
located on a cleared swamp with
numerous natural springs. In
response, the garden is comprised of
a raised plateau bordered by a series
of cascading ponds to avoid the
waterlogged soils. Two deeply incised
lobes provide a series of intimate
spaces for over 1,000 plant species,
including numerous rare and
endangered plants. Carved into the
sides of the plateau are five Fissure
Gardens for specialized horticultural
displays. A blue steel bridge spans
over the ponds, from the entrance to
the plateau, while cantilevered
concrete and steel stairs take visitors
into the gabion-lined Fissure Gardens.

Several sculptural elements are
used as formal counterpoints to
the plantings. Two steel 'clouds' are
planted with vines to form large
shade-giving forms. One sits above
an undulating lawn from which a fine
water mist rises – the Cloud Garden.
The second provides shade to the
Puddle Fountain – a folded inclined
plane from which water jets emerge
and where depressions set with
coloured glass beads collect water to
form puddles. The Puddle Fountain is
fed by three ponds which step down
the slope from the Bottle Tree Garden,
which features the uniquely bottom
heavy forms of the *Brachychiton
rupestris*. The Dragon Garden, on the
southern lobe, is planted with a rich
variety of succulents and cacti set in
an assortment of concrete water
pipes. Water is an ever-present
element in the garden, spilling through
water stairs, brass sills, splash ledges
and water chutes to animate each
cascade as it flows to the lower dam.

1 View across the
lowest cascade pond
and splash ledges
towards the raised
Plateau Garden. The
blue bridge leads visi-
tors from the entrance
to the left, to the
gardens on the right.
2 The Stepped Pond,
flanked on the left by
the Bottle Tree Garden.
The stepped water
body leads from the
highest point of the
garden to the Puddle
Fountain.
3 The Steel Cloud
leads the viewer
from the Blue Bridge
toward the Mist
Garden beyond.
4 Entrance to the
Pandanus Fissure,
where the precast
concrete walls that
wrap the Plateau
Garden are seen in
the foreground.
5 A steel and concrete
stair takes visitors up
and onto the Plateau
Garden, past plants
displayed on gabions
and custom built
stainless steel and
coconut fibre logs.

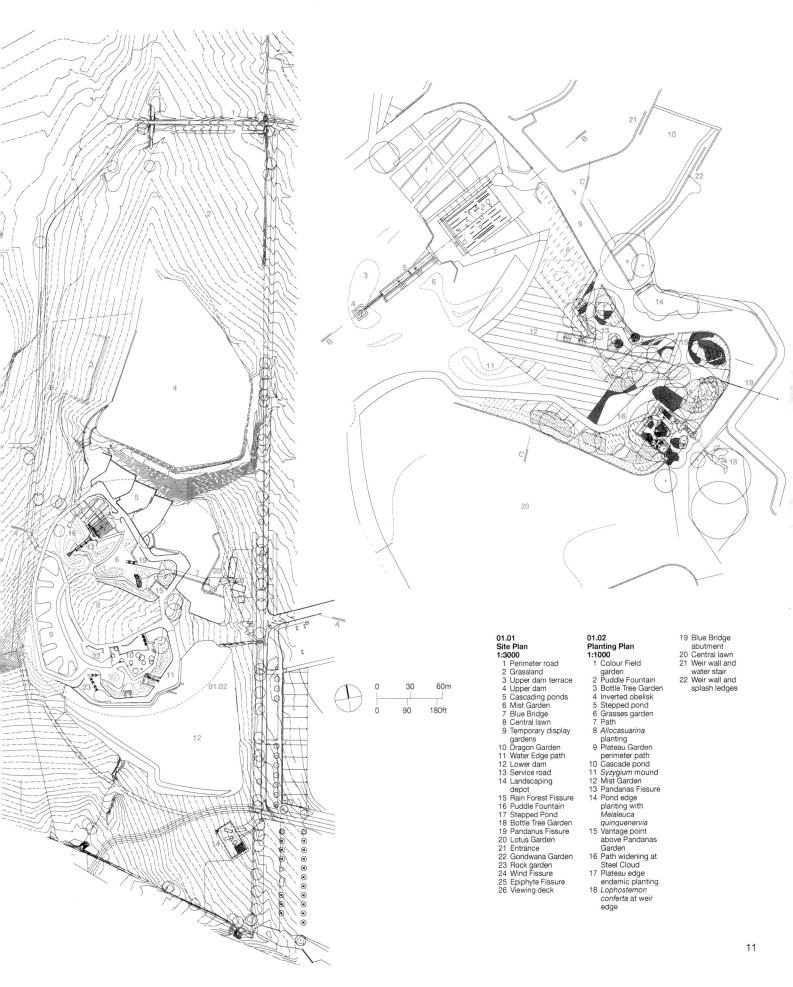

0   30   60m

0   90   180ft

01.01
Site Plan
1:3000
1 Perimeter road
2 Grassland
3 Upper dam terrace
4 Upper dam
5 Cascading ponds
6 Mist Garden
7 Blue Bridge
8 Central lawn
9 Temporary display gardens
10 Dragon Garden
11 Water Edge path
12 Lower dam
13 Service road
14 Landscaping depot
15 Rain Forest Fissure
16 Puddle Fountain
17 Stepped Pond
18 Bottle Tree Garden
19 Pandanus Fissure
20 Lotus Garden
21 Entrance
22 Gondwana Garden
23 Rock garden
24 Wind Fissure
25 Epiphyte Fissure
26 Viewing deck

01.02
Planting Plan
1:1000
1 Colour Field garden
2 Puddle Fountain
3 Bottle Tree Garden
4 Inverted obelisk
5 Stepped pond
6 Grasses garden
7 Path
8 *Allocasuarina* planting
9 Plateau Garden perimeter path
10 Cascade pond
11 *Syzygium* mound
12 Mist Garden
13 Pandanas Fissure
14 Pond edge planting with *Melaleuca quinquenervia*
15 Vantage point above Pandanas Garden
16 Path widening at Steel Cloud
17 Plateau edge endemic planting
18 *Lophostemon conferta* at weir edge

19 Blue Bridge abutment
20 Central lawn
21 Weir wall and water stair
22 Weir wall and splash ledges

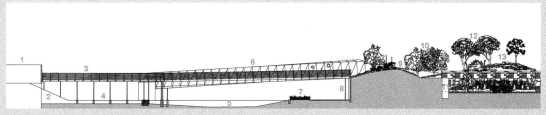

01.03
Bridge Section A–A
1:500
  1 Entry kiosk
  2 Bamboo planted
slope
3 Viewing deck
4 Lotus Garden
5 Cascading pond
(lowest pond)
6 Blue Bridge
box beam
7 Poa planting
8 Precast concrete
wall
9 Garden path
10 *Banksia robur*
11 Pandanas Fissure
gabion wall
12 *Cupaniopsis
anacardioides*
13 Ground cover
planting

01.04
**Puddle Fountain
Section B–B**
1:500
  1 *Brachychiton
discolor*
2 Inverted concrete
obelisk
3 Bottle Tree Garden
planted with
Brachychiton Rupestris
4 *Liriope* planting
5 Stepped pond
6 Steel Cloud 2
7 Colour Field garden
8 Puddle Fountain
9 *Bambusa lako*
10 *Eucalyptus*
haemastoma
11 Plateau perimeter
path
12 Cascading pond

01.05
**Mist Fountain Section
C–C**
1:200
  1 Plateau Garden
perimeter path
2 Precast concrete
wall
3 Earth undulations
and mist fountain
4 Stair and Pandanas
Fissure
5 Gymea Lily
(Doryanthes excelsa)
6 Carrotwood
*(Cupaniopsis
anacardioides)*
7 Mixed native
groundcover and
perenials
8 Steel Cloud 1
9 Plateau Garden
edge with endemic
planting
10 Precast concrete
wall and central lawn

01.06
**Cascade Elevation
and Plan Detail**
1:100
  1 Water level
  2 Off-form concrete
weir wall
  3 Concrete footing
  4 Concrete splash
edge
  5 Spitter with brass
plate to shape flow
  6 Splash ledge
  7 Brass rill
  8 Weir wall
  9 Weir wall
10 Splash ledge
11 Spitter with brass
plate to shape flow
12 Spitter with brass
plate to shape flow

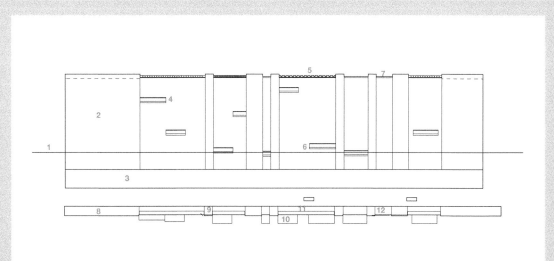

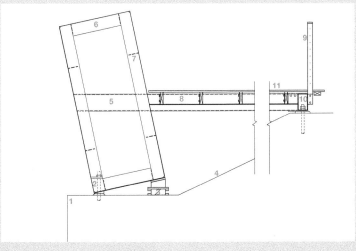

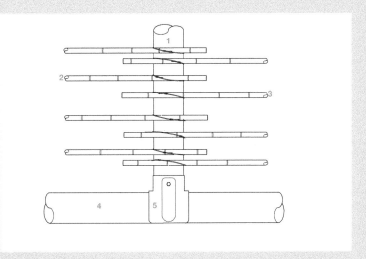

01.07
Bridge Section
1:50
　1 Concrete abutment
　2 Hold-down bolt
　3 Fastening bracket
　4 Ground level
　5 Rectangular hollow
section steel beam
　6 Blue twisted beam

　7 Internal diaphragm
　8 Steel joists
　9 Galvanized steel
ballustrade with
tensioned stainless
steel horizontal cables
　10 Hold-down bolt
　11 Timber decking

01.08
Cloud Detail
1:10
　1 90 mm (3½ inch)
galvanized tubing
　2 Bamboo canes
　3 Bamboo canes
　4 Cable ties
　5 Fixed angle pipe
connector

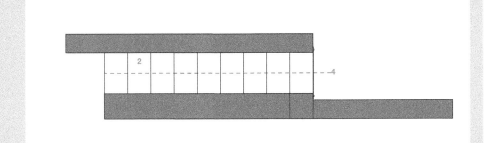

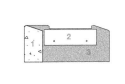

01.09
Water Stair Detail
Plan
1:50
　1 Concrete weir wall
　2 Water stair
　3 Sloped weir wall
　4 Brass plate to
control water flow
　5 Concrete weir wall

01.10
Water Stair Detail
Long Section
1:50
　1 Concrete weir wall
　2 Concrete footing
　3 Sloped weir wall
in foreground
　4 Brass plate to
control water flow
　5 Water level

01.11
Water Stair Detail
Cross Section
1:50
　1 Concrete weir wall
　2 Brass plate to
control water flow
　3 Concrete weir wall

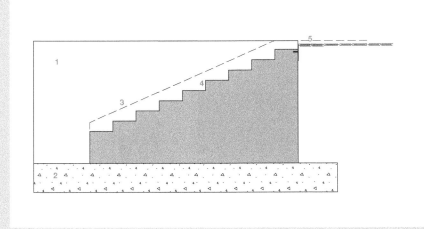

AP Atelier, Josef Pleskot

Pathway Through the Deer Moat
Prague, Czech Republic

Client
Prague Castle Administration /
Dagmar and Václav Havel VISION 97
Foundation

Area
160 square metres (1,720 square feet)

Project Team
Josef Pleskot, Jana Kantorová, Jitka
Svobodová, Jiří Trčka, Zdeněk Rudolf,
Isabela Grosseová

Structural Engineer
Metroprojekt Praha / Křístek,
Trčka a spol

Landscape Architect
Eva Vízková

Commissioned at the instigation of
Czech President Václav Havel, this
underground tunnel provides a route
from the Vlatava River to the grounds
of Prague Castle, forming a
connection between two sections of
the existing Deer Moat. The project
facilitates pedestrian movement along
the entire length of this unique natural
monument and makes the castle
accessible via a new system of
walkways. The tunnel follows the line
of an existing stream located below
the bastion walls used to protect the
original Renaissance Powder Bridge.
The massive open-cut concrete portal
entrances to the tunnel facilitate water
run-off to the stream, which continues
beneath the new tunnel.

   Once beyond the portals, the
orthogonal geometry is abandoned in
favour of a striking brick vault. The 84-
metre (275-foot) long cambered vault
was designed to necessarily narrow
dimensions, however the impression
of spaciousness is enhanced by
recessed floor lighting and glimpses
of the stream below through metal
grilles. The tunnel is clad in self-
supporting, hard-burnt, fair-faced
dark-red brick which, when lit, gives
the space a warm glow. The paving to
the floor of the tunnel is made from
pre-fabricated concrete elements with
a textured, non-slip surface treatment.
Elsewhere, grilles designed to reveal
the presence of the stream are
made from steel rods with slip-resistant
lugs. A Renaissance column rescued
during excavations for the tunnel is
dramatically displayed in a niche in
the arched tunnel.

1 The sophistication
of the brick vault
construction makes a
striking contrast with
the historic walls and
ramparts of the castle.
2 The project is
located in the grounds
of one of Prague's
most iconic historic
monuments – Prague
Castle (right). Two
sections of the existing
Deer Moat are linked
to create a new
pedestrian access
route to and from
the Castle.
3 View of one of the
cast in-situ concrete
portals that announce
the entrances to
the tunnel.
4 The floor of the
tunnel incorporates
steel grilles that reveal
the presence of the
stream below. Here,
the concrete portals
give way to the dark
red brick vaulted arch
of the tunnel.

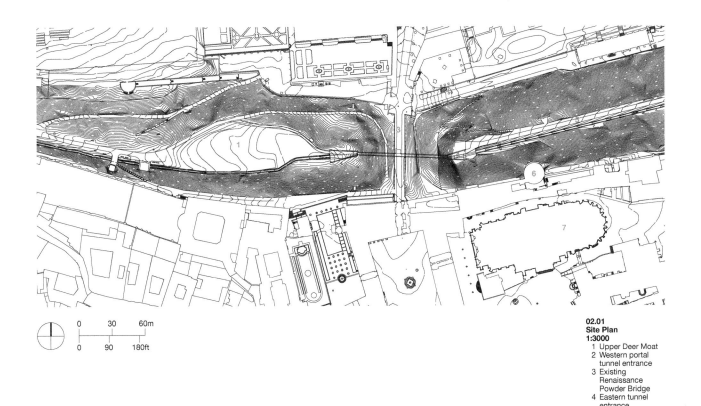

0 30 60m
0 90 180ft

02.01
Site Plan
1:3000
1 Upper Deer Moat
2 Western portal
   tunnel entrance
3 Existing
   Renaissance
   Powder Bridge
4 Eastern tunnel
   entrance
5 Lower Deer Moat
6 Mihulka Tower
7 St Vitus Cathedral

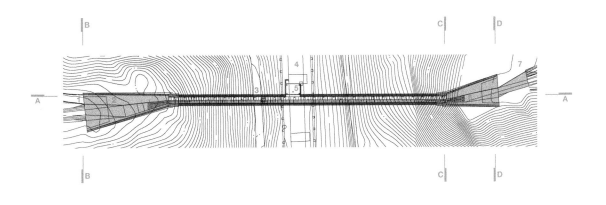

02.02
Deer Moat Tunnel
Plan
1:1000
1 Upper Deer Moat
2 West portal
   entrance to tunnel
3 Brick arched
   tunnel
4 Existing Powder
   Bridge
5 Recess leading to
   views of the
   original bridge pier
6 East portal
   entrance to tunnel
7 Lower Deer Moat

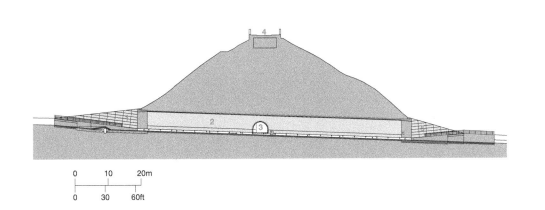

02.03
Section A–A
1:1000
1 West portal
   entrance to tunnel
2 Brick arched
   tunnel
3 Recess leading to
   views of the
   original bridge pier
4 Existing Powder
   Bridge
5 East portal
   entrance to tunnel

0 10 20m
0 30 60ft

15

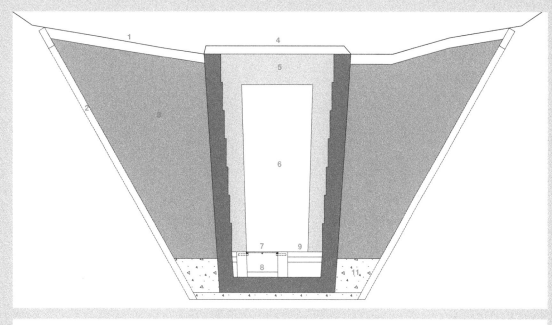

02.04
Tunnel Section B–B
1:100
 1 Topsoil to landscape above tunnel
 2 Reinforced concrete retaining wall
 3 Back-fill between retaining wall and tunnel
 4 Top of reinforced concrete tunnel opening
 5 Reinforced concrete tunnel doorway
 6 Tunnel opening
 7 Steel mesh grille over stream bed
 8 Quarry stone finish to stream bed
 9 Quarry stone paving to tunnel path
 10 Reinforced concrete tunnel opening in section
 11 Reinforced concrete foundation

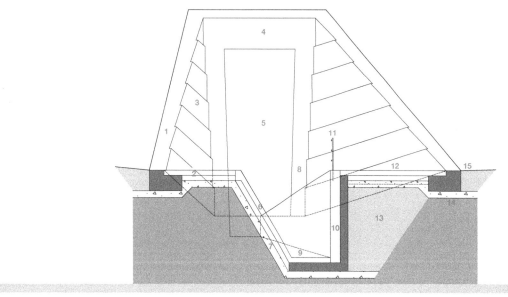

02.05
Tunnel Section C–C
1:100
 1 Reinforced cast in-situ concrete supporting wall
 2 Quarry stone block paving
 3 Profiled fair-faced concrete to inclined wall
 4 Reinforced concrete doorway surround to tunnel entrance
 5 Tunnel opening
 6 Stone dressing to stream bank
 7 Reinforced concrete foundation to stream bank
 8 Stone wall edge to tunnel opening
 9 Quarry stone finish to stream bed
 10 Stone wall to stream bank
 11 Stainless steel handrail

12 Quarry stone paving to tunnel path
13 Back-fill
14 Existing ground level
15 New ground level

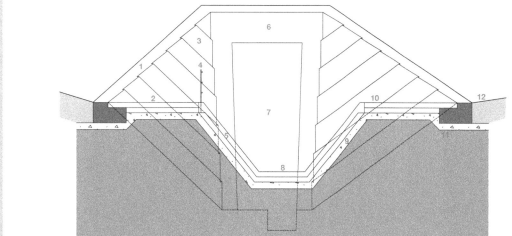

02.06
Tunnel Section D–D
1:100
 1 Cast in-situ reinforced concrete supporting wall
 2 Quarry stone block paving
 3 Profiled fair-faced concrete to inclined wall
 4 Stainless steel handrail
 5 Stone dressing to stream bank
 6 Reinforced concrete surround
 7 Tunnel opening
 8 Quarry stone finish to stream bed
 9 Reinforced concrete foundation to stream bank
 10 Quarry stone paving to tunnel path
 11 Existing ground level
 12 New ground level

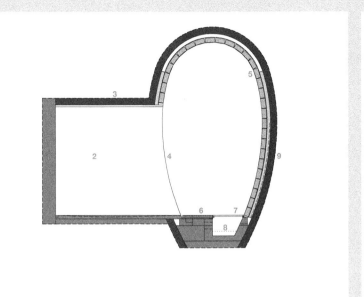

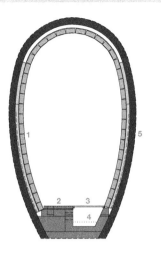

02.07
Tunnel Section at Sculpture Niche Detail
1:100
  1 Existing bridge pier
  2 Reinforced concrete frame to recess in tunnel beyond
  3 Shotcrete load-bearing structure
  4 Edge of reinforced concrete frame between tunnel recess and main tunnel
  5 Hard-burnt, fair-faced dark-red brick to tunnel interior
  6 75 mm (3 inch) thick concrete slab paving on 25 mm (1 inch) thick mortar bed
  7 30 mm (1 1/5 inch) diameter steel rod grating on 50 x 50 mm (2 x 2 inch) steel T-sections
  8 Stream bed
  9 Shotcrete load-bearing structure

02.08
Typical Tunnel Section
1:100
  1 Hard-burnt, fair-faced dark red brick to tunnel interior
  2 75 mm (3 inch) thick concrete slab paving on 25 mm (1 inch) thick mortar bed
  3 30 mm (1 1/5 inch) diameter steel rod grating on 50 x 50 mm (2 x 2 inch) steel T-sections
  4 Stream bed
  5 Shotcrete load-bearing structure

02.09
Tunnel Wall Detail
1:10
  1 Cement render finish to interior of tunnel wall
  2 Fair-face brick vault over crushed stone filling, perforated membrane and shotcrete load-bearing structure
  3 Reinforced shotcrete load-bearing structure

02.10
Tunnel Floor Detail
1:20
  1 Line of shotcrete load-bearing structure
  2 Drainage board
  3 Cement mortar bed
  4 Fair-faced brick vault
  5 Continuous cavity drainage system
  6 Concrete or crushed stone filling according to location in tunnel
  7 Concrete pavers on mortar bed
  8 Lighting recess
  9 Conduit with concealed lighting and wiring
  10 Continuous 50 x 50 x 5 mm (2 x 2 x 1/5 inch) steel T-section
  11 30 mm (1 1/5 inch) diameter steel rod grating on 50 x 50 mm (2 x 2 inch) steel

T-sections
12 Through-wall drainage
13 Continuous 50 x 50 x 5 mm (2 x 2 x 1/5 inch) steel T-section
14 Fair-face brick vault
15 Cement mortar bed
16 Drainage board
17 Continuous cavity drainage system
18 Through-wall drainage
19 Waterproof concrete to stream bed

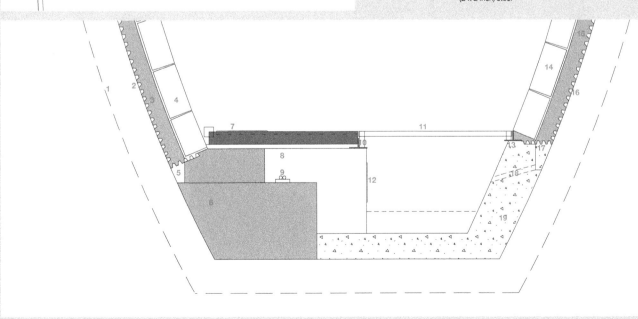

**Biosphere and Flower Pavilion
Potsdam, Germany**

Client
City of Potsdam, represented by
Entwicklungsträger Bornstedter Feld

Area
1.1 hectares (2.7 acres)

Project Team
Heiko Krech, Christian Helfrich,
Dietrich Bernstorf, Giuseppe Boezi,
Bernd Jürgens, Stephanie Kaindl, Jan
Kircher, Julien Monfort, Volkmar
Nickol, Karin Ocker, Andrea Pelzeter,
Florian Steinbächer

Structural Engineer
Hörnicke Hock Thieroff, Berlin

The Biosphere is located next to the
historical gardens of Frederick the
Great's Sanssouci Palace in Potsdam,
the former seat of Prussian military
power, and was used as a military
parade ground up until the Nazi era.
After the war, the Soviets occupied
the site and criss-crossed it with a
series of earth berms to protect the
barracks. Following the reunification
of Germany and the demolition of the
barracks, the berms remained. This
raw, defensive landscape provided the
conceptual basis for the design. The
pavilion is defined by four large berms
which enclose the space and form a
central valley. The new 'artificial'
berms are made from in-situ concrete,
covered in timber logs or grass sod.

The berms are excavated by cutting
into the central garden in order to
extend its vertical height. A steel and
glass façade completes the vertical
enclosure. Like a net, it adjusts to the
contours of the rising slopes, creating
a lightness in contrast to the massive
earthworks. The flat roof hovers over
a complex interior terrain of sloping
surfaces. The plan is organized within
the 200-metre (656-foot) long space
with a lobby at the entrance end and
an orangery at the other for public
events. A circulation loop is provided
by a series of ramps, suspended
bridges, platforms and boardwalks
so that one can experience the
gardens from multiple vantage points.
The gardens are complemented
by a restaurant, bar and a suspended
water basin, whose underwater
luminaires bring light into an
underwater exhibition space.

1 Grass-covered earth berms sit in contrast with the lightness of the glass pavilion.
2 Indoor and outdoor areas accommodate a range of local and exotic plants, protected both by the grass berms and by new artificial berms created from in-situ concrete.
3 The flat glazed roof has a slight incline in order to store rainwater, which humidifies the tropical plants inside.
4 Walkways take the form of paths at the lower levels and bridges at upper levels to provide visitors with varying outlooks over the planted areas.
5 Detail view of one of the planted interior berms.

03.01
Ground Floor Plan
1:1000
1 Orangery
2 Timber-clad berm
3 Paludarium (aquarium and terrarium) below
4 Berm clad with ivy
5 Berm clad with ivy (sectional view)
6 Paludarium plant room
7 Sectional view through berm
8 Exterior staircase

9 Cistern
10 Sectional view through berm
11 Lawn-covered berm
12 Heating and ventilation plant room
13 Employee changing room
14 Ice cave
15 *Ficus* plantation
16 Tropical garden plantation
17 Berm maintenance

to bar
18 Planted berm
19 Water basin cascade and mangrove
20 Steel and glass north façade
21 Sunken garden
22 Ramped path for maintenance
23 Exit
24 Slate-covered rock face
25 Hollow section of concrete berm structure

path
26 Foyer
27 Entrance
28 Cascade
29 Planted berm
30 Administration offices
31 Plant room
32 Sectional view of berm
33 Stock delivery area
34 Exterior staircase to restaurant at first floor
35 Lawn-covered berm

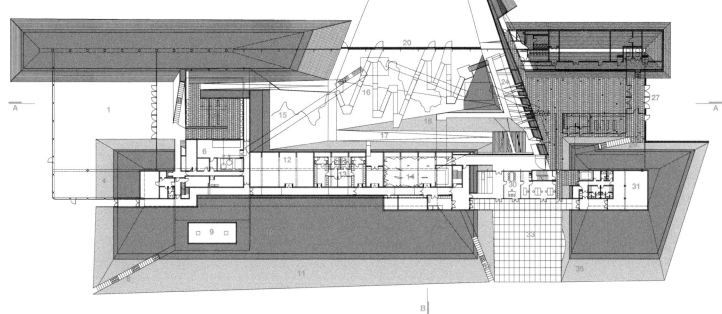

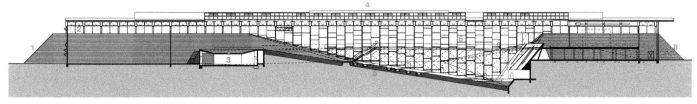

03.02
Section A–A
1:1000
1 Timber-clad berm
2 Operable windows for cross ventilation

3 Paludarium
4 Operable glazing to skylight roof
5 Tropical garden plantation
6 Steel and glass façade

7 Cave behind cascade
8 Existing concrete berm

03.03
Section B–B
1:1000
1 Slate-clad berm
2 Cantilevered steel roof
3 Steel and glass façade

4 Existing concrete berm
5 Operable glazing to skylight roof
6 Grass-covered berm

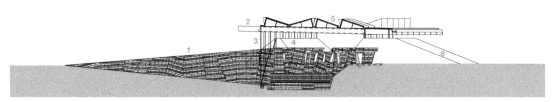

03.04
Interior Planted
Berm Detail
1:50
 1 Maintenance path
 2 Soil
 3 Back-filled topsoil
 4 200 mm (7⁹/₁₀ inch)
substratum
 5 Stainless steel
skeleton container
fixed to soil with
stainless steel nails
 6 Visitors trail

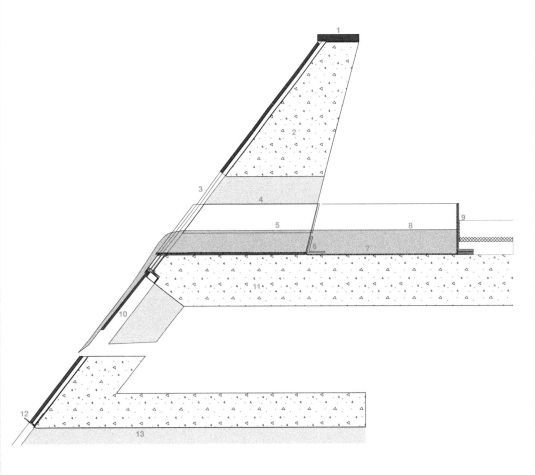

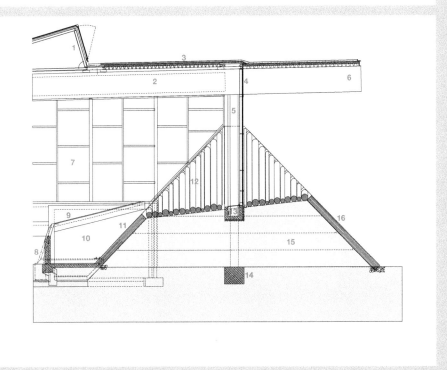

03.05
Water Slot Wall
Elevational Detail
1:100
1 Water spout
2 Water overflow slot
3 Impervious glazing to foyer area
4 20 mm (3/4 inch) thick slate set in mortar bed
5 Rock cave set back behind cascade
6 Stainless steel handrail with glass balustrade
7 Water basin constructed from waterproof concrete filled with gravel

03.06
Water Slot Wall
Sectional Detail
1:20
1 40 mm (1 1/2 inch) thick steel cover plate to top of balustrade
2 Fair-faced concrete balustrade
3 Water overflow slot
4 Top edge to steel water tank
5 10 mm (2/5 inch) thick galvanized steel water tank
6 100 x 100 x 10 mm (4 x 4 x 2/5 inch) hole-punched hot-dip galvanized steel L-angle to gravel

catchment
7 Composite sealing layer
8 Water level at 140 mm (5 1/2 inch) deep
9 Capped 300 x 280 mm (11 4/5 x 11 inch) hot dip galvanized U-profile capping
10 Sealed aluminium window frame with impervious glazing
11 Reinforced concrete ceiling
12 Stainless steel drain
13 Top of Rock Cave

03.07
Timber Berm Detail
1:200
1 Operable glazing to skylight roof
2 Reinforced concrete beam with hollow cross section
3 Roof system comprised of top layer of gravel, two-part sealing layer, flame-resistant thermal insulation, 120 mm (4 3/4 inch) thick rigid foam, welded bitumen sheet vapour proofing and trapezoidal profile sheet metal ceiling
4 Steel and glass façade
5 Composite steel column
6 Cantilevered

reinforced concrete beam with solid cross section
7 Steel and glass façade
8 Reinforced concrete wall
9 Line of ceiling over passageway to Paludarium
10 Passage from paludarium to botanic garden
11 300 mm (11 4/5 inch) diameter oak tree trunks to berm surface
12 300 mm (11 4/5 inch) diameter oak tree trunks to berm surface
13 Prefabricated heating duct
14 Composite steel column and concrete foundation
15 Reinforced earth mass retained by geotextile
16 300 mm (11 2/5 inch) diameter oak tree trunks to berm surface

04
Batlle i Roig Arquitectes

La Vall de'n Joan, Parc del Garraf
Barcelona, Spain

Client
Entidad Metropolitana de Serveis
Hidràilics del Àrea Metropolitana de
Barcelona

Area
20 hectares (49 acres)

Project Team
Enric Batlle, Joan Roig, Teresa Galí,
Jordi Nebot

Main Contractor
Ute Fomento, Comsa, Dragados y
Cespa

The Vall d'en Joan waste dump was opened in 1974 in the El Garraf natural park. As a result, existing vegetation was destroyed, the site was waterproofed and a drainage system was installed for the poisonous leachates. The waste was alternated with shallow layers of earth over several decades and the landfill eventually occupied 70 hectares (173 acres) with a depth of over 80 metres (262 feet) at some points. To begin the restoration process, a layer of earth was used to cover the refuse. The existing terrace formation necessitated the construction of massive retaining walls, requiring an enormous amount of imported earth which was used to form a layer of fertile land for the introduction of vegetation.

Layers of sand, geotextile, waterproof lining and a second layer of sand were used to separate the waste dump from new soil. Manure was applied to specific planted areas and plant compost to the terraces to improve the structure and texture of the soil. Crop rotation based on leguminous plants was established on the terraces in order to improve soil fertility. Three types of plants were employed in the restoration – rows of pine trees lining the drainage channels and paths, shrubs on the slopes and leguminous crops on the terraces. The ultimate aim is to encourage species that are native to the Garraf to grow, whether by means of direct introduction or by providing the conditions conducive to natural propagation. Proximity to urban areas, good access and parking facilities, and a connection with the long-distance GR pathway make it a perfect new recreation facility for the inhabitants of Barcelona.

1 Aerial view of the new park.
2 View from the access road with the waste dump to the left. To the right is one of the vegetal walls constructed from galvanized wire mesh with inclined panels.
3 After the basic structure of the terraces was in place, these were reinforced with retaining walls. The terraces are used for the introduction of vegetation, separated from the contaminated soil below with layers of sand, geotextile, waterproof lining and a second layer of sand.
4 Rows of pine trees and an assortment of shrubs will be planted on the slopes.
5 The new park features walls of garbage constructed from compacted PVC bottles which act as potent symbols of the old waste dump.

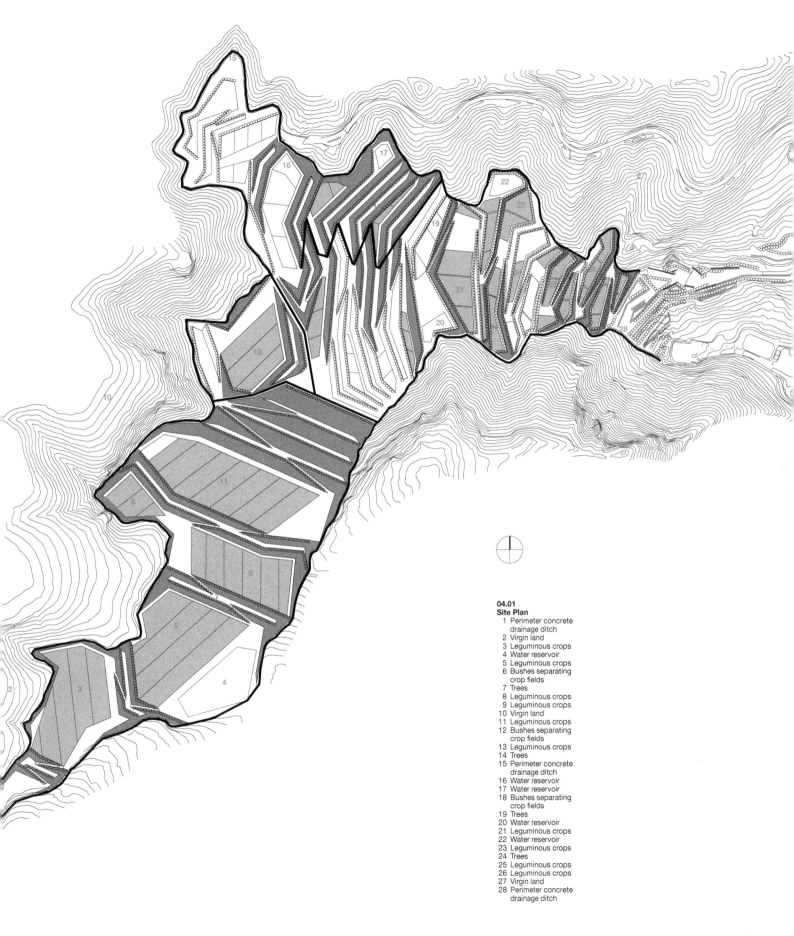

04.01
Site Plan
1 Perimeter concrete
  drainage ditch
2 Virgin land
3 Leguminous crops
4 Water reservoir
5 Leguminous crops
6 Bushes separating
  crop fields
7 Trees
8 Leguminous crops
9 Leguminous crops
10 Virgin land
11 Leguminous crops
12 Bushes separating
  crop fields
13 Leguminous crops
14 Trees
15 Perimeter concrete
  drainage ditch
16 Water reservoir
17 Water reservoir
18 Bushes separating
  crop fields
19 Trees
20 Water reservoir
21 Leguminous crops
22 Water reservoir
23 Leguminous crops
24 Trees
25 Leguminous crops
26 Leguminous crops
27 Virgin land
28 Perimeter concrete
  drainage ditch

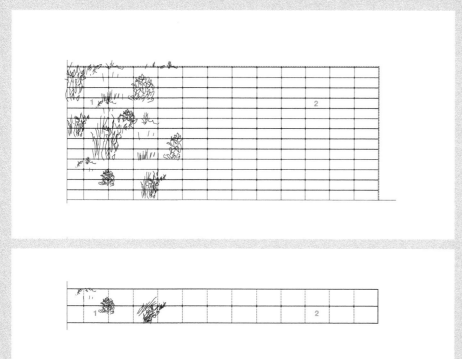

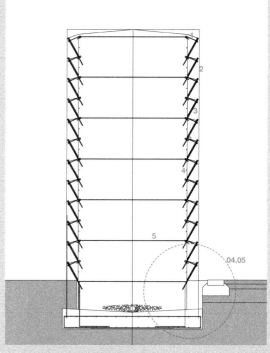

04.02
Vegetal Wall
Elevation
1:100
 1 Vegetation
 2 4 metre (13 feet)
high structure of
galvanized wire mesh
with inclined panels
of polyproplyene mesh
to take vegetation

04.03
Vegetal Wall
Plan
1:100
 1 Vegetation
 2 4 metre (13 feet)
high structure of
galvanized wire mesh
with inclined panels
of polyproplyene mesh
to take vegetation

04.04
Vegetal Wall
Cross Section
1:20
 1 Tensile hook
 2 Line of outer edge
of vegetal wall
 3 15 x 15 x 8 mm ($^3/_5$
x $^3/_5$ x $^1/_3$ inch) inclined
wire mesh panels with
outer layer of
polyproplyene mesh
 4 Galvanized
mesh wall
 5 Galvanized mesh
internal structure

04.05
Vegetal Wall
Sectional Detail
1:20
 1 Crushed aggregate
over PVC drainage
pipe
 2 Reinforced
concrete floor slab
 3 Timber edge beam
 4 Asphalt to new
ground surface
 5 200 mm ($7^9/_{10}$ inch)
artificial graded
aggregate sub-surface

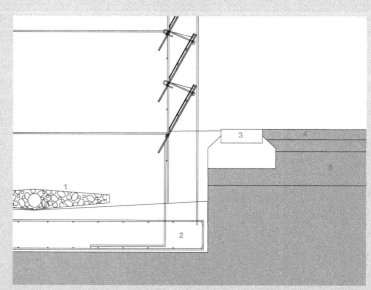

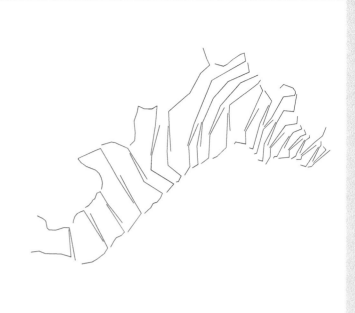

04.06
Vegetation: Crops
Leguminous crops
have been planted on
the terraces to improve
soil fertility. Traditional
crop rotation
methodology is used
to maximize yield.

04.07
Vegetation: Bushes
It was important to use
species that are native
to the Garraf, whether
by means of direct
introduction on the
slopes via planting,
irrigation and weeding,
or by providing the
conditions conducive
to natural propagation.
These plants help to
prevent further soil
erosion as well as
providing wind-breaks
for the crop fields.

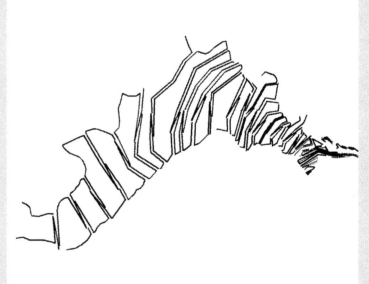

04.08
Vegetation: Slopes
To ensure that the
newly planted crops
and shrubs flourish in
the new park, compost
was added to the
terraces to improve the
structure and texture
of the soil.

04.09
Vegetation: Trees
Rows of pine trees
have been planted to
line the drainage
channels and paths as
part of the plan to
reintroduce only those
species that are native
to the Garraf region.

Burckhardt + Partner Architects

MFO Park
Zurich, Switzerland

Client
Grün Stadt Zürich

Area
0.85 hectares (2.1 acres)

Project Team
Roger Nussbaumer, Heinz Moser,
Oliver S. Gilbert, Roland Raderschall,
Sibylle Raderschall, Markus Fierz

Landscape Architect
Raderschall Landscape Architects

Structural Engineer
Basler Hofmann AG

This gigantic garden arbour is located
in the newly emerging district of
Zurich North. The government
department responsible for the
creation of the park intended to
design a series of open recreational
spaces on this heroically scaled
former industrial site. The architects
felt that a built volume was more
appropriate and sympathetic to the
context than simply landscaping the
open space. The architects used 290
tons of steel, 32 kilometres (20 miles)
of cable and 870 square metres (9,365
square feet) of timber and metal grids
to create a massive framework in the
open site, placed on an artificially
raised area on the slightly sloping plot.

The resulting theatrical nature of the
structure is a reminder of the lost
industrial identity of the site, as well as
offering a new spatial experience of
the park and the surrounding area.
Timber viewing platforms are
suspended from the frame at a height
of 17 metres (56 feet), providing
spectacular views and one of the most
popular meeting places in the area.
Narrow hedges connect the interior
and exterior spaces at ground level,
while creepers and climbers will
proliferate along the steel structure to
cover the whole height over time,
creating a living green 'fur coat'. An
irrigation system and batteries of
troughs on the roof ensure that the
green camouflage flourishes. A slightly
sunken rectangular field in the rear of
the space is covered in recycled green
glass chippings and features timber
benches and a circular pool to create
a more intimate, relaxing environment.

1 The climbers and
creepers are slowly
but surely reaching the
lofty heights of the
timber viewing gantries
at the top of the
structure.
2 The stone façade of
an existing industrial
building (scheduled
to be demolished),
currently forms the
fourth façade of the
gigantic arbour.
3 Throughout the
structure, walkways,
platforms and
benches provide
ample opportunities
to relax and enjoy the
progress of the
building as it
apparently grows.
4 The creepers and
climbers offer a
delicately filigreed
veil to the lightness
and complexity of the
steel frame.

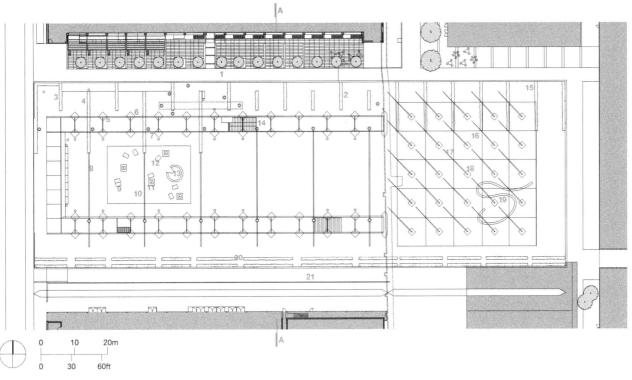

05.01
Site Plan
1:1000
1 James Joyce Weg
2 Box tree and Hornbeam hedge
3 Box tree and Hornbeam hedge
4 Box tree and Hornbeam hedge
5 Base with planting beds
6 Base with planting beds
7 Base with planting beds
8 Water chute
9 Steel and timber seating
10 Gravel ground surface
11 Stalactite sculpture with climbing plants
12 Steel and timber seating
13 Fountain
14 Steel staircase
15 Box tree and Hornbeam hedge
16 Pre-cast concrete paving slabs
17 Timber framing stick for climbing plants
18 Stainless steel planting base filled with humus and climbing plants
19 Snail-shaped sculptural plastic seating
20 Box tree and hornbeam hedge
21 Ricarda Huch Weg

0   10   20m
0   30   60ft

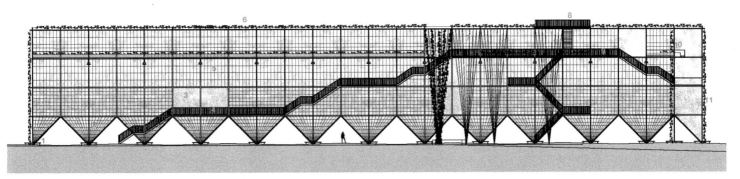

05.02
South Elevation
1:500
1 Stainless steel planting base filled with humus and climbing plants
2 5 mm (1/5 inch) diameter tensioned stainless steel rope for climbing plants attached to steel wind bracing structure
3 Window opening
4 Steel and timber handrail
5 5 mm (1/5 inch) diameter tensioned stainless steel rope for climbing plants
6 Planting to roof on 5 mm (1/5 inch) diameter tensioned stainless steel rope
7 Hanging 5 mm (1/5 inch) diameter tensioned stainless steel rope for climbing plants in stalactite formation
8 Handrail to viewing platform
9 Steel and timber handrail to platform and stair
10 Plastic planter tubs filled with humus and climbing plants
11 Climbing plants to exterior of structure on 5 mm (1/5 inch) diameter tensioned stainless steel rope

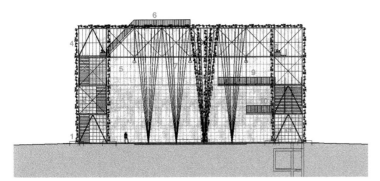

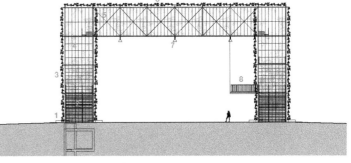

05.03
West Elevation
1:500
1 Planting base filled with humus and climbing plants
2 5 mm (1/5 inch) diameter tensioned stainless steel rope for climbing plants attached to steel wind bracing
3 5 mm (1/5 inch) diameter tensioned stainless steel rope for climbing plants attached to steel wind bracing over steel staircase
4 5 mm (1/5 inch) diameter tensioned stainless steel rope for climbing plants in stalactite formation
5 Green wall beyond
6 Viewing platform
7 Hanging 5 mm (1/5 inch) diameter tensioned stainless steel rope for climbing plants in stalactite formation
8 Plastic planter tubs filled with humus and climbing plants
9 Open-air gallery
10 Open-air gallery
11 Access way

05.04
Section A–A
1:500
1 Planting base filled with humus and climbing plants
2 5 mm (1/5 inch) diameter tensioned stainless steel rope for climbing plants
3 Climbing plants
4 5 mm (1/5 inch) diameter tensioned stainless steel rope for climbing plants
5 Steel wind bracing
6 Planting to roof on 5 mm (1/5 inch) diameter tensioned stainless steel rope
7 Pendant luminaire lighting
8 Open-air gallery at first floor

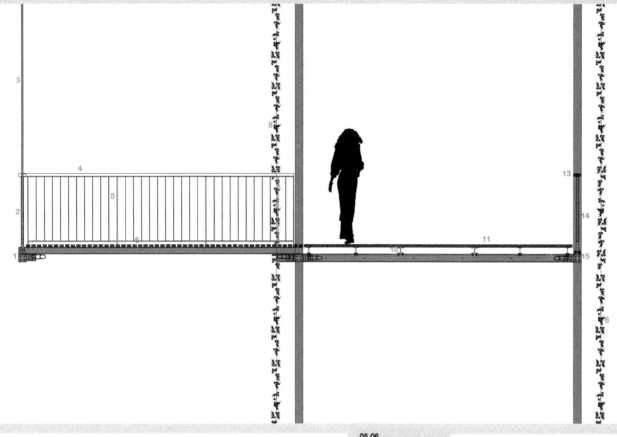

05.05
Walkway Detail 1
1:50
  1 Steel wind bracing
  2 40 x 15 mm (1³/5 x ³/5 inch) steel post balustrade
  3 5 mm (¹/5 inch) diameter tensioned stainless steel rope for climbing plants
  4 120 x 40 mm (4³/4 x 1³/5 inch) timber grab rail
  5 40 x 8 mm (1³/5 x ¹/3 inch) steel post handrail
  6 Timber decking to gallery
  7 Secondary steel structure of 120 mm (4³/4 inch) steel sections
  8 5 mm (¹/5 inch) diameter tensioned stainless steel rope for climbing plants
  9 Primary steel structure of 120 mm (4³/4 inch) steel sections
  10 Secondary steel structure of 120 mm (4³/4 inch) steel sections
  11 Timber decking to elevated walkway
  12 80 mm (3¹/10 inch) diameter steel wind bracing
  13 120 x 40 mm (4³/4 x 1³/5 inch) timber grab rail
  14 40 x 8 mm (1³/5 x ¹/3 inch) steel post balustrade
  15 Primary steel structure of 120 mm (4³/4 inch) steel sections

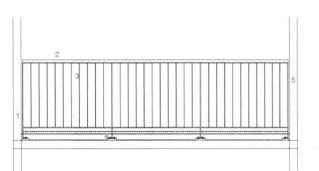

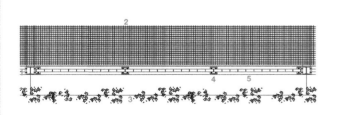

05.06
Walkway Detail 2
1:50
  1 Primary steel structure of 120 mm (4³/4 inch) steel sections
  2 120 x 40 mm (4³/4 x 1³/5 inch) timber grab rail
  3 40 x 8 mm (1³/5 x ¹/3 inch) steel post handrail
  4 Steel balustrade bolted mounting assembly
  5 Primary steel structure of 120 mm (4³/4 inch) steel sections

05.07
Walkway Detail 4
1:50
  1 Primary steel structure of 120 mm (4³/4 inch) steel sections
  2 Timber decking to gallery
  3 5 mm (¹/5 inch) diameter tensioned stainless steel rope for climbing plants
  4 40 x 15 mm (1³/5 x ³/5 inch) steel post balustrade
  5 40 x 8 mm (1³/5 x ¹/3 inch) steel post balustrade

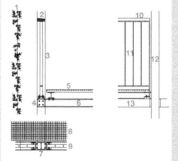

05.08
Walkway Detail 3
1:50
  1 5 mm (¹/5 inch) diameter tensioned stainless steel rope for climbing plants
  2 38 x 38 mm (1¹/2 x 1¹/2 inch) timber grab rail
  3 40 x 8 mm (1³/5 x ¹/3 inch) steel post balustrade
  4 Primary steel structure of 120 mm (4³/4 inch) steel sections
  5 Steel grate walkway surface
  6 Primary steel structure of 120 mm (4³/4 inch) steel sections
  7 Primary steel structure of 120 mm (4³/4 inch) steel sections
  8 Steel grate walkway surface
  9 40 x 8 mm (1³/5 x ¹/3 inch) steel post balustrade
  10 38 x 38 mm (1¹/2 x 1¹/2 inch) timber grab rail
  11 40 x 8 mm (1³/5 x ¹/3 inch) steel post balustrade
  12 Primary steel structure of 120 mm (4³/4 inch) steel sections
  13 Primary steel structure of 120 mm (4³/4 inch) steel sections

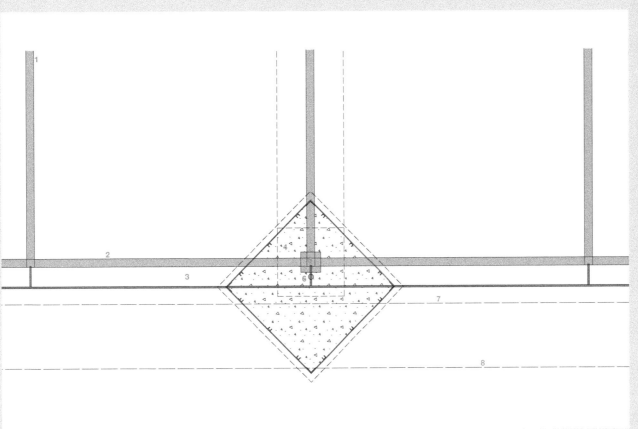

05.09
Steel Frame Plan Detail
1:50
1 Primary steel structure of 120 mm (4³/₄ inch) steel sections
2 Primary steel structure of 120 mm (4³/₄ inch) steel sections
3 5 mm (1/5 inch) diameter tensioned stainless steel rope for climbing plants
4 Planting base filled with humus and climbing plants
5 Primary steel structure of 120 mm (4³/₄ inch) steel sections
6 Tensioned stainless steel rope fixing point
7 Line of steel structure dotted over
8 Line of steel structure dotted over

05.10
Steel Frame Sectional Detail
1:50
1 Rubble underlayer to footpath
2 Gravel to ground surface
3 5 mm (1/5 inch) diameter tensioned stainless steel rope for climbing plants
4 5 mm (1/5 inch) diameter tensioned stainless steel rope for climbing plants
5 Primary steel structure
6 Topsoil
7 Tensioned stainless steel rope fixing point
8 Waterproof membrane
9 Concrete and steel column base
10 100 mm (4 inch) deep layer of humus substrate
11 80 x 60 x 4500 mm (3¹/₁₀ x 2¹/₃ x 177¹/₅ inch) reinforced concrete footing
12 100 mm (4 inch) deep layer of humus substrate
13 Compacted rubble substrate
14 100 mm (4 inch) diameter PVC drainage pipe
15 Existing building rubble left in place
16 Compacted rubble substrate
17 4220 mm (166¹/₄ inch) construction grid dotted
18 Box tree and hornbeam hedge
19 Topsoil

**Bureau B+B Stedebouw en
Landschapsarchitectuur**

**Waldpark
Potsdam, Germany**

Client
ETBF Potsdam

Area
16 hectares (39.5 acres)

Project Team
Frans Boots, Helene Hölzl,
Petrouschka Thumann

Structural Engineer
Buro Thomas M. Dietrich

Throughout the historic city of
Potsdam, parks and gardens are
being redesigned and refurbished
with the original aims of the
eighteenth-century Prussian
aristocracy that created them. Among
these is the Bornstedter Feld, a former
Russian military drill-ground. This new
city district accommodates a 60-
hectare (148-acre) park, where
the objective was to create a dynamic
recreational space offering sports
and game facilities to complement the
city's gardens. Bureau B+B won a
competition to design the Waldpark,
16 hectares (39 acres) of the
Bornstedter Feld, where trenches
and concrete installations attest to
its military past, and where, over
time, lush forests and meadows
have emerged.

The Waldpark encourages 30
different wildlife habitats to thrive. In
contrast to these carefully preserved
habitats, four sculptural 'play
terminals' encourage a plethora
of activities and relieve pressure on
the vulnerable wildlife areas. The
size and scale of the concrete
sculptures are not immediately
apparent, nor is their purpose
obvious. However, these brightly
coloured amorphous sculptures
accommodate various activities, such
as ball games, climbing, sliding,
skating and trampolining. The soft,
rounded shapes are also perfect
for sitting, gazing, sunbathing and
picnics, as well as serving as a
background for theatre performances
and outdoor concerts, while the
vertical walls offer a projection surface
for slides, light shows and movies.
The aesthetic strength of the objects
happily encourages visitors to
interpret their meaning and use at
their discretion.

1 One of the play
terminals. Four of
these amorphous
concrete sculptures
were built at the edges
of the park and are
points of concentration
for intensive
activities.
2 Seating terminal.
The terminals
intentionally appear
as unfamiliar objects
that seemingly have
landed in the park by
coincidence.
3 Glide terminal. The
appearance of the
terminals encourages
visitors to use them for
playing, hanging,
lying, skating, sliding,
climbing, jumping and
sitting.
4 Jump terminal.
Active visitors to the
park stay in the vicinity
of the terminals while
nature lovers can enjoy
the woodland
landscape elsewhere.

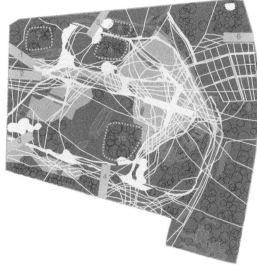

06.01
Concept Diagram
1 Play terminal
2 Play terminal
3 Play terminal
4 Play terminal
5 Play terminal
6 Play terminal
7 Ecological island
8 Ecological island
9 Ecological island
10 Ecological island

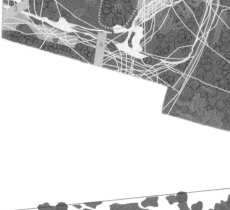

06.02
**High Ecological Value
Biotope Areas**

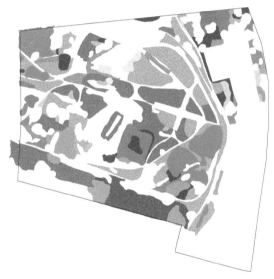

06.03
**Medium Ecological
Value Biotope Areas**

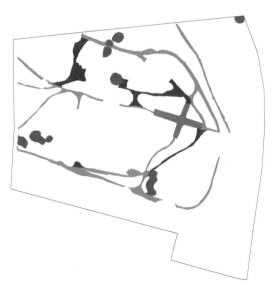

06.04
**Low Ecological Value
Biotope Areas**

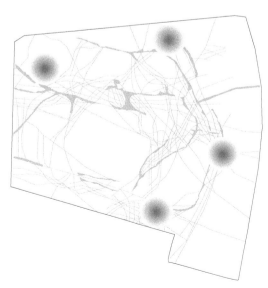

06.05
**Magnets and
Network Systems**

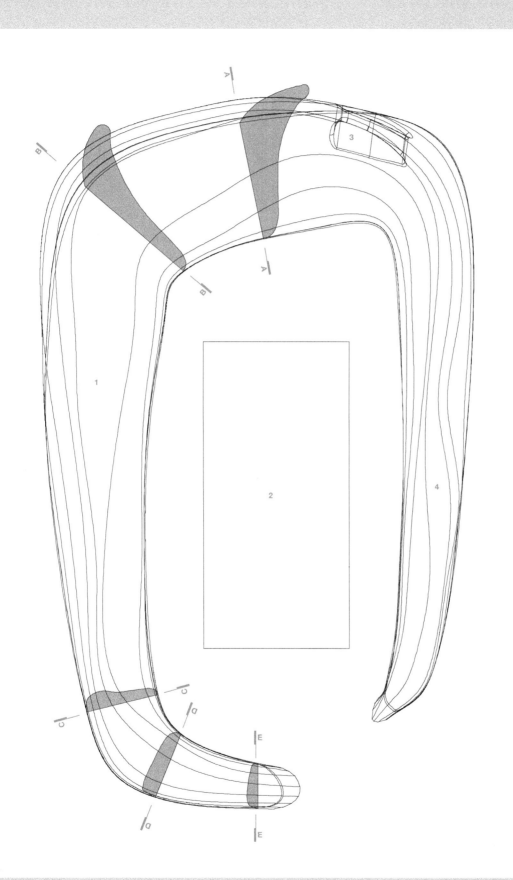

06.06
**Play Terminal Plan
1:200**
 1 Jetcrete concrete
surface
 2 Beach volleyball
court
 3 Hole-in-wall surface
 4 Jetcrete concrete
surface

06.07
**Play Terminal
Sections**
1:200
1 Section A–A
2 Section B–B
3 Section C–C
4 Section D–D
5 Section E–E

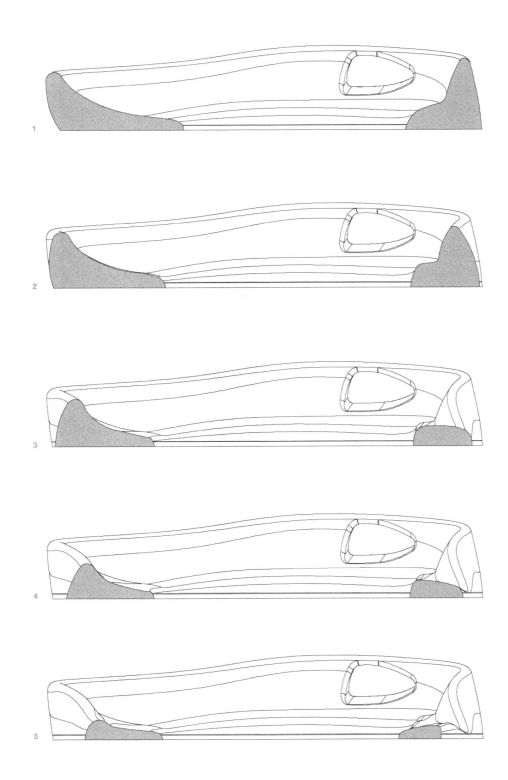

Donaldson + Warn, Architects

Bali Memorial, King's Park
Perth, Western Australia, Australia

Client
Department of Premier and Cabinet,
Western Australia

Area
400 square metres (4,305 square feet)

Project Team
Geoff Warn, Simon Pendal, Tom
Griffiths, and artists David Jones,
Sally Morgan, Kevin Draper

Structural Engineer
Capital House Australasia

Landscape Architect
Plan E

The Bali Memorial is the result of a
competition for the design of a
memorial commemorating the terrorist
bombing in Bali on October 12, 2002
in which 202 people died, of whom 88
were Australian, and to honour those
who assisted in the aftermath of the
tragedy. The memorial is nestled into
the native landscape of King's Park
escarpment, looking out across the
open expanse of the Swan River to
the distant Darling Range. The design
is dominated by two axes: the Swan
River axis is aligned with a framed
view to the ranges beyond, while
the Sunrise axis is positioned so that
a ray of light is captured within the
memorial at sunrise on October 12
each year, illuminating the victims'
names cast into a bronze plaque. This
plaque is fixed to a cut and polished
face of a large granite boulder sourced
from the distant hills.

The design celebrates relationships
between people, and as such is
designed as a casual meeting place
for the families, friends and visitors
who wish to reflect on this significant
event in the history of Australia.
The materials include stone from the
Kimberley region, weather-resistant
plate steel and granite paving. The
memorial was completed for the first
anniversary on October 12, 2003.

1 The site, chosen
by the families, is
an appropriately
contemplative place
for the memorial.
The careful use of
indigenous flora and
materials is reinforced
by images of local
botanical species
etched into a curved
steel wall by artist
David Jones and
sculptor Kevin Draper.
In addition, text by
writer Sally Morgan is
etched into stone
surfaces throughout
the design.
2 View through the
Sunrise axis towards
Darling Escarpment. A
massive granite block
(right) is etched with
the names of the 16
young West
Australians who died in
the Bali bombing.

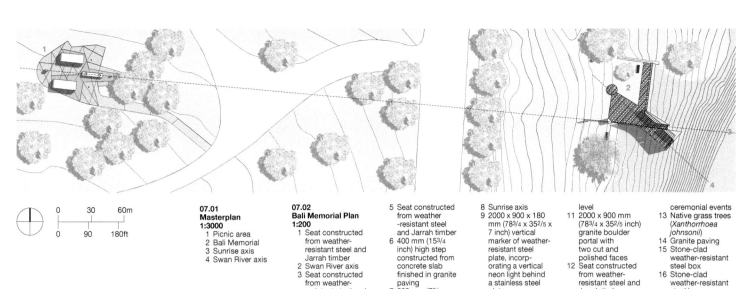

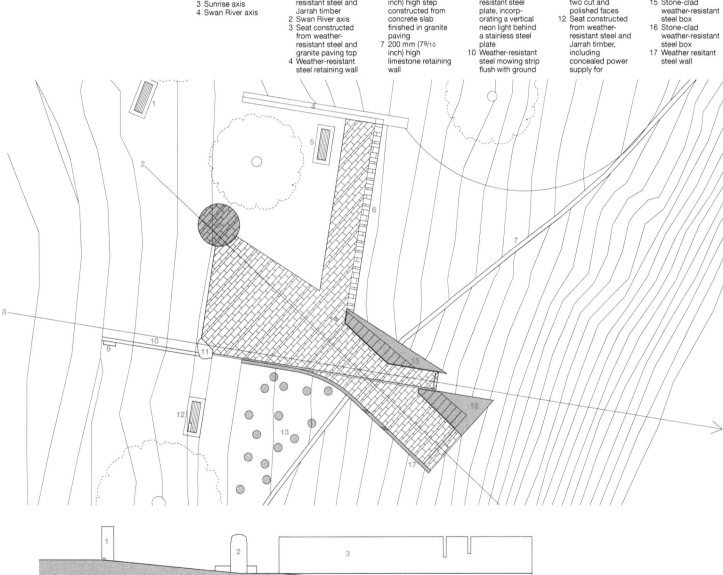

07.01
Masterplan
1:3000
1 Picnic area
2 Bali Memorial
3 Sunrise axis
4 Swan River axis

07.02
Bali Memorial Plan
1:200
1 Seat constructed from weather-resistant steel and Jarrah timber
2 Swan River axis
3 Seat constructed from weather-resistant steel and granite paving top
4 Weather-resistant steel retaining wall
5 Seat constructed from weather-resistant steel and Jarrah timber
6 400 mm (15³/₄ inch) high step constructed from concrete slab finished in granite paving
7 200 mm (7⁹/₁₀ inch) high limestone retaining wall
8 Sunrise axis
9 2000 x 900 x 180 mm (78³/₄ x 35²/₅ x 7 inch) vertical marker of weather-resistant steel plate, incorporating a vertical neon light behind a stainless steel plate
10 Weather-resistant steel mowing strip flush with ground
level
11 2000 x 900 mm (78³/₄ x 35²/₅ inch) granite boulder portal with two cut and polished faces
12 Seat constructed from weather-resistant steel and Jarrah timber, including concealed power supply for
ceremonial events
13 Native grass trees (*Xanthorrhoea johnsonii*)
14 Granite paving
15 Stone-clad weather-resistant steel box
16 Stone-clad weather-resistant steel box
17 Weather resistant steel wall

07.03
South Elevation
1:200
1 2000 x 900 x 180 mm (78³/₄ x 35²/₅ x 7 inch) vertical
marker of weather-resistant steel plate, incorporating a vertical neon light behind a stainless
steel plate
2 2000 x 900 mm (78³/₄ x 35²/₅ inch) granite boulder portal with two cut and
polished faces
3 Weather-resistant steel wall
4 15 mm (³/₅ inch) thick weather-resistant steel skirt

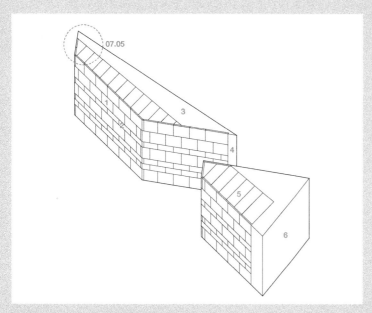

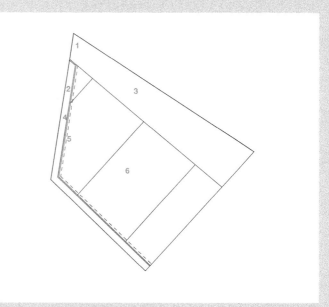

07.04
**Memorial Wall Stone
and Steel Cladding
Detail**
 1 600 x 400 mm
(23²/³ x 15³/⁴ inch)
Kimberly sandstone
cladding
 2 900 x 200 mm
(35²/⁵ x 7⁹/₁₀ inch)
Kimberly sandstone
cladding
 3 12 mm (1/2 inch)
thick weather-resistant
steel plate box
 4 12 mm (1/2 inch)
thick weather-resistant
steel plate box
 5 Kimberly sandstone
cladding
 6 Weather-resistant
steel box

07.05
**Memorial Box
Cladding Detail**
1:20
 1 12 mm (1/2 inch)
weather-resistant steel
box steps notched to
accept stone cladding
 2 40 mm (1¹/² inch)
thick Kimberly
sandstone cladding
 3 Weather-resistant
steel box
 4 15 mm (³/⁵ inch)
cavity
 5 Line of face of steel
below, dotted
 6 40 mm (1¹/² inch)
thick Kimberly
sandstone to top of
weather-resistant
steel box

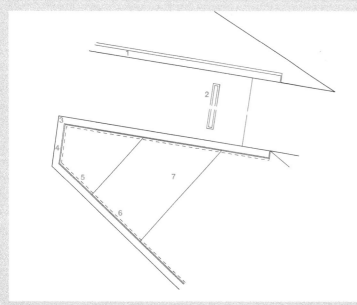

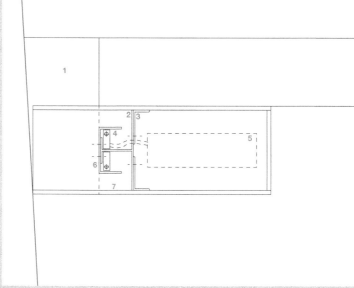

07.06
**Sunrise Axis
Plan Cladding
Detail**
1:20
 1 40 mm (1¹/² inch)
thick Kimberly
sandstone cladding
 2 Cantilevered glass
balustrade in stainless
steel perimeter
channel
 3 Stepped stone
corner detail
 4 40 mm (1¹/² inch)
thick stone Kimberly
sandstone cladding
 5 15 mm (³/⁵ inch)
cavity
 6 Face of steel below,
dotted
 7 40 mm (1¹/² inch)
thick Kimberly
sandstone to top of
weather-resistant
steel box

07.07
**Vertical Marker
Lighting Plan Detail**
1:10
 1 Single piece of
weather-resistant steel
mowing strip and
welded studs at 1200
mm (47¹/⁴ inch)
centres, chemset into
concrete edge beam
 2 4 mm (1/6 inch)
thick grade 316, No. 4
finished stainless steel
light housing, fixed
using countersunk
stainless steel tamper-
proof fixings
 3 Grade 304, 100 x
50 mm (4 x 2 inch)
cold-formed brackets
welded to weather-
resistant steel casing
at 500 mm (19³/⁵ inch)
centres
 4 Continuous neon
light tube
 5 Transformer
 6 4 mm (1/6 inch)
thick grade 316, No. 4
finished stainless steel
light housing, fixed
using countersunk
stainless steel tamper-
proof fixings
 7 12 mm (1/2 inch)
thick fully welded
weather-resistant steel
case

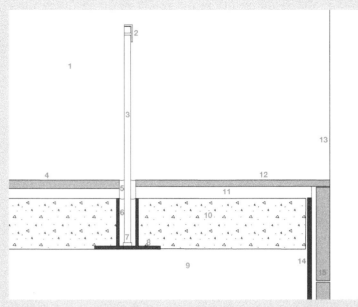

07.08
Detail Section
Through Sunrise Axis
Balustrade
1:10
  1 40 mm (1¹/2 inch)
thick stone cladding to
top of weather-
resistant steel
box beyond
  2 Stainless steel
perimeter framing
angle
  3 Cantilevered glass

balustrade in stainless
steel perimeter
channel
  4 25 mm (1 inch)
thick stone paving on
30 mm (1¹/5 inch)
mortar bed
  5 15 mm (³/5 inch)
wide black silicone
extending from top of
non-shrink grout to
finished paving level
  6 Non-shrink grout
packing

  7 Neoprene strip
packers and non-
shrink grout to level
glass sheet
  8 Cast-in stainless
steel pocket for
cantilevered glass
balustrade
  9 Void below
suspended
concrete slab
  10 150 mm (6 inch)
thick suspended
concrete slab

  11 30 mm (1¹/5 inch)
mortar bed
  12 25 mm (1 inch)
thick stone paving
  13 Edge of 12 mm (¹/2
inch) thick weather-
resistant steel box
  14 12 mm (¹/2 inch)
thick weather-resistant
steel skirt
  15 40 mm (1¹/2 inch)
thick Kimberly
sandstone cladding to
face of weather-

resistant steel skirt
across width of
Sunrise axis

07.09
Detail Section
Through Memorial
Edge Retaining Wall
1:10
  1 25 mm (1 inch)
thick stone paving on
30 mm (1¹/5 inch) deep
mortar bed
  2 12 mm (¹/2 inch)
thick weather-resistant
steel mowing edge
flush with paving
and grass

  3 12 mm (¹/2 inch)
thick weather-resistant
steel retaining wall
  4 Concrete slab
  5 12 mm (¹/2 inch)
thick weather-resistant
steel mowing edge
  6 New ground level
  7 Concrete strip
footing

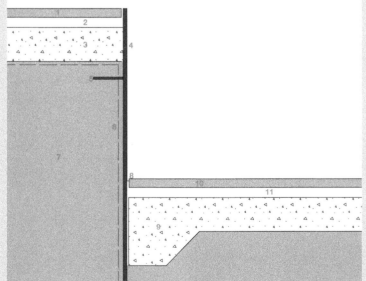

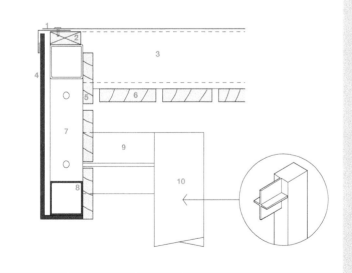

07.10
Detail Section at
Memorial Seat
1:10
  1 25 mm (1 inch)
thick stone paving
  2 30 mm (1¹/5 inch)
deep mortar bed
  3 100 mm (4 inch)
thick concrete slab
  4 12 mm (¹/2 inch)
thick weather-resistant
steel drum
  5 Weather-resistant

steel stiffening ring
  6 Waterproof sheet
membrane
  7 Compact fill
  8 5 mm (¹/5 inch)
silicone joint to paving
and steel interface.
Top of silicone 5 mm
(¹/5 inch) below top of
paving
  9 Concrete footing
  10 25 mm (1 inch)
thick stone paving
  11 30 mm (1¹/5 inch)

thick mortar bed

07.11
Detail Section at
Picnic Shelter Roof
1:10
  1 2 mm (¹/10 inch)
thick folded, powder
coated steel sheet
roofing directly fixed to
square hollow section
framing with fixings
through top surface
only. Steel double
folded at overhang
with single piece at

gable end overlapped
by main roof sheet
  2 Timber blocking
  3 Steel square hollow
section framing
  4 Weather-resistant
steel fascia – single
piece with concealed
fixings to mild
steel frame
  5 175, 150 or 125 x
25 mm (6³/4, 6 or 5 x 1
inch) skip-dressed,
prime-grade timber

Jarrah lining boards
with linseed oil finish
and self-tapping
counter-sunk
galvanized hexagonal-
head fixings
  6 175, 150 or 125 x
25 mm (6³/4, 6 or 5 x 1
inch) skip-dressed,
prime-grade timber
Jarrah lining boards
  7 90 x 45 mm (3¹/2 x
1³/4 inch) timber
framing bolted through

to steel frame
  8 Mild steel frame
  9 Cruciform mild
steel connection
assembly
  10 Rectangular hollow
section with cruciform
connection to mild
steel framework and
polyurethane finish
and flange located
on centre line of 20
mm (³/4 inch) open
board joint

08
Gustafson Guthrie Nichol

The Lurie Garden
Chicago, Illinois, USA

Client
Millennium Park, Inc

Area
1.2 hectares (3 acres)

Project Team
Kathryn Gustafson, Shannon Nichol,
Jennifer Guthrie, Gareth Loveridge,
David Nelson, Anita Madtes

Local Landscape Architect
Terry Guen Design Associates

Chicago built itself up from marshy origins and continues to rise ambitiously skyward. A refinement of nature and natural resources has accompanied Chicago's wilful development. Similarly, the site of the Lurie Garden has been built up over time. It has been elevated from wild shoreline to railroad yard to parking garage and finally to roof garden. The Lurie Garden celebrates the exciting contrast between the past and present that lies within this site. Part of Millennium Park, an ambitious new segment of Grant Park, the garden is located between a new band-shell by Frank O. Gehry & Associates and a renovation to the Chicago Art Institute by the Renzo Piano Building Workshop.

The entire garden is constructed over the roof deck of the Lakefront Millennium Parking Garage. The Shoulder Hedge, a 4.5-metre (15-foot) high topiary, encloses the garden on two sides and creates the illusion of solid 'shoulders' supporting the silvery forms of the band-shell beyond. The Shoulder Hedge also serves to protect the garden's interior from heavy pedestrian traffic moving throughout Millennium Park. Inside the hedge, two sculpted 'plates' are covered in perennial compositions of bold contrast. The plates seem to be punched up from the surface of the plaza-like a muscular torso. The Dark Plate references the moist, mysterious past of the site, offering an experience of dream-like immersion in a volume of robust perennial compositions. The Light Plate references Chicago's modern and artistic control of nature, providing an exhilarating experience of surveying a bright and clean, controlled landscape.

1 With the garden in its infancy, the muscular hedge that encloses the garden is in the process of growing into its steel-framed armature.
2 The steel frame of the hedge will, in time, provide a simple and convenient clipping guide for the mature plants.
3 At night, lighting brings an extra dimension to the park. Its proximity to the city makes it a popular recreation destination.
4 A woven steel gate creates a textured surface in contrast to the dense planting.
5 A stepped water-course runs the length of the 'plate' walls, bordered by a timber boardwalk allowing access to the water.
6 Detailed view of the limestone coping.

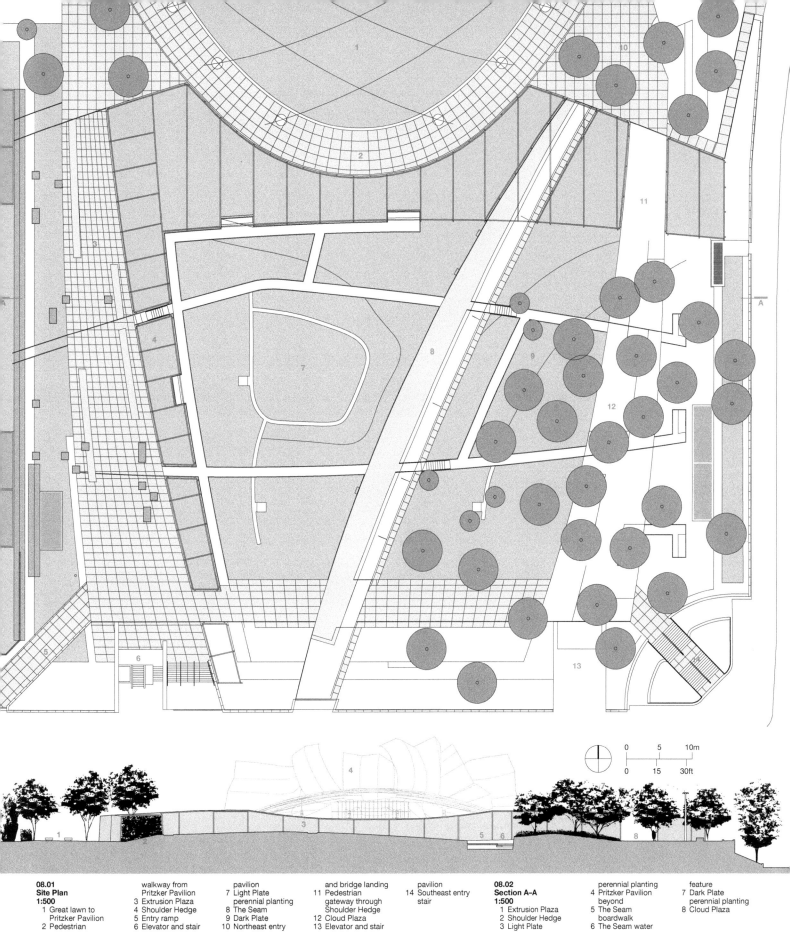

08.01
Site Plan
1:500
1 Great lawn to
   Pritzker Pavilion
2 Pedestrian

walkway from
Pritzker Pavilion
3 Extrusion Plaza
4 Shoulder Hedge
5 Entry ramp
6 Elevator and stair

pavilion
7 Light Plate
   perennial planting
8 The Seam
9 Dark Plate
10 Northeast entry

and bridge landing
11 Pedestrian
   gateway through
   Shoulder Hedge
12 Cloud Plaza
13 Elevator and stair

pavilion
14 Southeast entry
   stair

08.02
Section A–A
1:500
1 Extrusion Plaza
2 Shoulder Hedge
3 Light Plate

perennial planting
4 Pritzker Pavilion
   beyond
5 The Seam
   boardwalk
6 The Seam water

feature
7 Dark Plate
   perennial planting
8 Cloud Plaza

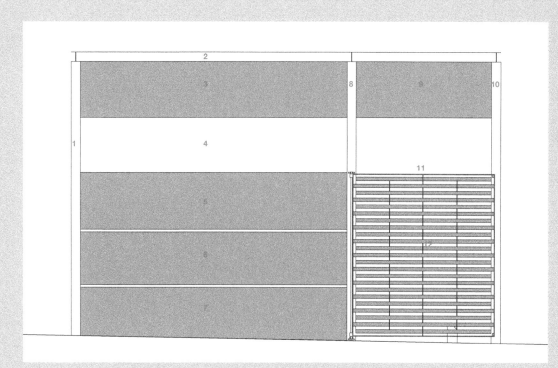

08.03
**Bronze Gate
Elevation Detail**
1:50
 1 Vertical structure of
127 x 127 mm (5 x 5
inch) steel T-section
with powdercoat finish
 2 Horizontal structure
of 127 x 127 mm (5 x 5
inch) steel T-section
with powdercoat finish
 3 812 mm (32 inch)
high bronze plate with
patinized finish bolted
to vertical armature
 4 Open section
in gate
 5 812 mm (32 inch)
high bronze plate with
patinized finish bolted
to vertical armature
 6 812 mm (32 inch)
high bronze plate with
patinized finish bolted
to vertical armature
 7 812 mm (32 inch)
high bronze plate with
patinized finish bolted
to vertical armature
 8 Vertical structure of
127 x 127 mm (5 x 5
inch) steel T-section
with powdercoat finish
 9 812 mm (32 inch)
high bronze plate with
patinized finish bolted
to vertical armature
10 Vertical structure of
127 x 127 mm (5 x 5
inch) steel T-section
with powdercoat finish
11 Bronze frame to
opening section
of gate
12 50 x 3 mm (2 x 1/8
inch) thick bronze
bands at 100 mm (4
inch) centres woven
between vertical
members of gate

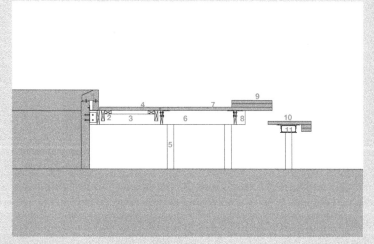

08.04
**Boardwalk Typical
Section Detail**
1:50
 1 150 x 250 mm (6 x
10 inch) limestone
coping with rough-
sawn face, mortar set
with stainless steel
dowel reinforcement
 2 Timber frame
 3 Steel deck joist
 4 914 mm (36 inch)
wide removeable
timber access panel
with steel frame flush
with boardwalk
 5 Structural steel
post
 6 Steel deck joist
 7 50 x 200 mm (2 x 8
inch) timber decking of
variable length
 8 Steel deck joist
 9 50 x 200 mm (2 x 8
inch) laminated timber
upper curb
10 50 x 200 mm (2 x 8
inch) laminated timber
decking to lower step
11 Continuous steel
tube beam

08.05
**Typical Seam Wall
Section Detail**
1:50
 1 Reinforced
concrete slab
 2 300 x 457 x 25 mm
(12 x 18 x 1 inch)
granite pavers to pool
floor
 3 Granite veneer with
rough-sawn face to
pool wall
 4 Mortar setting bed
 5 Waterproof
membrane
 6 Masonry clip
 7 15 mm (5/8 inch)
mortar joint with
12 mm (1/2 inch) rake
 8 Mankato Kasota
limestone veneer with
rough-sawn face
 9 Mankato Kasota
limestone coping with
rough-sawn sides
10 Topsoil
11 Reinforced
concrete retaining wall
12 Reinforced
concrete retaining wall
with varying finished
heights from 1520 to
2438 mm (5 to 7 feet)
13 Structural foam
filler

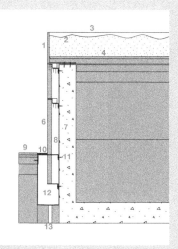

08.06
Typical Seat Wall Section Detail
1:50
  1 Bronze dam wall
  2 Water level
  3 Line of metal dam beyond
  4 300 x 457 x 25 mm (12 x 18 x 1 inch) granite pavers to pool floor
  5 Custom stainless steel water source channel
  6 300 x 457 x 25 mm (12 x 18 x 1 inch) granite pavers to pool floor
  7 Structural

reinforced concrete wall
  8 Waterproof membrane
  9 300 x 457 x 25 mm (12 x 18 x 1 inch) granite pavers to pool floor
  10 Metal grille over basin
  11 Masonry clip
  12 Stainless steel basin
  13 Water feature drainage pipe

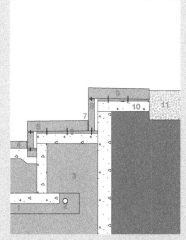

08.07
Typical Stone Seating Step Section Detail 1
1:50
  1 Crushed stone aggregate
  2 Drain cast into structural concrete footing
  3 Compacted structural fill
  4 Pre-cast concrete pavers
  5 Mankato Kasota limestone coping with saw cut finish and rough-sawn sides
  6 Masonry clip
  7 Backing rod and sealant

  8 Mankato Kasota limestone veneer with rough-sawn face, pinned to structural slab
  9 Mankato Kasota limestone coping with saw-cut finish and rough-sawn sides
  10 Reinforced concrete slab
  11 Topsoil

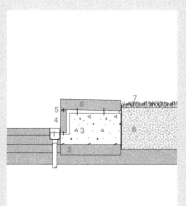

08.08
Typical Stone Step Section Detail 2
1:50
  1 Trench drain
  2 Crushed stone aggregate
  3 Structural reinforced concrete wall
  4 Mankato Kasota limestone veneer with rough-sawn face
  5 15 mm (5/8 inch) mortar joint
  6 Mankato Kasota limestone coping with saw-cut finish and rough sawn sides
  7 Turf or planting bed

  8 Topsoil

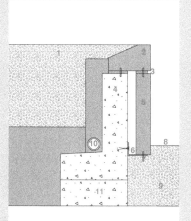

08.09
Typical Stone Wall Section Detail
1:20
  1 Topsoil
  2 150 x 250 mm (6 x 10 inch) Mankato Kasota limestone coping with rough-sawn face, mortar set with stainless steel dowel reinforcement
  3 Mortar joint
  4 Reinforced concrete retaining wall
  5 Mankato Kasota limestone veneer with rough-sawn face
  6 Stainless steel stone anchor bracket

  7 Stainless steel dowel
  8 Finished grade
  9 Topsoil
  10 Drain cast into structural concrete footing
  11 Reinforced concrete footing

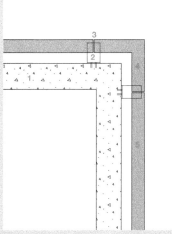

08.10
Typical Stone Wall Corner Section Detail
1:20
  1 Reinforced concrete wall
  2 Masonry clip
  3 Mortar joint
  4 Hooked Mankato Kasota limestone veneer cut to wrap corner
  5 Mankato Kasota limestone veneer with rough-sawn face

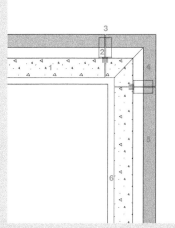

08.11
Typical Stone Wall Plan Detail
1:20
  1 Reinforced concrete wall
  2 Masonry clip
  3 Mortar joint
  4 Hooked Mankato Kasota limestone veneer cut to wrap corner
  5 Mankato Kasota limestone veneer with rough-sawn face
  6 Overlapped coping stone

**Enric Miralles i Benedetta
Tagliabue, EMBT**

**Diagonal Mar Park
Barcelona, Spain**

Client
Diagonal Mar/HINES

Area
14 hectares (34.6 acres)

Project Team
Elena Rocchi, Lluis Cantallops, Fabián
Asunción

Landscape Architects
Enric Miralles i Benedetta Tagliabue,
EMBT + Edaw, London

Engineers
Europroject Consultores Asociados

In the lead-up to the Olympic Games
in 1992, massive investment and
development served to reconnect
Barcelona to the coast – previously
used almost entirely for heavy
industry. Following the Olympics, the
Mediterranean coast continued to
be rehabilitated, and by 1996 Diagonal
Mar was one of the last brownfield
sites to be developed. Including
housing, a convention centre, offices
and retail, the 86-hectare (212-acre)
development is organized around this
park. The brief stated that the park
was to recapture the site's natural
attributes, transforming it into an area
of great scenic, recreational and
cultural value.

The park is designed as a gateway
between the city and the sea. In plan it
symbolizes a tree that was born from
the sea, branching out into an open
hand. Rather than using trees for
shade, vast networks of winding steel
pipes criss-crossed by wire cables
and huge tiled flowerpots, many of
which are suspended in mid-air,
support a growing fabric of vines.
Emphasizing water, the park includes
lakes, a waterfall and fountains.
Wetland plantings filter the water, and
carp help to reduce algae. Three areas
are specifically designed with children
in mind. The play area closest to the
sea is for children under six years old.
A second area, known as Magic
Mountain, includes slides built into the
side of a hill. The third, for older
children, includes basketball courts
and an amphitheatre for
neighbourhood events.

1 The park is
characterized by the
spiralling coils of steel
pipe that meander
through the site,
connecting a series of
waterways, fountains,
play areas and paths.
Areas of ceramic tile
paving bring detail and
focus to the pathways
and seating areas.

2 The park is
surrounded by the
Diagonal Mar
development,
consisting of housing,
a conference centre,
retail and offices, the
centrepiece of which is
the park. Lakes are
supplied not from town
water but from water
collected directly from

the high water table
in an underground
reservoir.
3 Areas of shallow
water are available for
paddling, and reeds
filter the water,
reducing reliance on
mechanical filtering
devices.
4 Smooth concrete
mounds for climbing

and playing on are
etched with the shapes
of sea creatures.
Behind, gabion walls
create the edges to
raised areas formed by
using spoil from
surrounding
construction sites.

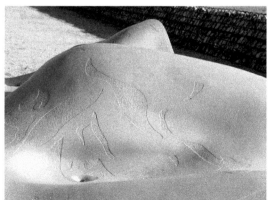

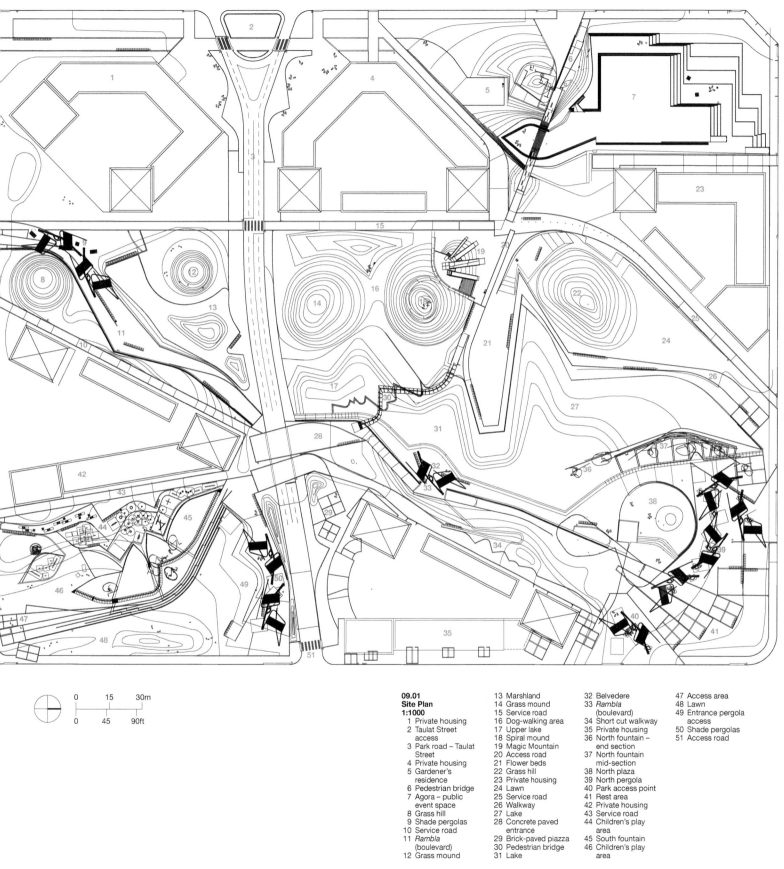

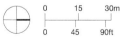

09.01
Site Plan
1:1000

1 Private housing	13 Marshland	32 Belvedere	47 Access area
2 Taulat Street access	14 Grass mound	33 *Rambla* (boulevard)	48 Lawn
3 Park road – Taulat Street	15 Service road	34 Short cut walkway	49 Entrance pergola access
4 Private housing	16 Dog-walking area	35 Private housing	50 Shade pergolas
5 Gardener's residence	17 Upper lake	36 North fountain – end section	51 Access road
6 Pedestrian bridge	18 Spiral mound	37 North fountain mid-section	
7 Agora – public event space	19 Magic Mountain	38 North plaza	
8 Grass hill	20 Access road	39 North pergola	
9 Shade pergolas	21 Flower beds	40 Park access point	
10 Service road	22 Grass hill	41 Rest area	
11 *Rambla* (boulevard)	23 Private housing	42 Private housing	
12 Grass mound	24 Lawn	43 Service road	
	25 Service road	44 Children's play area	
	26 Walkway	45 South fountain	
	27 Lake	46 Children's play area	
	28 Concrete paved entrance		
	29 Brick-paved piazza		
	30 Pedestrian bridge		
	31 Lake		

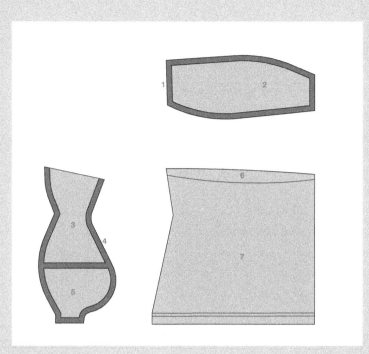

 1 Tubular water
spray nozzles
 2 Concrete bulkhead
 3 Tubular water spray
nozzles
 4 Handrail
 5 Belvedere
 6 Fountain basin
 7 Water spray jet
 8 Bird-shaped metal
tube fountain structure
and water conduit
 9 Tubular water spray
nozzles
10 Tubular water spray
nozzles
11 Bird-shaped
sculptural form
12 Bird-shaped
sculptural form
13 Tubular water spray
nozzles

09.02
Concrete Flowerpot
Details
1:50
 1 Glazed reinforced
concrete shell
 2 Soil reservoir
 3 Soil reservoir
 4 Glazed reinforced
concrete shell
 5 Void below soil
reservoir
 6 Top opening to pot
 7 Glazed reinforced
concrete shell
structure finished with
ceramic tiles

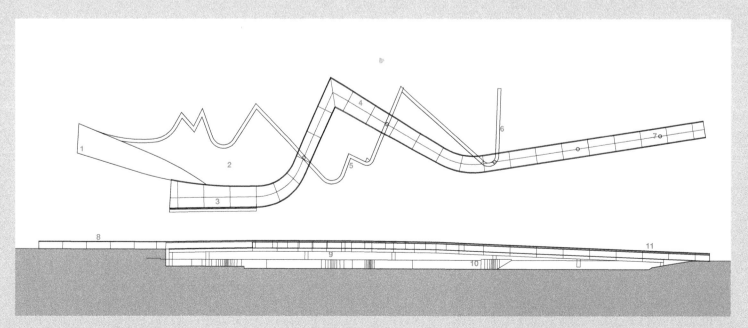

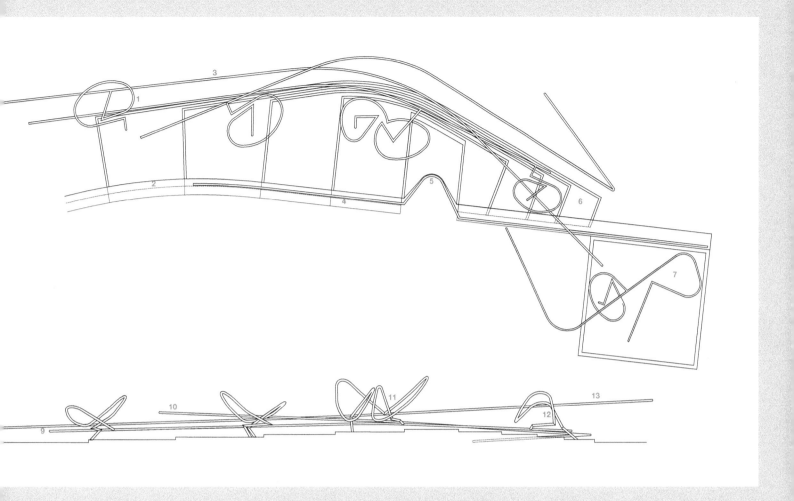

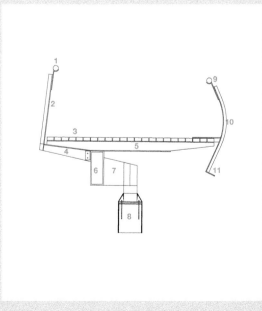

09.04
Bridge
Plan and Elevation
1:500
1 Earth bank
2 Lower lake
3 Concrete perimeter wall
4 Steel and timber bridge
5 Cascade wall from precast concrete panels
6 Precast concrete panels
7 Structural concrete column
8 80 mm (3^1/$_8$ inch) circular timber handrail
9 Steel beam
10 Structural steel column
11 80 mm (3^1/$_8$ inch) circular timber handrail

09.05
Bridge Cross Section
1:50
1 80 mm (3^1/$_8$ inch) circular timber handrail
2 1000 x 120 x 10 mm (39^1/$_8$ x 4^3/$_4$ x ^{2}/$_5$ inch) timber balustrade panels from pine, screw-fixed to steel structure
3 Timber deck
4 Secondary steel beam
5 Steel beam
6 Steel box beam
7 Steel structure
8 Reinforced concrete column
9 80 mm (3^1/$_8$ inch) circular timber handrail
10 1000 x 120 x 10 mm (39^1/$_8$ x 4^3/$_4$ x ^{2}/$_5$ inch) timber balustrade panels from pine, screw-fixed to steel structure
11 Steel lip to end of balustrade

**Noel Harding Studio, Neil Hadley,
Landscape Architect**

**The Elevated Wetlands
Toronto, Ontario, Canada**

Client
Canadian Plastics Industry
Association and The City of Toronto

Area
0.44 hectares (1 acre)

Project Team
Noel Harding, Neil Hadley, Al Mattes,
David Acheson, Ian Lazarus, Peter
North, David Toledano, Guy Walter,
Eric Aurandt, Eric Fehlberg, Suzanne
Meyer, Nick Scali

The Elevated Wetlands is bisected by
a major freeway and adjacent to a
polluted urban river. The project
appears to grow out of the earth, with
its animal-like forms sprouting
vegetation, and a constructed wetland
at its base. The sculptures, consisting
of six giant polystyrene containers,
utilize recycled plastics as a
hydroponic soil matrix (plastic bottles,
waste auto plastics, shredded
consumer plastics) to maintain plant
life. Water from the polluted Don River
is pumped via solar voltaic systems
into ponds, then directed into a
continuous cascade through the
containers. The cleansed water
eventually finds its way back to the
river and on to Lake Ontario.

The containers and ponds sustain
indigenous plants that target the
toxins in the river so that water returns
to the river significantly cleansed. The
planting of the elevated containers
and the constructed wetlands at their
base uses only native plants from the
Don Valley ecosystem, and is a
symbolic representation of the local
plant communities, including alpine
forest, alpine meadow, mixed forest,
mixed lowland forest, cedar and
shrub swamp, prairie meadow edge,
short grass prairie, and bog. The
wetlands at the base of the sculptures
mimic natural wetlands, including
upper shoreline, lower shoreline and
emergent plant associations, and
provide habitat to native species
including waterfowl, frogs, turtles
and mammals. The Elevated Wetlands
has established itself with ducks,
frogs, herons and an abundance of
wild flowers. The City of Toronto
has identified and designated the site
as one of seven green tourism
locations.

1 This most eye-catching of landscapes features giant polystyrene containers that are reminiscent of elephants or perhaps rhinoceros.
2+3 The wetlands are bisected by the Don Valley Parkway, from where they are viewed by tens of thousands of motorists daily, and enjoyed by cyclists and joggers using the regional trail system cutting through the site.
4+5 Commissioned by the Canadian Plastics Industry Association, the work draws attention to the importance of wetland ecosystems with plastic as an environmental benefit.

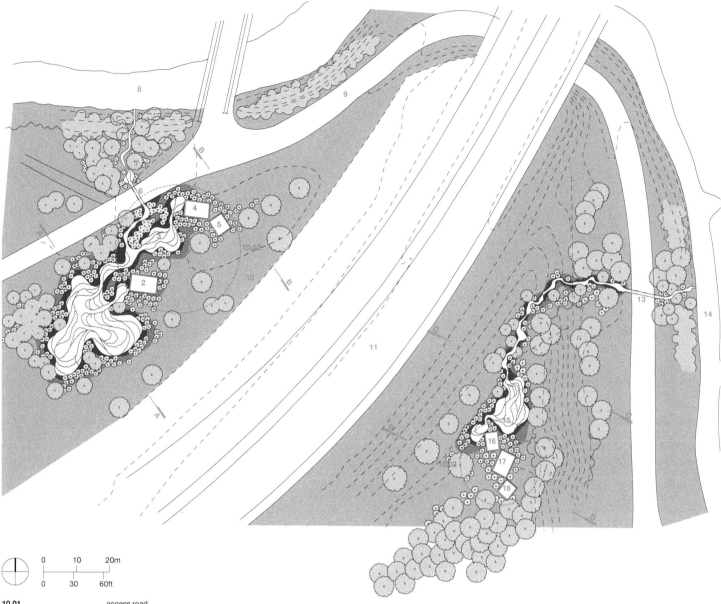

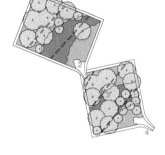

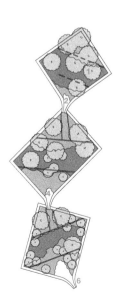

10.01
Site Plan
1:1000
1 Ground level wetland, lower pool
2 Elevated Wetland, container B
3 Ground level wetland, upper pool
4 Elevated Wetland, lower container C
5 Elevated Wetland, upper container C
6 Culvert under access road
7 Rivulet connection from wetland to Don River
8 Don River
9 Taylor Creek Park

10 Proposed meadow planting at Don Valley Parkway cloverleaf intersection
11 Don Valley Parkway
12 Rivulet connection from Wetland to Taylor creek
13 Culvert under access road
14 Taylor Creek
15 Ground level wetland pool
16 Elevated Wetland, lower container A
17 Elevated Wetland, middle container A
18 Elevated Wetland, upper container A

10.02
Planting Site B + C
Scale 1:50
1 Site C – mixed forest shrub edge, shrub grassland and swamp native planting
2 Sculpture spout overflow to lower container
3 Site C – mixed lowland forest shrub edge, grassland and cedar shrub swamp native planting
4 Sculpture spout overflow to ground level wetland
5 Site B – mixed forest shrub edge, short grass prairie and bog native planting
6 Sculpture spout overflow to ground level wetland

10.03
Planting Site A
Scale 1:50
1 Alpine forest, alpine meadow and alpine marsh native plantings
2 Sculpture spout overflow to middle container
3 Mixed woodland, prairie meadow edge and bog native planting
4 Sculpture spout overflow to lower container
5 Mixed lowland forest, short grass prairie and bog native planting
6 Sculpture spout overflow to ground level wetland

10.04
Planting Detail
Section A–A
Scale 1:100
 1 Culvert under Taylor Creek access road
 2 Catchment area
 3 Wet meadow
 4 Emergent vegetation
 5 Open water
 6 Submergent and emergent vegetation
 7 Wet meadow with short and tall grass prairie
 8 Shrub edge
 9 Existing tree

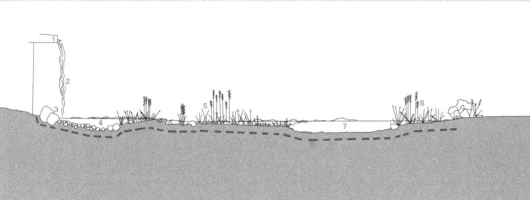

10.05
Planting Detail
Section B–B
Scale 1:100
 1 Sculpture spout
 2 Water from sculpture spout
 3 Large, randomly placed limestone boulders
 4 Open water
 5 Rapids and pools with emergent vegetation
 6 Geomembrane liner with an average depth of 450 mm (17³/₄ inch)
 7 Submergent vegetation and open water
 8 Emergent vegetation and wet meadow

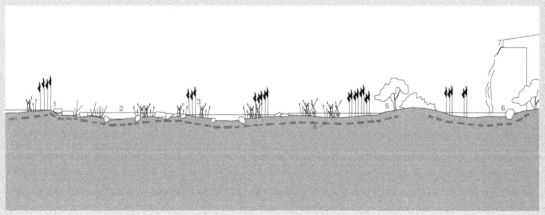

10.06
Planting Detail
Section C–C
Scale 1:100
 1 Open water with submergent and emergent native plant species
 2 Rapids and pools with emergent plant species
 3 Open water with emergent plant species
 4 Geomembrane liner with an average depth of 450 mm (17³/₄ inch)
 5 Wet meadow
 6 100 – 200 mm (4 – 8 inch) riverstones at a depth of 200mm (8 inches)
 7 Sculpture spout

10.07
Planting Detail
Section D–D
Scale 1:100
 1 Riverstone wetland bottom at sculpture outflow
 2 Wet meadow with randomly placed boulders at edge
 3 Open water
 4 Geomembrane liner with an average depth of 450 mm (17³/₄ inch)
 5 Submergent and emergent vegetation
 6 Shrub edge and existing forest edge

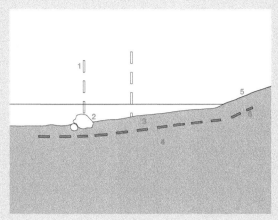

10.08
Detail Section at Wetland Planting
Scale 1:50
1 Native submergent species planted 300–500 mm (11⅘–19¾ inches) deep
2 Limestone boulder edge adjacent to open water and submergent vegetation
3 Pea, gravel and sand mix
4 Growing medium and topsoil mix
5 Native emergent species planted at 0–300 mm (0–11⅘ inches) deep
6 450 mm (17¾ inch) thick geomembrane liner

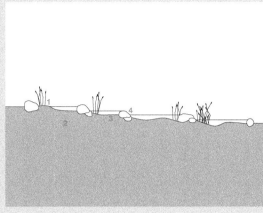

10.09
Planting Detail Section at Rivulet
Scale 1:50
1 Pools with native emergent plantings
2 Existing native soil
3 Geomembrane liner with an average depth of 450 mm (17¾ inch)
4 Limestone ledgerock rapids at random placement in steeper portions of rivulet

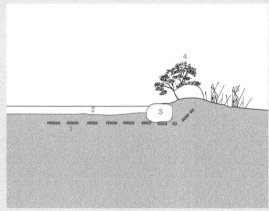

10.10
Limestone Ledgerock at Wetland Edge Detail
Scale 1:50
1 Geomembrane liner with an average depth of 450 mm (17¾ inch)
2 Open water
3 Randomly placed boulder edge
4 Shrub edge
5 Meadow

10.11
Limestone Ledgerock at Sloped Planting Detail
Scale 1:50
1 Geomembrane liner with an average depth of 450 mm (17¾ inch)
2 Emergent vegetation
3 Wet meadow
4 Large, randomly placed limestone boulders
5 Shrub edge

10.12
Sculptural Planter System Section Detail
1 Solar panel for irrigation attached to container
2 Native plantings in containers
3 Shredded automobile tires
4 Recycled plastic pellets
5 Automobile fluff (shredded plastics)
6 Plastic soda bottles
7 Sculpture spout overflows
8 Geomembrane liner
9 Water fall – outflow from containers
10 Irrigation supply line
11 Solar pump for irrigation
12 Native wetland pool
13 Native planting – emergent and submergent species
14 Rivulet connection from wetland to Don River
15 Irrigation water source – polluted Don River water

11
Schweingruber Zulauf
Landschaftsarchitekten

Oerliker Park
Zurich, Switzerland

Client
Municipal Department of Gardens and
Agriculture, Zurich

Area
2 hectares (5 acres)

Project Team
Christoph Haerle, Sabina Hubacher

Oerlikon has been one of
Switzerland's most important
industrial centres since the nineteenth
century. However, by the 1980s, the
old machine-based industries were
disappearing. Since then, a new
mixed-use district has started to
emerge on a massive 29-hectare
(72-acre) site, including around 2.4
hectares (6 acres) of open space, of
which Oerliker Park is part. At the
outset, the site posed serious
challenges, not least of which was the
high level of contamination of the
subsoil, meaning that the entire space
had to be covered in asphalt to seal it
off, so the park has been designed
as if it were sitting on a tray of topsoil.
In addition, the Oerliker district was
planned to grow and expand over
several decades, so it was decided to
develop a very simple design concept
that would fit the level of inhabitation
at every stage.

This concept involved the planting
of 800 young trees in a grid that would
eventually grow into a great green
hall. The dominant species of ash
saplings, sourced from nurseries all
over Switzerland, as well as The
Netherlands, Italy and Germany, are
supplemented by sweet gum trees,
river birch, wild cherry and princess
trees to provide a range of blossom
highlights. A series of striking
concrete elements are embedded
in the growing park – a red pavilion,
a green fountain table and a blue
viewing tower that serves as a lookout
over the trees and surrounding urban
landscape. Forestry methods will
be used to thin out the dense stand of
trees gradually until the year 2025,
when the grid of trees, competing for
light and growing taller each year,
will eventually form the intended hall,
with columnar narrow trunks and a
roof of leafy green.

1 In front of the red
pavilion, a timber deck
offers an alternative
ground surface as well
as forming a visual link
between the eastern
and western parts of
the park.
2 The eastern half of
the park (bottom) is
characterized by a
carpet of turf, in
contrast to the western
half (top), which
features hard surfaces.
A red steel folly is
available for visitors to
inhabit and utilize as
they wish.
3 Each of the 800
young ash saplings
are held in place by
numbered marker
poles.
4 The 33-metre (108-
foot) high viewing
tower with its steel
spiral staircase makes
it possible to climb up
through what will be a
leafy canopy for
spectacular views over
the rooftops of
northern Zurich.

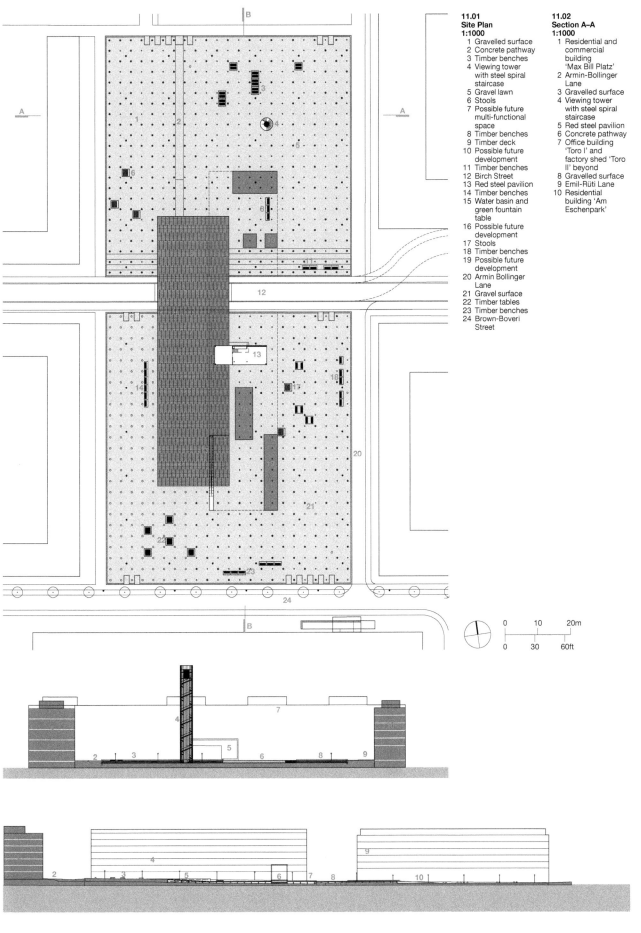

11.01
Site Plan
1:1000
1 Gravelled surface
2 Concrete pathway
3 Timber benches
4 Viewing tower
 with steel spiral
 staircase
5 Gravel lawn
6 Stools
7 Possible future
 multi-functional
 space
8 Timber benches
9 Timber deck
10 Possible future
 development
11 Timber benches
12 Birch Street
13 Red steel pavilion
14 Timber benches
15 Water basin and
 green fountain
 table
16 Possible future
 development
17 Stools
18 Timber benches
19 Possible future
 development
20 Armin Bollinger
 Lane
21 Gravel surface
22 Timber tables
23 Timber benches
24 Brown-Boveri
 Street

11.02
Section A–A
1:1000
1 Residential and
 commercial
 building
 'Max Bill Platz'
2 Armin-Bollinger
 Lane
3 Gravelled surface
4 Viewing tower
 with steel spiral
 staircase
5 Red steel pavilion
6 Concrete pathway
7 Office building
 'Toro I' and
 factory shed 'Toro
 II' beyond
8 Gravelled surface
9 Emil-Rüti Lane
10 Residential
 building 'Am
 Eschenpark'

11.03
Section B–B
1:1000
1 Office building
 'Toro I' and factory
 shed 'Toro II'
2 Brown-Boveri
 Street
3 Gravelled surface
4 Residential
 building 'Am Park'
5 Relaxation zone
 with timber
 benches
6 Red steel pavilion
7 Birch Street
8 Gravelled surface
9 Residential
 building 'Am
 Eschenpark'
10 Concrete ramps

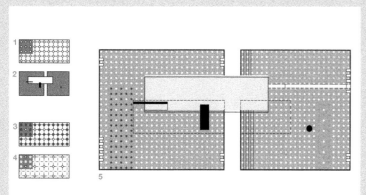

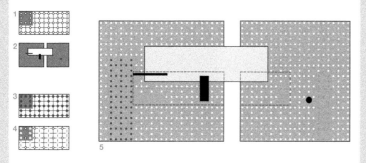

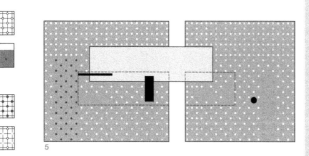

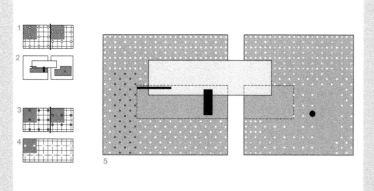

11.04
Planting Scheme
2000–2005
 1 Planting of young ash trees 3-4 metres (9–13 feet) high in 4 metre (13 feet) grid
 2 Planting zone
 3 Supplementary species A
 4 Supplementary species B
 5 Thinned out supplementary species field

11.05
Planting Scheme
2005–2015
 1 First thinning out of trees across the site
 2 Planting zone
 3 Supplementary species A
 4 Supplementary species B
 5 Further thinning out of trees

11.06
Planting Scheme
2015–2025
 1 Optional second thinning out of trees
 2 Planting zone
 3 Supplementary species A
 4 Supplementary species B
 5 Further thinning out of trees

11.07
Planting Scheme
2025 onwards
 1 Optional third thinning out of trees
 2 Planting zone
 3 Supplementary species A
 4 Supplementary species B
 5 Further thinning out of trees

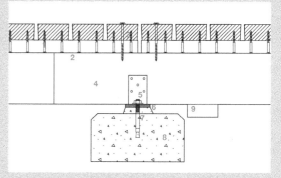

11.08
Timber Deck Beam
Detail 1
1:10
 1 50 x 100 mm (2 x 4 inch) Douglas fir floor decking
 2 40 x 80 mm (1³/5 x 3¹/8 inch) Douglas fir bracing
 3 Stainless steel floor

plank anchor
 4 100 x 200 mm (4 x 8 inch) timber beam
 5 60 mm (2¹/3 inch) flat steel angle joist bearing
 6 10 mm (²/5 inch) flat steel in mortar bed anchorage
 7 High-tension anchor bolt

 8 Reinforced concrete strip foundation
 9 Bracing element

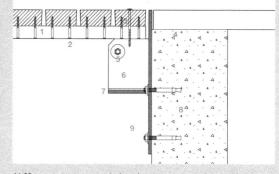

11.09
Timber Deck Beam
Detail 2
1:10
 1 50 x 100 mm (2 x 4 inch) Douglas fir floor decking
 2 40 x 80 mm (1³/5 x 3¹/8 inch) Douglas fir bracing
 3 Stainless steel floor

plank anchor
 4 Birch Street
 5 16 mm (³/5 inch) drilled hole in steel
 6 130 x 160 mm (5¹/10 x 6³/10 inch) steel web plate with bearing plate
 7 5 mm (¹/5 inch) weld line
 8 Reinforced

concrete strip foundation
 9 High-tension anchor bolt

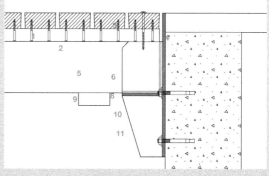

11.10
Timber Deck Beam
Detail 3
1:10
 1 50 x 100 mm (2 x 4 inch) Douglas fir floor decking
 2 40 x 80 mm (1³/5 x 3¹/8 inch) Douglas fir bracing
 3 Stainless steel floor

plank anchor
 4 Birch Street
 5 100 x 200 mm (4 x 8 inch) timber beam
 6 130 x 160 mm (5¹/10 x 6³/10 inch) steel web plate with 120 x 90 mm (4³/4 x 3¹/2 inch) bearing plate
 7 Reinforced concrete strip

foundation
 8 5 mm (¹/5 inch) weld line
 9 Bracing element
 10 Steel bearing plate
 11 High-tension anchor bolt

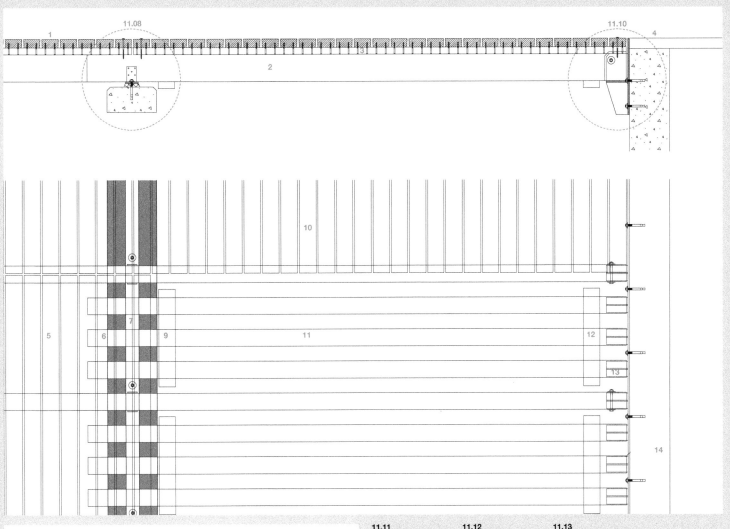

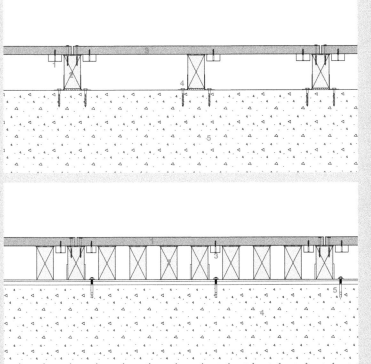

11.11
Timber Deck Section and Plan
1:20
  1 50 x 100 mm (2 x 4 inch) Douglas fir floor decking
  2 100 x 200 mm (4 x 8 inch) timber beam
  3 40 x 80 mm ($1^3/5$ x $3^1/8$ inch) Douglas fir bracing
  4 Birch Street
  5 50 x 100 mm (2 x 4 inch) Douglas fir floor decking
  6 100 x 200 mm (4 x 8 inch) timber beam
  7 60 mm ($2^1/3$ inch) flat steel angle joist bearing
  8 Reinforced concrete strip foundation
  9 Bracing element
10 Normal grating
11 Sidewalk grating
12 Bracing element
13 Steel web plate with bearing plate
14 Birch Street

11.12
Longitudinal Section Through Grating
1:20
  1 40 x 80 mm ($1^3/5$ x $3^1/8$ inch) Douglas fir bracing
  2 100 x 200 mm (4 x 8 inch) timber beam
  3 50 x 100 mm (2 x 4 inch) Douglas fir floor decking
  4 High-tension anchor bolt
  5 Reinforced concrete strip foundation

11.13
Longitudinal Section Through Grating Sidewalk
1:20
  1 50 x 100 mm (2 x 4 inch) Douglas fir floor decking
  2 100 x 200 mm (4 x 8 inch) timber beam
  3 40 x 80 mm ($1^3/5$ x $3^1/8$ inch) Douglas fir bracing
  4 Reinforced concrete strip foundation
  5 High-tension anchor bolt

12
SWECO FFNS Architects

Dania Park
Malmö, Sweden

Client
City of Malmö

Area
2 hectares (5 acres)

Project Team
Thorbjörn Andersson, PeGe Hillinge, Veronika Borg, Peter Ekroth, Clotte Frank, Sven Hedlund, Kenneth Hilldén, Anders Lidström

Structural Engineer
VBB, Lennart Knutsson

Main Contractor
Skanska

The Dania Park is located along the shoreline of the Öresund Sound that divides Sweden and Denmark. The original site was landfill – an industrial desert of contaminated mud. While discernible departure points for the design were difficult to establish at the outset, qualities such as the light, the horizon, long views and the sea informed the approach. The immense scale of the coastal landscape contrasts with developments in the city nearby.

The principal features of the park are the 'Scouts' – three tilted concrete planes that penetrate the boulder lining and allow access to the sea. A 40 by 40 metre (131-foot) flat table called the 'Bastion' is elevated above the sea, leaving visitors totally exposed to the elements. In addition, the 'Balconies' – three wooden boxes – overlook the vast, slightly sunken grass meadow, called the 'Lawn'. This activity field is protected from the elements by a double row of trees and low, salt-resistant shrubs. The park is, to a great extent, about social activity and is comprised of spaces of different sizes and qualities which address the various forms of park life. The spaces range from the smallest within the 'Scouts', which accommodate 10 to 15 people, to the multi-use lawn, which provides space for several thousand people. In the multicultural city of Malmö, on sunny days the park is inhabited by thousands of users.

1 A view from one of the 'Scouts' towards the 'Bastion', which allows visitors to the park to stand directly over the sea.
2 The inclined façades of the 'Bastion', clad in rough timber, are a popular place to enjoy the water.
3 The park includes many opportunities to sit and contemplate the maritime landscape, including beds of coastal shrubs and flowering plants.
4 Robust detailing of smaller scale elements, including benches and ground surface treatments, complement the industrial scale of the park components.
5 View from the 'Meadow' where three timber shingle-clad platforms (the 'Balconies') stand sentinel.

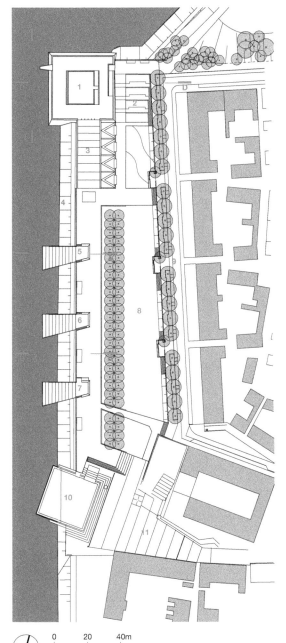

12.01
Site Plan
1:2000
1 The Bastion
2 Perennial terraces
3 Large granite ramp
4 Wave breaker from a lining of natural boulders from previous beach
5 The Scouts jetty 1
6 The Scouts jetty 2
7 The Scouts jetty 3
8 The Meadow
9 The Balconies
10 The Sea Plaza
11 Granite-surfaced entrance walkway

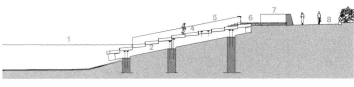

12.02
Scout Section A–A
1:500
1 Sea level
2 Reinforced concrete foundation
3 Concrete anchor foundation
4 Concrete stair with

sloped treads
5 Concrete parapet
6 Granite slab walkway
7 Granite block stone wall
8 Gravel shore promenade

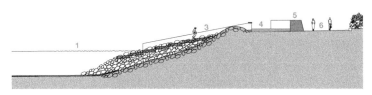

12.03
Scout Section B–B
1:500
1 Sea level
2 Wave breaker from a lining of natural boulders from previous beach
3 Concrete parapet
4 Granite slab

walkway
5 Granite block stone wall
6 Gravel shore promenade

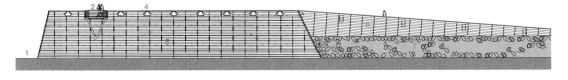

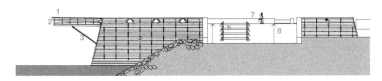

12.04
Bastion Section C–C
1:500
1 Sea level
2 Outpost Bridge
3 Supporting steel structure to Outpost Bridge
4 Lighting armature
5 Inclined tar-treated pine timber planks with stainless steel dividers at regular intervals
6 Vertical timber-clad wall to ramp
7 Wave breaker from natural boulders

12.05
Bastion Section D–D
1:500
1 Outpost Bridge
2 Stainless steel balustrade to Outpost Bridge
3 Supporting steel structure to Outpost Bridge
4 Inclined tar-treated pine timber planks with stainless steel dividers at regular intervals
5 Wave breaker from natural boulders
6 Massive larch timber benches
7 Bastion plateau
8 Ramp from pre-cast concrete flagstones ascending to the upper level
9 Inclined tar-treated pine timber planks with stainless steel dividers at regular intervals

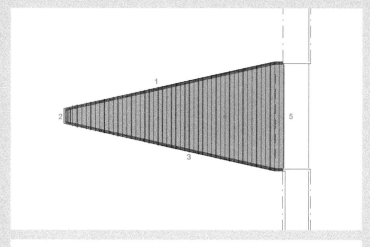

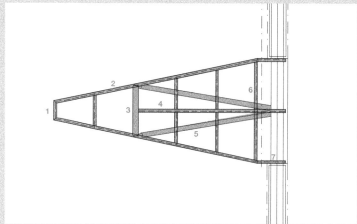

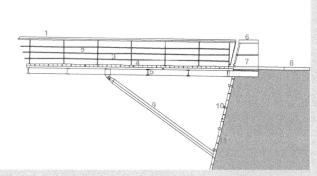

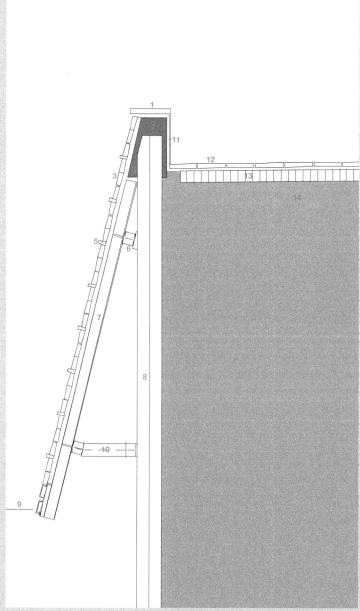

12.06
Outpost Bridge
Plan Detail
1:100
  1 Type A railing
consisting of 1200 mm
(4 feet) long straight
steel sections
  2 Type B railing
consisting of 1200 x
650 x 1200 mm
(4 x 2 x 4 feet)
U-shaped steel
sections
  3 Type C railing
consisting of 1064 x
274 mm (3¹/₂ feet x
10³/₄ inch)) diagonal
steel sections
  4 Bridge surface from
azobé timber
  5 Concrete tiles

12.07
Outpost Bridge
Structure Plan Detail
1:100
  1 100 x 200 mm
(4 x 8 inch) secondary
steel cross T-beam
  2 100 x 200 mm
(4 x 8 inch) primary
steel T-girder
  3 200 x 200 mm
(8 x 8 inch) primary
steel cross T-beam
with truss joint
  4 100 x 200 mm
(4 x 8 inch) steel
T-stringer / secondary
girder
  5 150 mm (6 inch)
diameter steel truss
  6 100 x 200 mm
(4 x 8 inch) secondary
steel cross T-beam
  7 Concrete wall
abutment

12.08
Outpost Bridge
Section Detail
1:100
  1 Teak handrail
  2 Horizontal steel
balustrade
  3 Hardwood azobé
planks to bridge
surface
  4 Vertical steel
balusters
  5 Steel beam to
Outpost Bridge
  6 Granite parapet cap
to top of wall
  7 Interior wall clad
with granite slabs
  8 Pre-cast granite
flagstones
  9 Structural steel
truss to Outpost
Bridge
  10 Stainless steel
dividers to inclined
wall of tar-treated
timber planks
  11 Tar-treated timber
planks

12.09
Bastion Parapet
Detail
1:20
  1 Granite parapet
cap
  2 Cement render
finish
  3 Tar-treated timber
planks
  4 Cement render
finish
  5 Stainless
steel dividers
  6 Stainless
steel support
  7 Steel mounting
rail for timber cladding
  8 Concrete
supporting wall
  9 Sea level
  10 Steel supporting
arm
  11 Interior wall clad
with granite slabs
  12 Pre-cast concrete
pavers
  13 Load-bearing
surface on sand layer
  14 Gravel filling with
drainage cavities

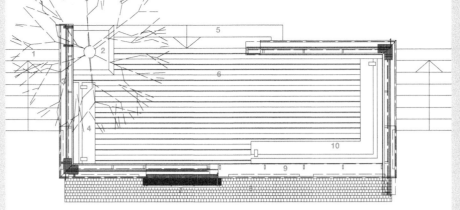

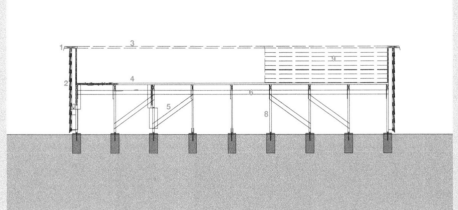
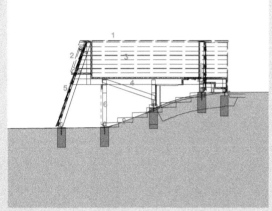

12.10
Balcony Plan Detail
1:100
 1 Solid granite steps with rough vertical and smooth horizontal surfaces
 2 Planting bed for hawthorn tree
 3 Teak wall cladding
 4 Solid teak bench
 5 Solid granite steps
 6 Timber decking
 7 Stainless steel mesh balustrade
 8 Inclined panel of tar-treated larch shingles
 9 Tubular light fixtures under wall capping
 10 Solid teak corner bench

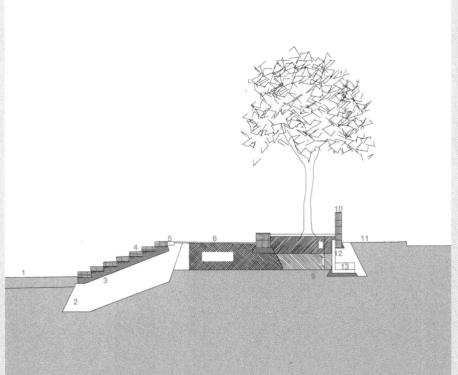

12.11
Balcony Structure Detail 1
1:100
 1 Teak wall capping
 2 Vertical panel of tar-treated larch shingles
 3 Line of stainless steel mesh balustrade
 4 Timber decking
 5 Timber truss
 6 Timber beam
 7 Concrete anchor foundation with U-shaped connector
 8 Timber column
 9 Inclined panel of tar-treated larch shingles

12.12
Balcony Structure Detail 2
1:100
 1 Teak wall capping
 2 Stainless steel mesh balustrade
 3 Vertical panel of tar-treated larch shingles
 4 Timber truss
 5 Inclined panel of tar-treated larch shingles
 6 Timber column
 7 Concrete anchor foundation with U-shaped connector
 8 Solid granite steps with rough vertical and smooth horizontal surfaces

12.13
Balcony Stair Detail
1:100
 1 Lawn over topsoil
 2 Load-bearing material packed below to frost-free depth
 3 Soil
 4 Solid granite steps with rough vertical and smooth horizontal surfaces
 5 Strip of tactile finished flagstones
 6 Gravel surface to upper promenade level
 7 Crushed stone filling
 8 Edge to tree planting area (*Querqus palustris*) of zig-zag granite blocks with rough vertical surfaces
 9 Existing sub-grade fill
 10 Granite block wall
 11 Street pavement of pre-cast concrete pavers
 12 Concrete foundation for granite wall
 13 Load-bearing fill

Northside Park
Denver, Colorado, USA

Client
City and County of Denver,
Department of Parks and Recreation

Area
5.3 hectares (13 acres)

Architecture and Structure
Stabilization
Semple Brown Design

Civil Engineering and Surveying
J. F. Sato and Associates

The Northside Park site originally contained the vandalized and graffiti-covered remains of Denver's outdated sewage treatment plant. Completely removing the plant was cost-prohibitive, so the challenge was to leave as many elements in place while creating a neighbourhood park. Elements of the structure were removed or modified to function within the park's new programme. Grading and drainage were alternately manipulated to conceal and reveal the structure and to further define park spaces. The park has galvanized neighbourhood support, and has provided a vehicle for directing funding to an area of need in the city.

Northside is also one of the final pieces of the city's 'Greening of the Platte' initiative, aimed at reclaiming the South Platte River as an open space corridor. Northside Park is a successful and sensitive example of how to carve park space from derelict industrial areas in older cities, which would otherwise lack land for recreational amenities. Nearly 27,500 metres (30,000 yards) of the plant's concrete were crushed and used as fill, and a wildlife viewing area was created from recycled concrete. This reuse strategy helped to achieve a 30 per cent reduction in demolition costs. The park draws on, but also significantly extends, earlier precedents in adaptive reuse, setting a precedent of its own, both in effecting a transformation of this scale and in solving the problems related to making it a completely functional part of the city's parks and recreation system.

1 The remnants of the treatment plant make an unexpected and spectacular new park environment. The '0 1 0 0' structures in the foreground make a memorable and iconic supergraphic suitable for the public image of the park.
2 The Northside Park site in its derelict state before rehabilitation.
3 The seemingly random forms of the retained concrete structures make perfect seating and climbing apparatus, and a foil to the soft planes of grass.
4 Detail view of the 'supergraphic' concrete structures that are located on one of the parks' main pathway thoroughfares.

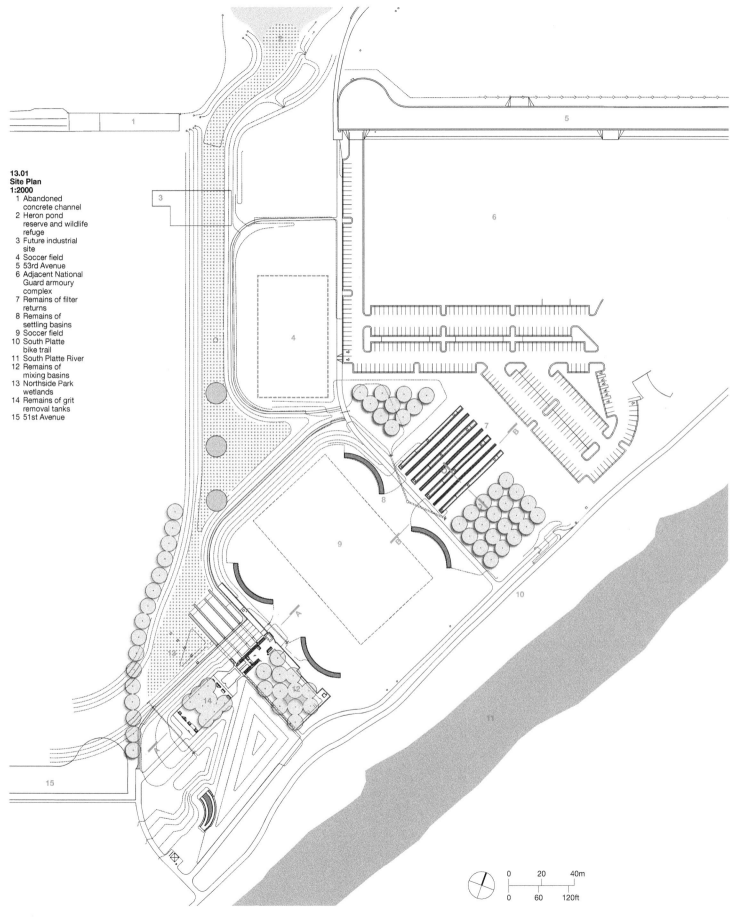

13.01
Site Plan
1:2000

1 Abandoned concrete channel
2 Heron pond reserve and wildlife refuge
3 Future industrial site
4 Soccer field
5 53rd Avenue
6 Adjacent National Guard armoury complex
7 Remains of filter returns
8 Remains of settling basins
9 Soccer field
10 South Platte bike trail
11 South Platte River
12 Remains of mixing basins
13 Northside Park wetlands
14 Remains of grit removal tanks
15 51st Avenue

0   20   40m
0   60   120ft

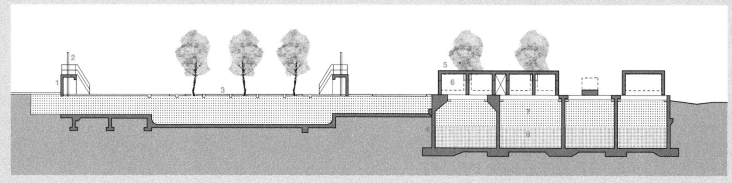

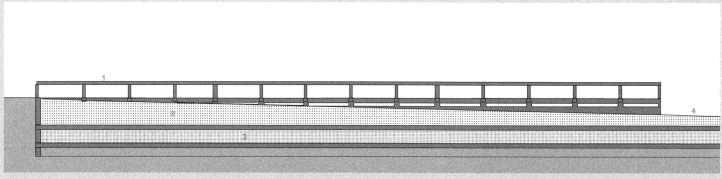

13.02
Section A–A Through
Grit Chambers and
Mixing Basins
1:200
 1 Remaining grit
chamber
superstructure
 2 Removed grit

chamber
superstructure
 3 Tree planting in grit
chamber openings
 4 Grit chamber and
mixing basin walls,
below grade
 5 Remaining mixing
basin superstructure

 6 Removed mixing
basin superstructure
 7 Soil backfill
 8 Demolition rubble

13.03
Section B–B Through
Filter Return
1:200
 1 Remaining
filter returns
 2 Fill under
filter returns
 3 Filter return

foundation below
grade
 4 Finished grade

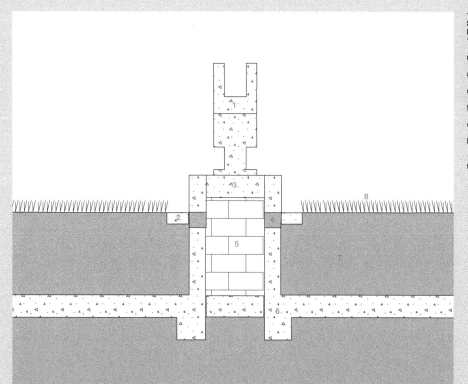

13.04
Section C–C Through
Filter Return
1:50
 1 Filter return,
remaining section
 2 Stone mowing edge
adjacent to turf
 3 Remaining section
of filter return
 4 Earth-filled voids in
filter return structure
 5 Blocked ends and
openings on side walls
 6 Existing structure
below grade
 7 Earth fill
 8 Finished grade in
turfed area

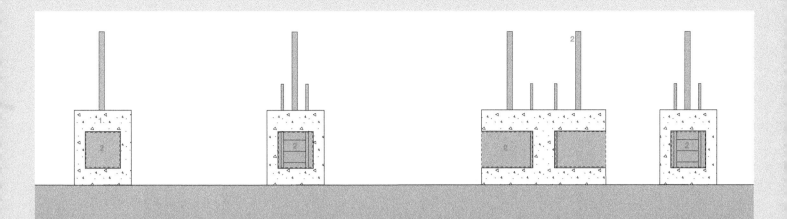

13.05
Elevational Detail of
Grit Chamber
Superstructure
1:100
  1 Remaining grit
chamber
superstructure
  2 Removed grit
chamber
superstructure

13.06
Grit Chamber
Superstructure
Section Details
1:50
  1 Removed grit
chamber
superstructure
  2 Removed railings
  3 Remaining grit
chamber
superstructure
  4 Removed grit
chamber
superstructure
  5 Valve gate
(removed)
  6 Removed valve
gate
  7 Compacted backfill
  8 Remaining grit
chamber
  9 Remaining grit
chamber
superstructure
10 Removed grit
chamber
superstructure

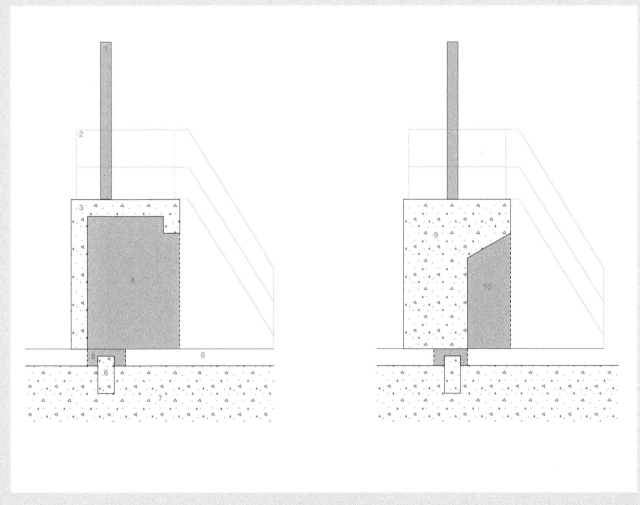

AEGON Square
The Hague, The Netherlands

Client
AEGON

Area
1.5 hectares (3.7 acres)

Project Team
Adriaan Geuze, Edzo Bindels, Edwin
van der Hoeven, Guido Marsille, Inge
Breugem, Rudolph Eilander, Sabine
Müller, Freek Boerwinkel, Paul Deibel

Structural Engineer
BRS, ABT Delft, IBDH

AEGON Square is the result of an
international design competition in
which the neighbourhood tram,
bus, and parking stations were to be
upgraded into a public park.
The design cleverly incorporates
the bus loops, the access area and
tram tracks into a poetic and
functional layout. While the space acts
as a public square, it is also a much-
needed green space for the inner
city, including trees, follies, seating
facilities and two kiosks. Unlike many
public squares, this area is based on
a well thought out 20-year
management plan in which a high
level of maintenance is guaranteed.

The square's two kiosks, one for
flowers and a snack bar, operate from
early in the morning till late at night,
ensuring that the square is activated
outside peak travel hours, helping the
space to become part of the
neighbourhood. The square features
seven green follies placed on carpets
of red gravel, which are constructed
from delicate cable structures with
finely woven mesh upon which ivy
and honeysuckle grow. The seventh
folly, in the centre of the square,
contains a water curtain that
disappears with a thundering sound
into an opening illuminated in red.
The kiosks are also imposing
presences on the square, with large
corrugated zinc roofs from which the
hydraulic awnings protrude.

1 View of the square where, despite its primary function as a transport interchange, the designers have created an uplifting park environment for the neighbourhood.

The kiosk (upper right) helps to create a sense of liveliness and activity throughout the day and evening.
2 View of one of the follies with its water spout. The steel cables

anchoring the structure to the ground emphasize the dramatic, deliberately precarious geometry.
3 Detail view of the top of one of the follies. A cable net

provides support for an array of climbing plants.

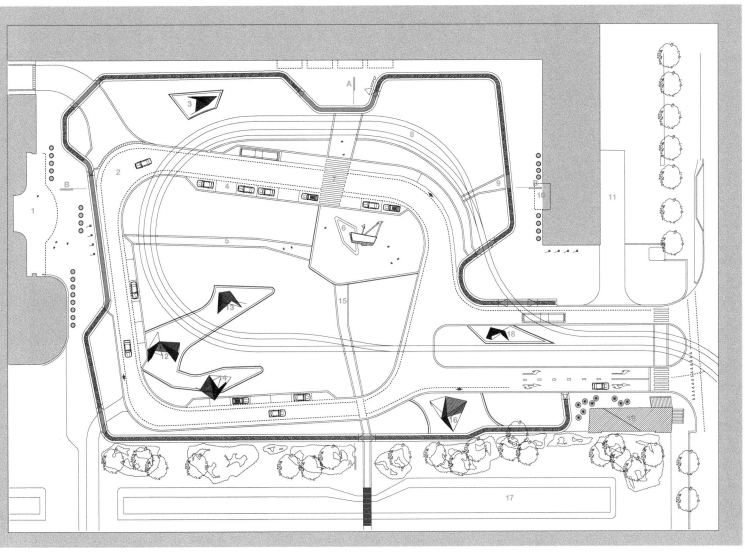

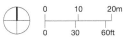

0 10 20m
0 30 60ft

14.01
Site Plan
1:1000
1 Building entrance
2 Asphalt roadway
3 Folly of steel poles
  with cast iron
  heads and support
  wire, grown over
  with ivy
4 Parking area of
  asphalt with
  thermoplastic
  markings
5 Concrete paving
  stones to path
6 Steel water folly
  with granite
  waterfall, ending in
  basin with steel
  grating
7 Pedestrian
  crossing
8 Tram tracks
  embedded in grass
9 Concrete paving
  stones to path
10 Building entrance
11 Building entrance
12 Folly of steel poles
   with cast iron
   heads and support
wire, grown over
   with ivy
13 Steel folly
14 Steel folly
15 Concrete paving
   stones to path
16 Steel folly
17 Water feature
18 Steel folly
19 Kiosk with snack
   bar and flower stall

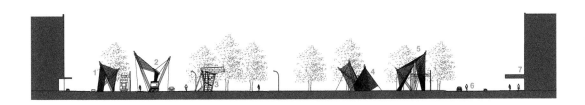

14.02
Section A–A
1:1000
1 Neighbouring
  building façade
2 Tram
3 Water folly
4 Folly of steel poles
  with cast iron
  heads and support
  wire, grown over
  with ivy
5 Tram
6 Folly of steel poles
  with cast iron
  heads and support
  wire, grown over
  with ivy
7 Water feature
  with bridge
8 Neighbouring
  building

14.03
Section B–B
1:1000
1 Folly of steel poles
  with cast iron
  heads and support
  wire, grown over
  with ivy
2 Folly of steel poles
  with cast iron
  heads and support
  wire, grown over
  with ivy
3 Water folly
4 Folly of steel poles
  with cast iron
  heads and support
  wire, grown over
  with ivy
5 Folly of steel poles
  with cast iron
  heads and support
  wire, grown over
  with ivy
6 Road
7 Building entrance

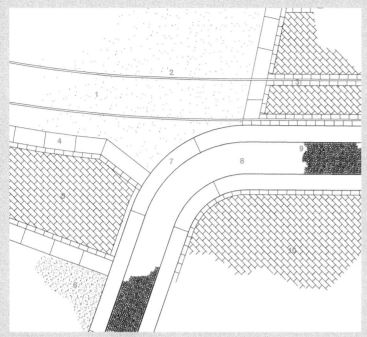

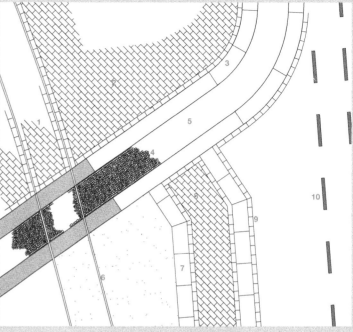

**14.04
Granite Strip to
Paving Detail
1:100**
1 Grass
2 Tram tracks
embedded in grass
3 150 x 300 mm (6 x
12 inch) concrete tiles
to pavement, laid

diagonally
4 Concrete kerb
stone
5 150 x 300 mm (6 x
12 inch) concrete
paving tiles to
pavement, laid
diagonally
6 Gravel
7 Concrete kerb

8 Granite blocks
9 Granite blocks
10 150 x 300 mm (6 x
12 inch) concrete
paving tiles to
pavement, laid
diagonally

**14.05
Paving Detail
1:100**
1 150 x 300 mm
(6 x 12 inch) concrete
paving tiles to
pavement, laid
diagonally
2 150 x 300 mm
(6 x 12 inch) concrete

paving tiles to
pavement, laid
diagonally
3 500 mm (19¾ inch)
wide concrete kerb
4 Granite blocks
5 Granite blocks
6 Tram tracks in
grass
7 500 mm (19¾ inch)

wide concrete kerb
8 150 x 300 mm
(6 x 12 inch) concrete
paving tiles to
pavement, laid
diagonally
9 Tiles to asphalt
edge
10 Thermoplastic
markings to asphalt

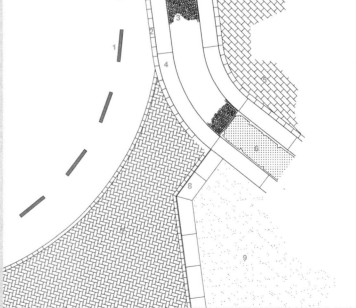

**14.06
Paving Detail at Tram
Line Crossing
1:100**
1 100 mm (4 inch)
concrete kerb
2 Grass
3 Tram tracks
4 500 mm (19¾ inch)
wide concrete kerb

5 150 x 300 mm (6 x
12 inch) concrete
paving tiles to
pavement, laid
diagonally
6 Grass
7 150 x 300 mm (6 x
12 inch) concrete
paving tiles to
pavement, laid

diagonally
8 500 mm (19¾ inch)
wide concrete kerb
9 500 mm (19¾ inch)
wide concrete kerb
10 Gravel
11 150 x 300 mm (6 x
12 inch) concrete
paving tiles to
pavement, laid

diagonally
12 500 mm (19¾ inch)
wide concrete kerb

**14.07
Paving Detail at
Granite Strip and
Planting
1:100**
1 Thermoplastic
markings to asphalt
2 Tiles to asphalt
edge
3 Granite blocks

4 500 mm (19¾ inch)
wide concrete kerb
5 150 x 300 mm (6 x
12 inch) concrete
paving tiles to
pavement, laid
diagonally
6 Maple hedge
7 Brick paving
8 Concrete kerbstone

9 Grass

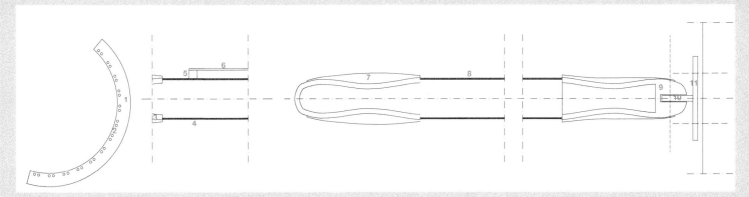

14.08
Cast Iron Pole Ends at Folly Detail
1:20
 1 Steel ring for attachment of wire grid mesh
 2 Drilled holes for attachment of wire grid mesh
 3 Section through pole head
 4 Pole head

component
 5 Steel element for attachment of wire grid mesh
 6 Steel pole for attachment of wire grid mesh
 7 Pole head component
 8 Section through pole
 9 Section through pole head

10 Ground plate with ring for attachment, vertical element
11 Ground plate with ring for attachment, horizontal element

14.09
Cast Iron Pole End to Folly Detail: Sectional Views
1:20

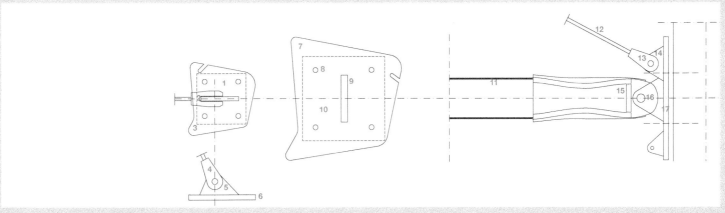

14.10
Folly Construction Detail
1:20
 1 Steel ground plate
 2 Steel attachment ring
 3 Edge of steel ground plate
 4 Steel ring with steel wire attachment
 5 Ground plate element with ring for

attachment
 6 Ground plate
 7 Edge of ground plate
 8 Holes for ground connection fixtures
 9 Attachment ring
10 Ground plate
11 Section through pole
12 Steel wire
13 Attachment ring
14 Attachment ring

on ground plate
15 Section through cast iron pole head
16 Steel ring
17 Ground plate

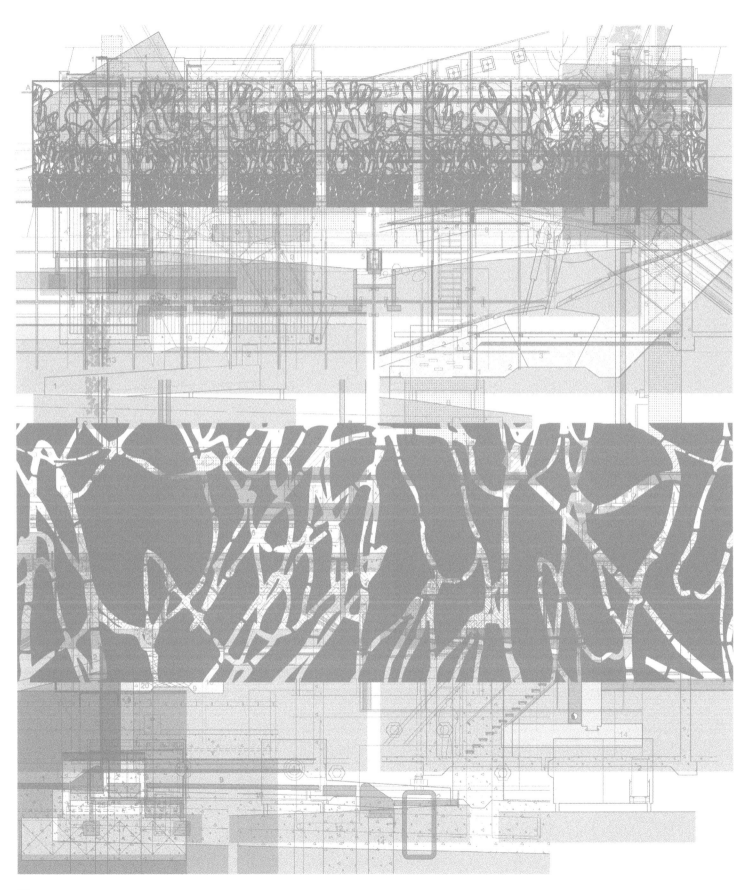

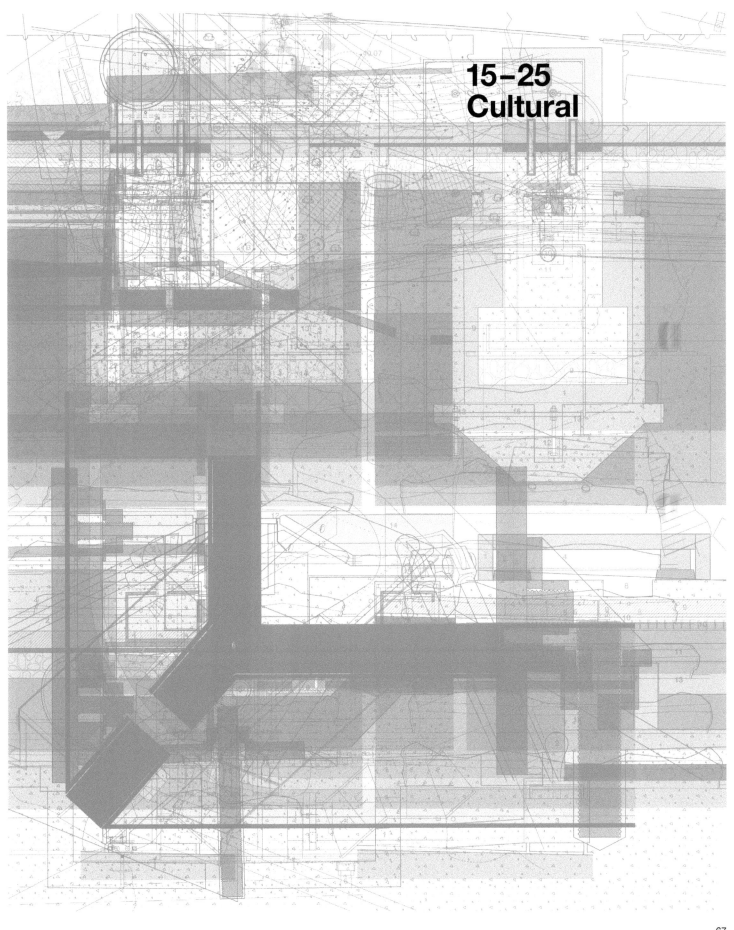

15–25
Cultural

15
Atelier Kempe Thill

Hedge Pavilion
Rostock, Germany

Client
International Flower Bulb Centre (IBC)

Area
120 square metres (1,291 square feet)

Project Team
André Kempe, Takashi Nakamura,
Cornelia Sailer, Ruud Smeelen,
Oliver Thill

Structural Engineer
ABT Velp

Landscape Architect
Niek Roozen

This intriguing project demonstrates the logic and rationality of Dutch architecture and agriculture. A new building element known as the 'smart screen' is employed to dramatic effect. The smart screen is an ivy hedge grown in greenhouses in sections of 1.2 by 1.8 metres (4 by 6 feet). Normally, it takes years for ivy to grow and cover a building, however, the smart screen makes a green building possible instantly. The Hedge Pavilion is entered through four-metre (13 feet) high doors, giving the building the enclosed character of a house, which is balanced by the semi-transparent character of the ivy.

A steel framework creates five rows of channels filled with earth from which the smart screens grow. A computer-controlled system of pipes provides irrigation for the hedges. The structure has no conventional diagonal bracing but is stabilized by four star-shaped corner columns that can withstand all horizontal loads. Vertical loads are carried by a multitude of slender columns. The hedges are visually continuous and look as if they support the structure, partly concealing the star-shaped columns and making them appear less substantial. Interesting light conditions characterize the interior. Light enters through the translucent plastic ceiling as well as filtering through the walls of hedges. The light from above makes the space feel like an interior, while the light entering through the hedges gives the space the character of an exterior space.

1 The walls of the Hedge Pavilion are enclosed by 10-metre (33-foot) high walls of 'smart screen' ivy. The initial impression is of a substantial building, however, on closer inspection, the building has a transparent quality more like a living plant which, in fact, it is. **2** With the sun shining through the panels of ivy, the quality of light in the interior is soft and diffused – perfect for exhibitions and displays. **3** View of an exhibition in the pavilion. The translucent plastic ceiling lets in more diffused light. **4** Detail view of one of the steel-framed entry doors located on each of the long façades.

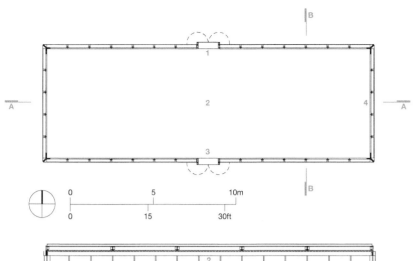

15.01
Floor Plan
1:200
 1 North entrance
 2 Exhibition space
 3 South entrance
 4 'Smart screen'
   ivy panels on steel
   frame

0   5   10m
0   15   30ft

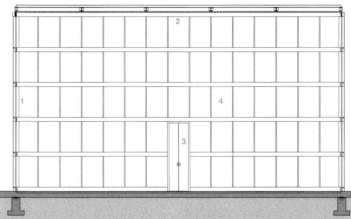

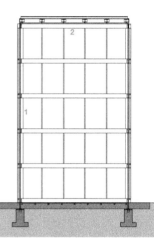

15.02
Section A–A
1:200
 1 'Smart screen'
   ivy panels on steel
   frame
 2 Translucent plastic
   ceiling and roof on
   steel structure
 3 Steel entrance
   door
 4 'Smart screen'
   ivy panels on steel
   frame
 5 Concrete footing

15.03
Section B–B
1:200
 1 'Smart screen'
   ivy panels on steel
   frame
 2 Translucent plastic
   ceiling and roof on
   steel structure
 3 Concrete footing

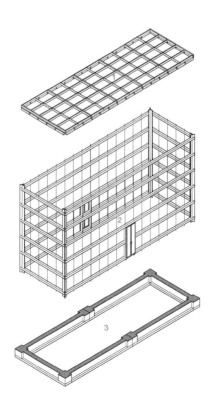

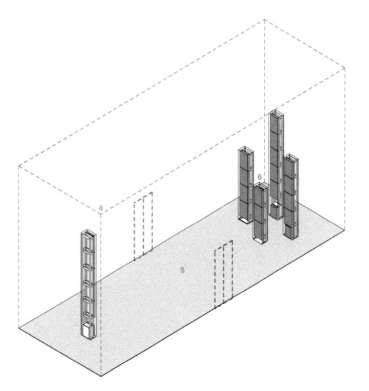

15.04
Axonometric
Diagram
 1 Steel roof structure
 2 Steel wall structure
 3 Concrete footing
   structure
 4 Line of 'smart
   screen' wall
 5 Timber floor
 6 Exhibition
   installation

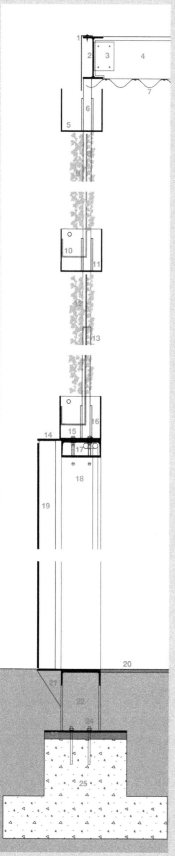

15.05
Wall Detail
1:20
 1 2 mm (1/16 inch)
thick aluminium corner
cover plate
 2 200 mm (73/4 inch)
steel I-beam
 3 Steel connection
plate
 4 200 mm (73/4 inch)
timber roof beam
 5 3 mm (1/8 inch)
thick steel planter
trough
 6 50 mm (2 inch)
diameter steel column
 7 Corrugated profile
clear polycarbonate
ceiling
 8 5 mm (1/4 inch)
steel planting grid
 9 Ivy
 10 Folded steel plant
trough
 11 Steel connection
plate between column
and plant trough
 12 Ivy
 13 5 mm (1/5 inch)
steel planting grid
 14 Steel plate door
lintel
 15 Screw connection
between plant trough
and door frame
 16 Steel connection
plate between column
and plant trough
 17 Steel door frame
with integrated
irrigation system
 18 Steel door frame
 19 5 mm (1/4 inch)
thick steel door plate
 20 Timber tongue and
groove floor boards
 21 Steel stabilization
flange
 22 200 mm (73/4 inch)
steel column
 23 Steel plate to top
of concrete footing
 24 Steel bolts to
secure connection
between steel column
and concrete footing
 25 Reinforced
concrete foundation

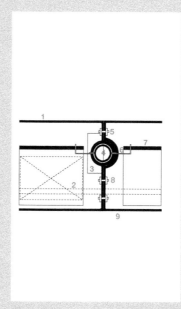

15.06
Column Plan Detail
1:10
 1 3 mm (1/8 inch)
thick steel planter
trough
 2 Line of ivy within
planter trough
 3 Steel connection
plate between column
and planter trough
 4 50 mm (2 inch)
diameter steel column

 5 Bolted connection
between plant troughs
 6 3 mm (1/8 inch)
connection between
steel ivy screen
elements
 7 5 mm (1/5 inch)
steel planting grid
 8 Bolted connection
between plant troughs
 9 3 mm (1/8 inch)
thick steel planter
trough

15.07
Column Sectional
Detail
1:10
 1 Ivy
 2 50 mm (2 inch)
diameter steel column
 3 Irrigation system
pipe
 4 Bolted connection
between plant troughs
 5 3 mm (1/8 inch)
thick steel planter

trough
 6 Bolted connection
between steel column
and steel plant troughs
 7 Line of earth and
potting mix in steel
trough
 8 5 mm (1/5 inch)
steel planting grid

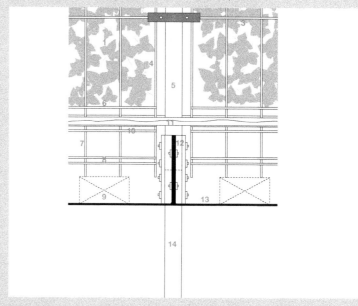

15.08
Column Elevational
Detail
1:10
 1 Ivy
 2 3 mm (1/8 inch)
thick steel connection
plate between sections
of steel planting grid
 3 Horizontal
component of 5 mm
(1/5 inch) steel planting
grid
 4 Vertical component
of 5 mm (1/5 inch) steel

planting grid
 5 50 mm (2 inch)
diameter steel column
 6 Horizontal
component of 5 mm
(1/5 inch) steel planting
grid
 7 Vertical component
of 5 mm (1/5 inch) steel
planting grid
 8 Steel planting grid
 9 Timber spacer
 10 Steel planting grid
 11 Line of earth and
potting mix in steel

planter trough
 12 Bolt connected
assembly between
column and steel
planter grid
 13 Finished floor level
 14 50 mm (2 inch)
diameter steel column

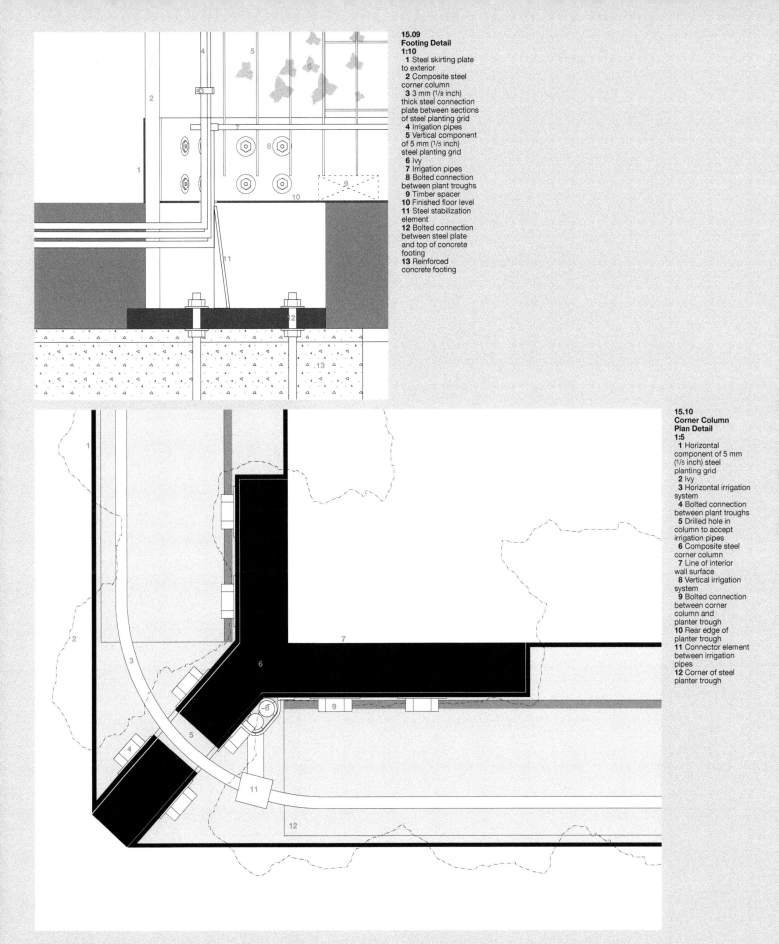

15.09
Footing Detail
1:10
 1 Steel skirting plate
to exterior
 2 Composite steel
corner column
 3 3 mm (1/8 inch)
thick steel connection
plate between sections
of steel planting grid
 4 Irrigation pipes
 5 Vertical component
of 5 mm (1/5 inch)
steel planting grid
 6 Ivy
 7 Irrigation pipes
 8 Bolted connection
between plant troughs
 9 Timber spacer
10 Finished floor level
11 Steel stabilization
element
12 Bolted connection
between steel plate
and top of concrete
footing
13 Reinforced
concrete footing

15.10
Corner Column
Plan Detail
1:5
 1 Horizontal
component of 5 mm
(1/5 inch) steel
planting grid
 2 Ivy
 3 Horizontal irrigation
system
 4 Bolted connection
between plant troughs
 5 Drilled hole in
column to accept
irrigation pipes
 6 Composite steel
corner column
 7 Line of interior
wall surface
 8 Vertical irrigation
system
 9 Bolted connection
between corner
column and
planter trough
10 Rear edge of
planter trough
11 Connector element
between irrigation
pipes
12 Corner of steel
planter trough

16
Gigon / Guyer Architekten

**Kalkriese Museum and Park
Kalkriese, Germany**

Client
Varusschlacht im Osnabrücker Land

Area
13 hectares (32 acres)

Project Team
Annette Gigon, Mike Guyer, Volker
Mencke

Landscape Architect
Zulauf, Seippel, Schweingruber

Kalkriese is the location of important
archaeological evidence of the
remains of a battle between the
Teutons and the Romans in 9 AD. No
building remains were found other
than an earthen rampart, so the
design acts as a tool with which to
interpret the archaeology. A series of
paths reveal the Roman legion's route
along the rampart, retraced in
irregularly placed iron plates with
historical, Roman or contemporary
written fragments. In contrast, narrow
wood-chip paths represent the
Teutons' positions in the forest. A
further series of paths represents
contemporary agriculture. Together,
these three path systems reveal the
layers of time and cultures that have
had an impact on the site.

The rampart is marked by means of
iron poles – where the rampart's
existence is evident, the iron bars are
close together. Where they are further
apart, the location of the rampart is
speculative. The forest has been
supplemented with trees to the south
in order to trace its former edge,
while to the north, it has been partially
cleared to reveal the former moor
landscape. Three pavilions act as
'perception instruments'. 'Seeing'
projects the exterior world through a
camera obscura onto a glowing half-
sphere. 'Hearing' has an acoustic
pipe that transmits amplified sounds
from outside an acoustically insulated
room. 'Questioning' consists of a wall
with slit-like openings opposite nine
television monitors where current
news broadcasts highlight that
conflicts continue to be fought. The
museum is a single-storey volume
raised above the ground, with a tower-
like structure on top, from which
visitors can enjoy spectacular views of
the landscape and the battlefield.

1 The museum serves to highlight the culture of the Romans and the Teutons through artefacts, images, films, drawings, photographs and maps. Panels of glazing set into the rusted steel exterior reveal views of the landscape and the battlefield.
2 A series of poles reveal the location of the Teutonic rampart.
3 The 'Questioning' pavilion makes it terrifyingly clear that, 2000 years later, conflicts continue to be fought with aggression and violence.
4 The 'Seeing' pavilion projects the world in reverse via a camera obscura so that it appears upside down.

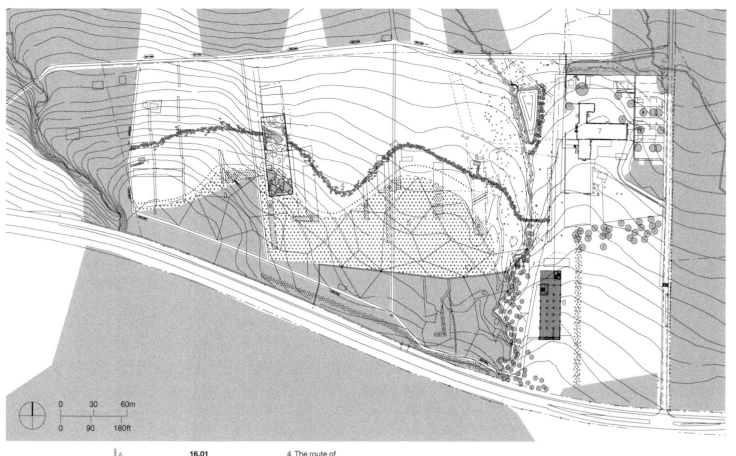

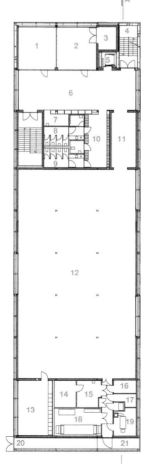

16.01
Site Plan
1:3000
  1 Questioning
    pavilion
  2 Hearing pavilion
  3 Reconstruction
    of the historic site

  4 The route of
    the Romans
  5 Paths of the
    Germans
  6 Seeing pavilion
  7 Visitors' centre
  8 Museum

16.02
Museum Floor Plan
1:500
  1 Lecture room 1
  2 Lecture room 2
  3 Storeroom
  4 Stair tower
  5 Lift
  6 Main entrance
    and shop
  7 Shop store
  8 Female toilets
  9 Male toilets
 10 Cloak room

 11 Lobby
 12 Exhibition space
 13 Teaching space
 14 Ancillary space
 15 Ancillary space
 16 Ancillary space
 17 Ancillary space
 18 Ancillary teaching
    space
 19 Office
 20 Entrance ramp
 21 Entrance lobby

16.03
Section A–A
1:500
  1 Entrance ramp
  2 Teaching spaces
  3 Exhibition space
  4 Lobby
  5 Line of emergency
    stairs beyond
  6 Main entrance
    and shop
  7 Stair tower
  8 Viewing platform

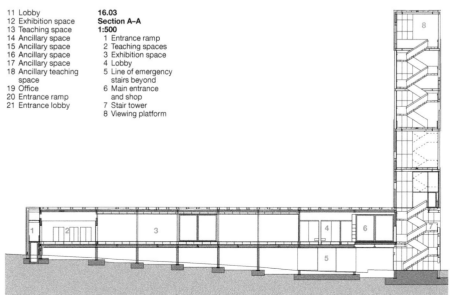

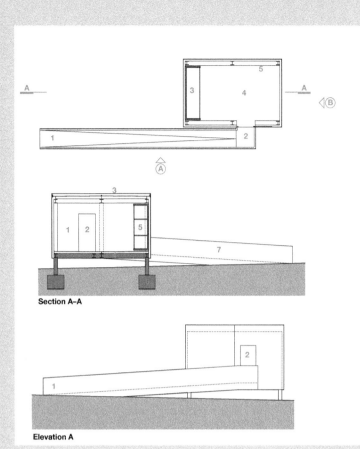

Section A–A

Elevation A

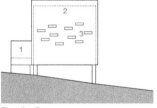
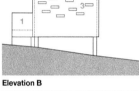

Elevation B

16.04
Questioning Pavilion
1:200
In the Questioning pavilion, a wall with slit-like openings stands opposite a wall with nine television monitors. A compilation of current news broadcasts makes it terrifyingly clear that to this day, 2000 years later, conflicts continue to be fought with aggression and violence.

Floor Plan
1 Entrance ramp
2 Entrance
3 Audiovisual monitor screen
4 Timber floor
5 Timber-clad, black-painted interior wall

Section A–A
1 Timber-clad, black-painted interior wall
2 Entrance
3 Steel-framed, steel-clad roof
4 Steel-framed floor structure with timber board floor
5 Audio visual monitor screen
6 Reinforced concrete footing
7 Steel-clad ramp

Elevation A
1 Steel-clad balustrade to entrance ramp
2 Entrance

Elevation B
1 Steel-clad balustrade to entrance ramp
2 Steel-clad exterior wall
3 Glazed viewing slots

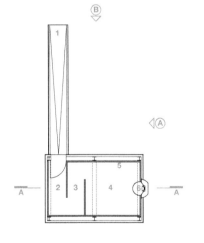

16.05
Seeing Pavilion
1:200
This pavilion shows the exterior world in reverse by means of a camera obscura projecting information from the outside onto a glowing half-sphere. The world is upside down – sky below and the ground above. Similar to the way the human eye functions, what is seen is displayed on the glass 'retina'. The camera obscura functions without electricity, however the glass half-sphere lightens the darkened room in a mystical manner.

Floor Plan
1 Ramp
2 Entrance
3 Timber-framed partition walls
4 Main space
5 Timber-framed and clad interior wall
6 Camera obscura

Section A–A
1 Entrance
2 Timber-framed partition wall
3 Steel-framed, steel-clad roof
4 Main space
5 Camera obscura
6 Timber floor
7 Reinforced concrete footing

Elevation A
1 Camera obscura
2 Steel-clad exterior wall
3 Steel cladding to ramp balustrade

Elevation B
1 Camera obscura
2 Steel-clad exterior wall
3 Entrance

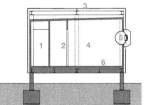

Section A–A

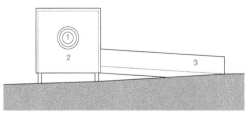

Elevation A

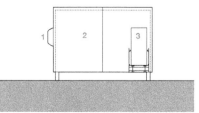

Elevation B

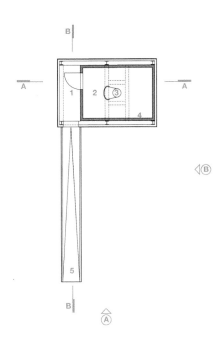

16.06
Hearing Pavilion
1:200
The Hearing pavilion is equipped with a large acoustic pipe that transmits the amplified sounds of the outside world into an acoustically insulated room. The pipe can be turned by hand and directed towards sources of sounds in order to listen, to eavesdrop and to interpret the aural context of the historic site from within the insulated shelter.

Floor Plan
1 Entrance
2 Main space
3 Acoustic pipe
4 Timber-framed, black painted interior wall
5 Ramp

Section A–A
1 Entrance
2 Acoustic pipe
3 Steel-framed, steel-clad roof
4 Timber-clad, black-painted interior wall
5 Steel-framed floor with timber board floor
6 Reinforced concrete footing

Section B–B
1 Steel-clad exterior wall
2 Timber-clad, black-painted interior partition wall
3 Acoustic pipe
4 Steel-framed, steel-clad roof
5 Steel-framed floor with timber boards
6 Reinforced concrete footing
7 Steel-framed ramp

Elevation A
1 Entrance
2 Acoustic pipe
3 Steel-clad exterior wall

Elevation B
1 Steel balustrade to entrance ramp
2 Acoustic pipe
3 Glazed slot window to exterior wall
4 Steel-clad exterior wall

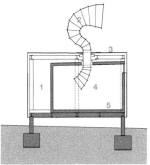

Section A–A

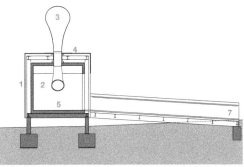

Section B–B

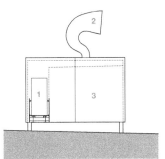

Elevation A

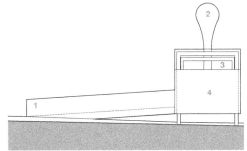

Elevation B

Shaw Center for the Arts
Baton Rouge, Louisiana, USA

Client
The Baton Rouge Area Foundation

Area
1.2 hectares (3 acres)

Project Team
George Hargreaves, Glenn Allen,
Kirt Rieder

Fountain Consultant
Dan Euser Waterarchitecture

General Contractor
The Lemoine Company

The Shaw Center for the Arts offers
innovative solutions to the challenge
of an unusual institutional hybrid.
The center includes an art museum,
theatre, performing arts centre,
and the Center for the Arts, all of
which were in need of an improved
civic identity. The project
encompasses the landscape for the
museum entry plaza, redesign of the
adjacent Lafayette Park, and
streetscape improvements to the
entire city block. The objective was to
establish a new and visually distinct
precinct in what was a waning
downtown core. This is achieved by
extending the lobby across the plaza,
through the street and toward the river
with a vocabulary of pavers clearly
legible as distinct from a standard
city streetscape.

   In effect, the ground plane appro-
priates a city street and combines
with a small park to establish a unified
Shaw Center identity. The paving
strategy includes four distinct colours
of concrete pavers in irregularly
sized and overlapping rectangles
parallel to the river. Rectangular bands
of planting within the paving contain
a variety of Louisiana native plants.
Trees punctuate the plaza or
are alternately aligned with the kerb,
channelling pedestrians across the
plaza. Two fountains feature sudden
vertical bursts of water, orchestrated
to emphasize the integration of
Lafayette Park and the Shaw Center.
The two fountains are choreographed
to spray aerated columns of water
at random intervals. The sound of
the water hitting the pavement mutes
adjacent traffic and creates an
immersive environment.

1 The dominant mate-
rial is a 150 x 300 x
100 mm (6 x 12 x 4
inch) concrete unit
paver configured in a
running bond pattern
parallel to the river. A
series of drawings
identified each paver
and its respective
colour, allowing teams
of paving contractors
to replicate the design
by moving outward
from the building
through the park.
2 The planting palette
takes a few of the
classic elements of a
Deep South garden
and configures them in
an unfamiliar way, allo-
cating a single species
to each lengthy, but
narrow, interlocking
rectangular bed.
3 The fountain nozzles
are flush with over-
sized concrete pavers
set on fibreglass-
reinforced polyester
grating that allows
the water to be
captured through open
joints to a below-
grade reservoir for
recirculation.

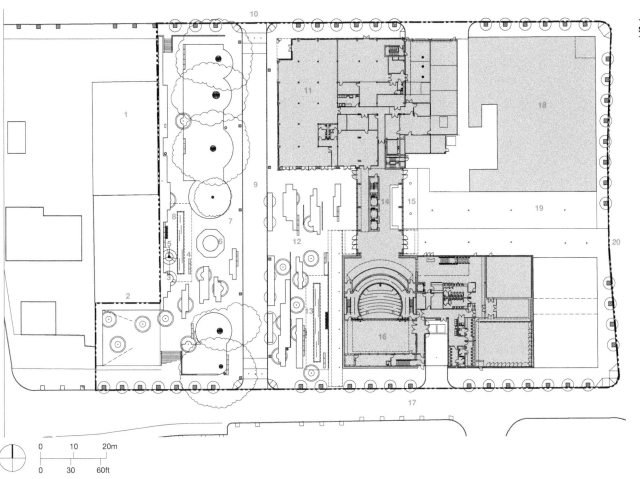

17.01
Site Plan
1:0000
1 Existing
  waterworks
2 Limit of landscape
  works
3 Existing magnolia
  tree
4 Stone bench
5 Existing magnolia
  tree
6 Water tower
7 Lafayette Park
8 Park fountain
9 Lafayette Street
10 Convention Street
11 Auto Hotel
12 Museum Plaza
13 Plaza fountain
14 Museum lobby
15 Sculpture garden
16 Theatre
17 North Boulevard
18 Onyx building
19 Landscape buffer
20 Third Street

0   10   20m
0   30   60ft

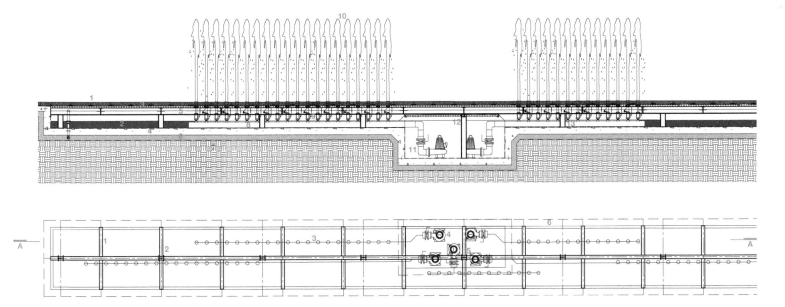

17.02
Plaza Fountain
Section A–A
1:100
1 Paver spacers
2 Concrete
  encasement
3 Removeable
  pavers

4 Waterproofing
  layer
5 Composite fibre
  reinforced plastic
  and steel I-beam
6 Compacted
  aggregate
7 Compacted soil
8 Fountain manifold

9 Water spray jets
10 Water spray
11 Submersible
  pumps
12 Concrete H-beam
  located to avoid
  pump locations
13 Vertically
  positioned H-beam

mechanically
fastened to
reservoir slab with
fibre-reinforced
plastic plate and
anchor bolts

17.03
Plaza Fountain Plan
1:100
1 Fibre-reinforced
  plastic transverse
  support beam
2 Fibre-reinforced
  plastic vertical
  H-beam

3 Spray jet layout
4 Fountain
  mechanical
  equipment
5 Concrete H-beam
  located to avoid
  pump locations
6 Concrete wall to
  fountain edge

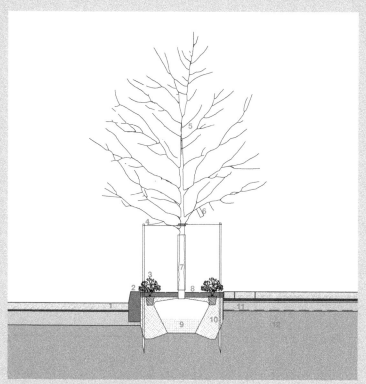

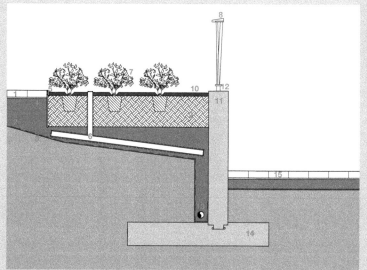

17.04
**Street Tree Planting
in Unit Pavers Detail**
1:50
 1 Vehicular load
paving
 2 Concrete kerb
 3 Ground cover
planting
 4 Secure aluminium
T-bars drilled to

receive aluminium
wire threaded through
rubber hose to
support tree
 5 Tree branches
protected from
damage during
planting
 6 Tree tag removed at
substantial completion
 7 Trunk guard

removed after planting
 8 50 mm (2 inch) of
mulch around tree
 9 Burlap and wire
basket removed from
top half of root ball
10 Raised sub-grade
pedestal
11 965 mm (38 inch)
deep planting mix
12 Compacted

sub-grade

17.05
**Typical Individual
Tree Planting on
Slopes Detail**
1:50
 1 Five per cent fall
away from root ball
 2 Raised sub-grade
pedestal
 3 Wire basket and
burlap removed from

top half of root ball
 4 50 mm (2 inch) of
mulch around tree
 5 Topsoil
 6 Roughened slope
of excavation

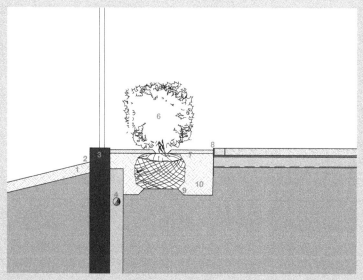

17.06
Hedge Planting Detail
1:50
 1 Topsoil
 2 Existing grass slope
 3 Existing retaining
wall with chain
link fence
 4 Perforated drain
 5 Burlap and wire
basket removed from

top half of root ball
 6 Hedge plant
 7 50 mm (2 inch)
of mulch cover
around plant
 8 Steel edge restraint
and pavers
 9 Bottom of root ball
set on compacted or
undisturbed sub-grade
10 Minimum 610 mm

(24 inch) of topsoil

17.07
**Concrete Retaining
Wall and Planter
Detail**
1:50
 1 Concrete paver
 2 Top of existing
grade
 3 Geotextile layer
 4 Sand bed
 5 Steel edge

restraints and pavers
 6 75 mm (3 inch)
diameter perforated
PVC aeration pipes
with black slotted PVC
cap and wrapped in
filter fabric
 7 Planting bed
 8 Guardrail to
top of wall
 9 Minimum 300 mm

(12 inch) of topsoil
10 50 mm (2 inch) of
mulch cover
11 Concrete
retaining wall
12 Height of
wall varies
13 Perforated
sub-drain pipe
14 Concrete footing
15 Concrete pavers

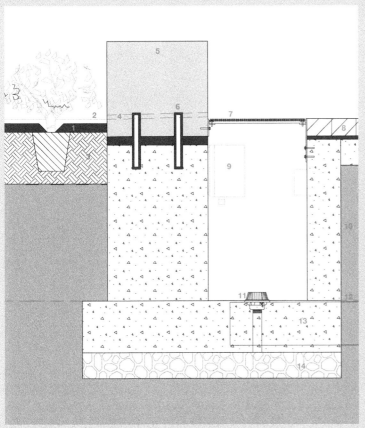

17.08
Granite Seat Wall and Illuminator Pit Detail
1:20

1 50 mm (2 inch) mulch layer
2 Top of plaza surface beyond
3 300 mm (12 inch) minimum of topsoil
4 38 mm (1½ inch) weep hole
5 Granite seat wall with thermal finish to all sides
6 Rows of stainless steel dowels epoxy set into granite block, set in grout-filled footing
7 Stainless steel removeable grate
8 Concrete plaza pavers
9 Fibre optic illuminator and junction box
10 Compacted subgrade
11 Drain
12 Frost line
13 Concrete footing
14 Compacted aggregate

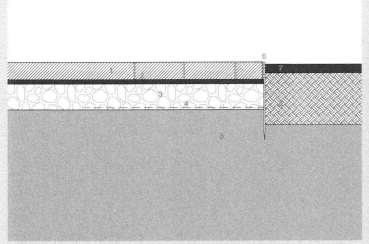

17.10
Paver Restraining Edge Detail
1:20

1 Concrete unit pavers
2 19 mm (¾ inch) sand bed
3 Compacted aggregate
4 Geotextile layer
5 Compacted sub-grade
6 Steel edging and interface with planting beds
7 50 mm (2 inch) layer of mulch finished 6 mm (¼ inch) below top of paver
8 Minimum of 300 mm (12 inches) of planting soil

17.09
Granite Seat Wall and Paving Detail
1:20

1 Concrete plaza pavers
2 Granite seat wall with thermal finish to all sides
3 38 mm (1½ inch) weep hole
4 50 mm (2 inch) mortar setting bed
5 Two rows of 25 x 300 mm (1 x 12 inch) stainless steel dowels epoxy set into granite block, set in grout filled footing
6 Concrete footing
7 Frost line
8 Compacted sub-grade
9 Compacted aggregate

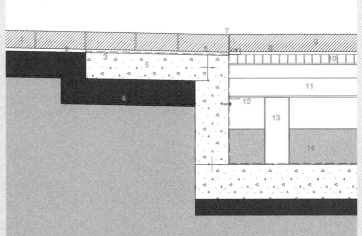

17.11
Pedestrain Unit Pavers at Fountain Detail
1:20

1 150 x 300 x 100 mm (6 x 12 x 4 inch) plaza unit pavers
2 19 mm (¾ inch) sand bed
3 Waterproofing layer
4 Geotextile layer
5 150 mm (6 inch) reinforced concrete slab
6 19 mm (¾ inch) mortar setting bed
7 Paver spacer
8 Waterproofing layer
9 300 x 600 x 100 mm (12 x 24 x 4 inch) fountain unit pavers
10 Fibre reinforced plastic grate
11 Transverse fibre reinforced plastic I-beam
12 Waterproofing layer
13 Fibre reinforced plastic H-beam
14 Concrete encasement

18
Gustafson Porter

Cultuurpark Westergasfabriek
Amsterdam, The Netherlands

Client
Westerpark District Council and City
of Amsterdam

Area
13 hectares (32 acres)

Architect
Mecanoo

Structural Engineer
Ove Arup

Westergasfabriek is a partially disman-
tled former industrial site where gas
production has been replaced by a
new park. A central promenade, 'The
Axis', serves as a central nervous
system that carries all of the park's
main functional requirements.
The Axis is accompanied by four less
distinct east-west paths: the canal
promenade; the gas-holder walk; the
woods–theatre way; and the wet
garden path. These are interconnected by a series of north-south
routes and bisected by 'Broadway'
– a path that connects all elements
of the site, and is lined with interactive
lighting triggered by pedestrian
movement.
   To the north of The Axis and
Broadway, a large grass area, the
'Field of Events', is framed by a
terraced amphitheatre and lake, where
a series of wind sculptures from which
sheets of water flow are located. The
lake empties into the 'Wet Gardens',
where it is recycled and cleaned as it
passes through the Willow Pool, Reed
Bed, Cascade and Stream. To the
south of The Axis and Broadway, the
site's history shapes the landscape.
For example, a Colour Field encircles
the Stadsdeelraad, using changing
colour through the seasons as a
compositional element, while a Market
Square defines the space between the
Stadsdeelraad and the Gas Factory
complex where the brick-paved
streets enhance public interaction
between the cultural facilities and the
activities in the park. In addition, the
Canal Promenade
acts as the main visual entrance into
the park from the city and is defined
by two water-filled basements of
former gas holders, one filled with
aquatic plants, and one a deep
fish pond.

1 Reclaimed 'Stelcon'
paving at the new
Market Square and
entrance to the park
contrasts with the
planted mound on
which 'Broadway'
bisects the park.
2 Aerial view of the
park showing the new
water features that
define the north
boundary, the town
hall facing the new
park to the east, and
the gas holder pools to
the west.
3 A boardwalk
seemingly floats
across the surface of
the water terrace reed
beds.
4 Detail view showing
the weir between two
water terraces among
the reed beds.

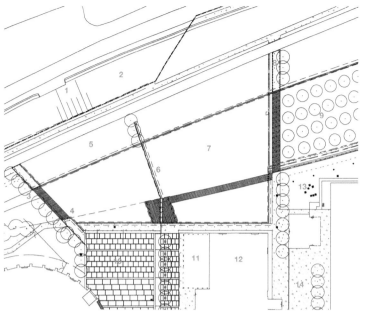

18.01
Site Plan 1
1 Existing grass mound to the 'overbracker polder'
2 Existing grass mound to the 'overbracker polder'
3 Water garden stream
4 Timber boardwalk
5 Willow bed
6 Weir
7 Reed bed
8 Boardwalk
9 Taxodium pool
10 Theatre square
11 Café
12 Transformer housing
13 Ornamental grass bed
14 Korfbal Square

18.02
Site Plan 2
1 Existing 'overbracker polder'
2 Existing sculpture
3 Mound planted with willows
4 Railway lines
5 Belvedere
6 Cycle path
7 Grass mound backdrop to lake
8 Willow wind break
9 Taxodium pool
10 Events lake
11 Beach edge of granite to lake

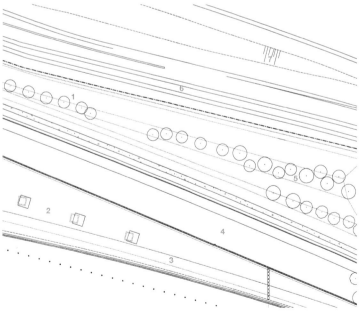

18.03
Site Plan 3
1 Grass mound screen to railway
2 Events lake
3 Beach edge of granite to lake
4 Grass mound
5 Grass mound
6 Railway lines
7 Gingko belvedere

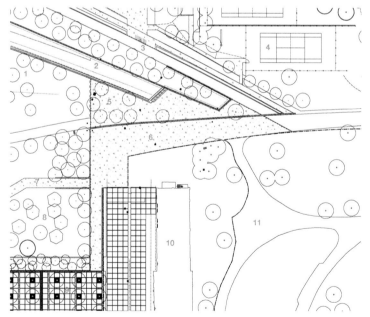

18.04
Site Plan 4
1 Grassed play area
2 Events lake paddling pool
3 Cycle route
4 Tennis centre
5 North-east entrance plaza
6 Bound gravel path
7 Broadway
8 Broadway East Rhododendron plantation
9 Market Square
10 Town Hall
11 Existing Westerpark

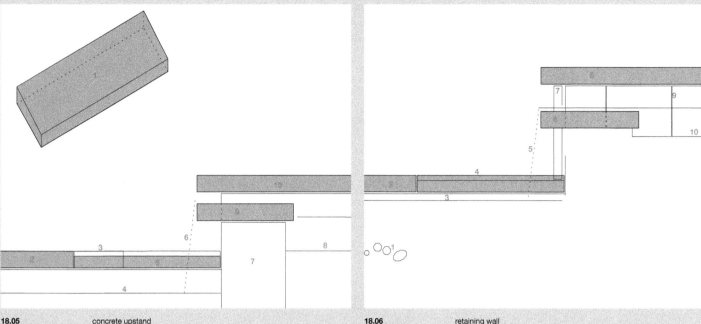

18.05
Weir Detail 1
1:20
 1 Granite seat
 2 Pool retaining wall
and coping stone
 3 Ground level
 4 Water level
 5 Sloped coping
stone at weir edge
 6 Linear weir cascade
 7 Reinforced

concrete upstand
 8 Pool base with
aquatic soil
 9 Weir coping stone
10 Pool retaining wall
and coping stone

18.06
Weir Detail 2
1:20
 1 Pebbles laid over
aquatic soil
 2 Pool retaining wall
and coping stone
 3 Water level
 4 Ground level
 5 Linear weir cascade
 6 Weir coping stone
 7 Granite cladding to

retaining wall
 8 Granite coping
stone
 9 Granite cladding to
retaining wall
10 Soil level in
taxodium pool

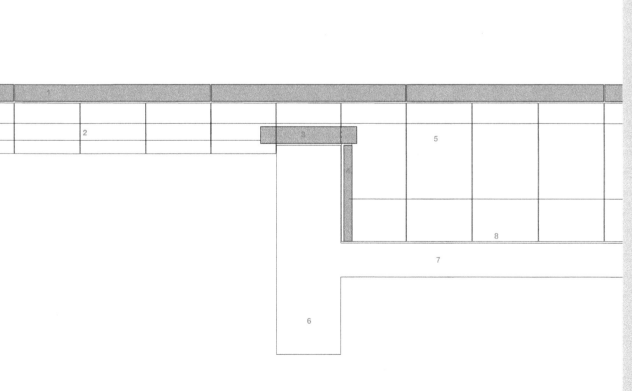

18.07
Weir Detail 3
1:20
 1 Granite coping
stone to retaining wall
 2 Granite cladding
stone
 3 Granite coping
dividing taxodium pool
from events lake
 4 Granite cladding
stone
 5 Granite cladding
 6 Reinforced
concrete foundation
and upstand
 7 Reinforced
concrete raft
foundation
 8 Black concrete
screed finish

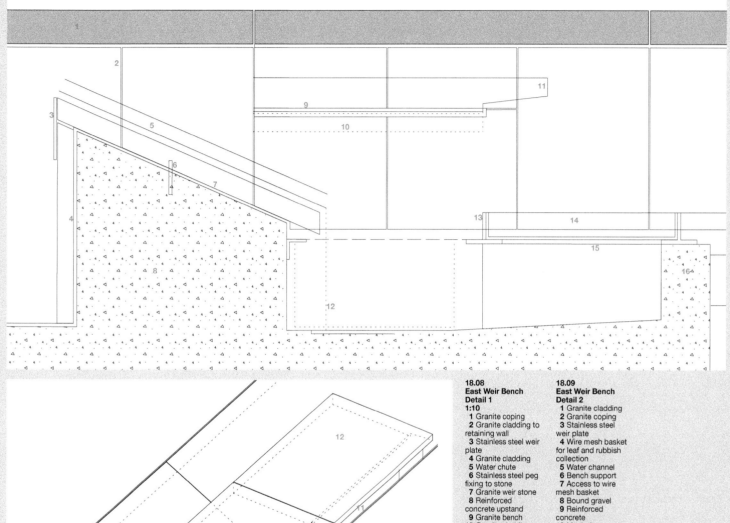

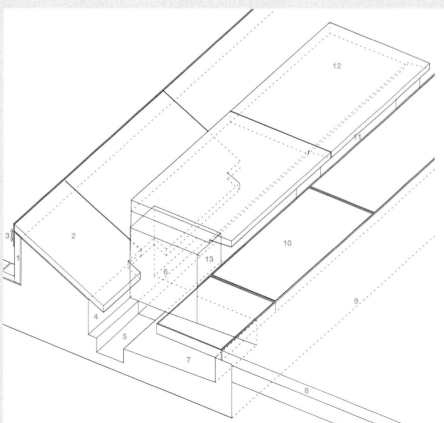

18.08
East Weir Bench
Detail 1
1:10
1 Granite coping
2 Granite cladding to
retaining wall
3 Stainless steel weir
plate
4 Granite cladding
5 Water chute
6 Stainless steel peg
fixing to stone
7 Granite weir stone
8 Reinforced
concrete upstand
9 Granite bench
10 Granite cladding
set in front of stainless
steel bracket
11 Bench nosing
12 Wire mesh basket
for leaf and rubbish
collection
13 Manhole cover
support
14 Manhole cover to
access wire basket
15 Access to wire
mesh basket
16 Reinforced
concrete upstand

18.09
East Weir Bench
Detail 2
1 Granite cladding
2 Granite coping
3 Stainless steel
weir plate
4 Wire mesh basket
for leaf and rubbish
collection
5 Water channel
6 Bench support
7 Access to wire
mesh basket
8 Bound gravel
9 Reinforced
concrete
10 Manhole cover
11 Bench nosing
12 Granite bench
13 Bench support

The Eden Project
Cornwall, England, UK

Client
The Eden Project

Area
2.3 hectares (5.7 acres)

Project Team
Sir Nicholas Grimshaw, Andrew Whalley, Jolyon Brewis, Vincent Chang, David Kirkland, Michael Pawlyn

Structural Engineer
Anthony Hunt Associates

Services Engineer
Ove Arup & Partners

Landscape Architect
Land Use Consultants

The Eden Project, a showcase for global biodiversity, is one of the most innovative and high-profile millennium projects. It is the largest plant enclosure in the world and represents a significant environmental improvement for the site – a defunct china clay pit. The biomes, a sequence of great transparent domes that encapsulate humid tropic and warm temperate regions, and the building which links them together are the highlight of the project. The biomes are a sinuous sequence of eight interlinked geodesic domes threading around the site, ranging from 18 to 65 metres (59 to 213 feet) in radius in order to accommodate the varying heights of the plants.

Structurally, each dome is a space frame reliant on two layers. The first, an icosahedral geodesic skin, is made up of hexagonal modules. Each comprises six straight, compressive, galvanized steel tubes. The primary layer is joined to a secondary one by diagonal circular hollow sections at the node points. Structural stability is guaranteed by the meeting of inner and outer structural members to form pinned connections. These are anchored to reinforced concrete strip foundations at the perimeter. The biomes are clad with ETFE (ethylene tetrafluoroethylene) foil, which is highly transparent to a wide spectrum of light, ensuring that the maximum amount of daylight filters through to nourish the plant life within. The foil is triple-layered within the frame of each hexagon, so that heat is retained.

1 The exact location of the biomes on site has been determined by solar modelling, a sophisticated technique that indicates where structures will benefit most from passive solar gain.
2 The biomes represent the perfect fulfilment of Buckminster Fullers' vision of the maximum enclosed volume within the minimal surface area.
3 ETFE represents less than one per cent of the dead weight of equivalent glass as well as being strong, anti-static and recyclable.
4 There is an active heating system in place in the biomes, but this is supplementary – a means of fine-tuning the natural passive system.

19.01
Site Plan
1:2000
1 Site contours, open space
2 Temporary car parking
3 Site contours, open space
4 Humid Tropics Biome, transparent roof section 1
5 Humid Tropics Biome, transparent roof section 2
6 Humid Tropics Biome, transparent roof section 3
7 External amphitheatre
8 Warm Temperate Biome, transparent roof section 1
9 Warm Temperate Biome, transparent roof section 2
10 Warm Temperate Biome, transparent roof section 3
11 Eden Foundation building
12 Approach road
13 Car park
14 Car park
15 Car park
16 Landscape feature
17 Lake
18 Horticultural compound
19 Fill from disused quarry
20 Site contours, open space

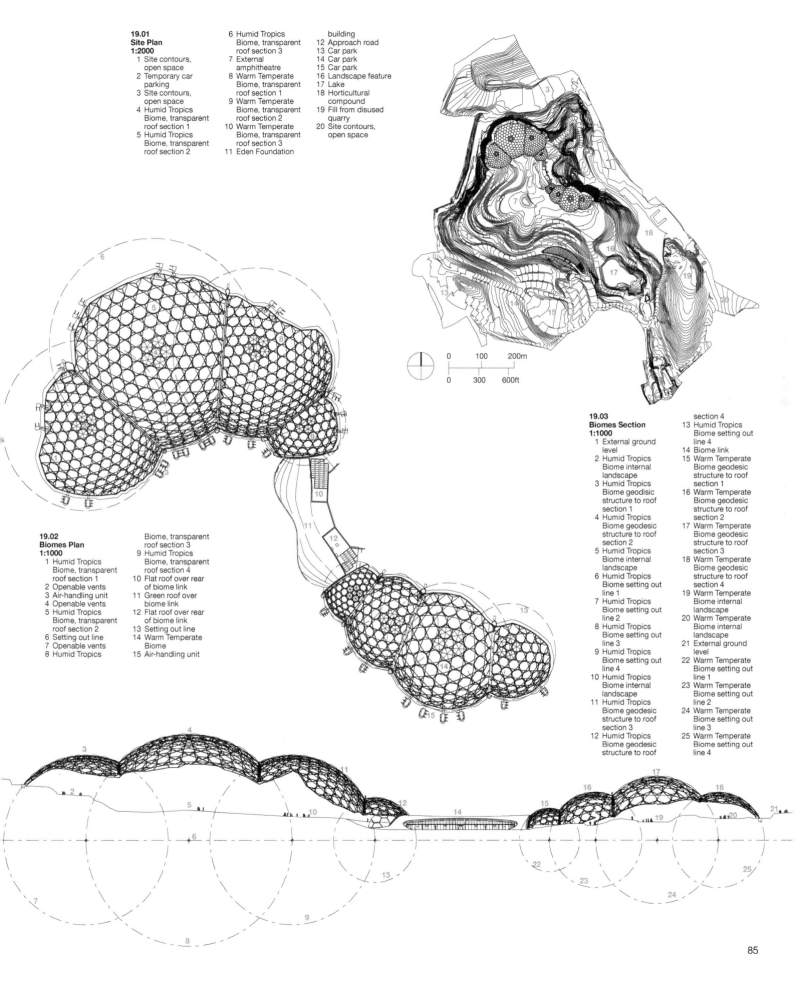

19.02
Biomes Plan
1:1000
1 Humid Tropics Biome, transparent roof section 1
2 Openable vents
3 Air-handling unit
4 Openable vents
5 Humid Tropics Biome, transparent roof section 2
6 Setting out line
7 Openable vents
8 Humid Tropics Biome, transparent roof section 3
9 Humid Tropics Biome, transparent roof section 4
10 Flat roof over rear of biome link
11 Green roof over biome link
12 Flat roof over rear of biome link
13 Setting out line
14 Warm Temperate Biome
15 Air-handling unit

19.03
Biomes Section
1:1000
1 External ground level
2 Humid Tropics Biome internal landscape
3 Humid Tropics Biome geodisic structure to roof section 1
4 Humid Tropics Biome geodesic structure to roof section 2
5 Humid Tropics Biome internal landscape
6 Humid Tropics Biome setting out line 1
7 Humid Tropics Biome setting out line 2
8 Humid Tropics Biome setting out line 3
9 Humid Tropics Biome setting out line 4
10 Humid Tropics Biome internal landscape
11 Humid Tropics Biome geodesic structure to roof section 3
12 Humid Tropics Biome geodesic structure to roof section 4
13 Humid Tropics Biome setting out line 4
14 Biome link
15 Warm Temperate Biome geodesic structure to roof section 1
16 Warm Temperate Biome geodesic structure to roof section 2
17 Warm Temperate Biome geodesic structure to roof section 3
18 Warm Temperate Biome geodesic structure to roof section 4
19 Warm Temperate Biome internal landscape
20 Warm Temperate Biome internal landscape
21 External ground level
22 Warm Temperate Biome setting out line 1
23 Warm Temperate Biome setting out line 2
24 Warm Temperate Biome setting out line 3
25 Warm Temperate Biome setting out line 4

0   100   200m
0   300   600ft

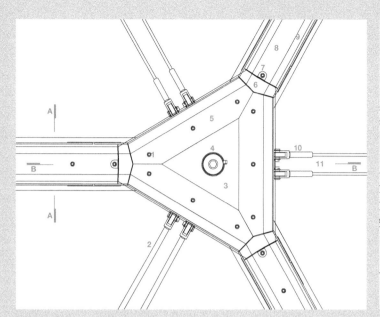

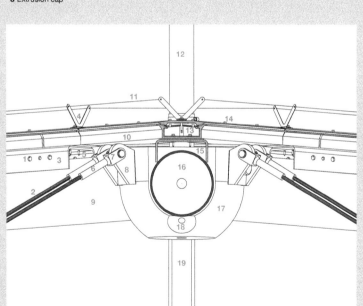

19.04
Node Detail Plan
1:10
1 Steel bolt fixing
2 Stainless steel
cables
3 Membrane
4 Access fixing point
5 Extrusion cap
6 Extrusion junction
7 Steel bolt fixing for
bird wire fixing
8 Extrusion cap
9 Extrusion cap
10 Stainless steel
cable anchor
11 Stainless steel
cables

19.05
Node Detail
Perspective
1:10
1 Steel circular
hollow section
2 Saddle plate
3 Stainless steel
cable
4 Stainless steel
cable anchor
5 Cast steel node
6 Cable fixing point
7 Bird wire
8 Membrane seal
9 Access fixing point
10 Bird wire anchor
point
11 Extrusion cap
12 Steel bolt fixing
13 Membrane
14 Extrusion cap
15 Movement joint
16 Bird wire

19.06
Node Detail Section
A–A
1:10
1 Steel bolt fixing
2 Stainless steel
cables
3 Saddle plate
4 Bird wire
anchor point
5 Saddle plate
6 Stainless steel
cable anchor
7 Cable fixing point
8 Steel plates
9 Steel circular
hollow section
10 Aluminium
extrusion for
ETFE (ethylene
tetrafluoroethylene)
roof
11 Bird wire
12 Access fixing point
13 ETFE carrier
extrusion
14 Extrusion cap
15 Saddle plate
16 Steel circular
hollow section
17 Cast steel node
18 Fixing for
lower chords
19 Stainless steel
cables

19.07
Node Detail Section
B–B
1:10
1 Steel circular
hollow section
2 Saddle plate
3 Bird wire
4 Bird wire anchor
point
5 Aluminium
extrusion for ETFE
(Ethylene Tetra Fluoro
Ethylene) roof
6 Stainless steel
cables
7 Insulation
8 Sealing cap
9 Access fixing point
10 Steel post
11 Fixing for steel
tubes
12 Cast steel node
13 Fixing for steel post
14 Bird wire anchor
point
15 Bird wire
16 Cable fixing
17 Steel bolt fixing
18 Stainless steel
cable fixing point
19 Saddle plate
20 Stainless steel
cable anchor
21 Cast steel node

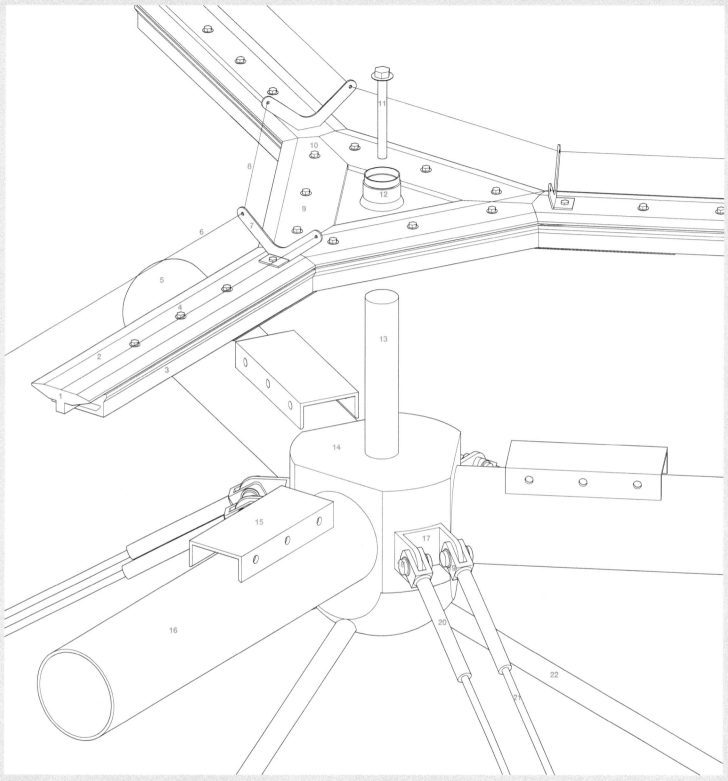

19.08
Node Exploded
Axonometric
1:5
1 Extrusion cap
2 Extrusion cap
3 Aluminium
extrusion for
ETFE (ethylene
tetrafluoroethylene)
roof
4 Steel bolt fixing
5 Steel circular

hollow section
6 Bird wire
7 Bird wire anchor
point
8 Bird wire
9 Extrusion cap
10 Steel bolt fixing
11 Sealing cap
12 Membrane seal
13 Steel post access
fixing point
14 Cast steel node
15 Saddle plate

16 Steel circular
hollow section
17 Fixing plate
18 Cable fixing bolt
19 Cable fixing
assembly
20 Stainless steel
cable anchor
21 Stainless steel
cables
22 Lower geodisic
chord

Bordeaux Botanical Gardens
Bordeaux, France

Client
City of Bordeaux

Area
4.6 hectares (11.4 acres)

Project Team
N. Leroy, C. Mosbach, T. M. T.
N'Guyen, J. Saint-Chély, L. Sciascia,
M. Talagrand, Jean-Paul Bonroy,
Laurent Berger, Emmanuel Helme
Guizon

The Botanical Garden of Bordeaux
inaugurates the urban connection
between the Bastide neighbourhood
on the right bank of the Garonne River
and the old city on the left bank. A
modular structure based on the major
functions of the garden – exotic
('Urban Garden'), ethno-botanic ('Field
of Crops'), ecological ('Environment
Gallery'), and topical ('Aquatic
Garden') – opens up an unlimited
range of possible combinations of
gardens. The phenomena of nature
and culture – mankind's relationship
with the vegetal world – is shown
through the sciences, the arts and
economics. For the Field of Crops,
gardeners make their imprint on the
soil by digging and seeding the
furrows and the repeated flow of
irrigation determines the root pattern.
Alternating expanses of wheat, oats,
rice and flax contrast with the other
areas of the garden.

In the Environment Gallery, the
stratifications of the ground determine
the processes of environmental
transformation in terms of geology,
soil and plant cover. The evolution of
this environment is linear so that a
gradual installation of natural
environments will be built in miniature.
Confined within the limits of the
separate areas they pass through,
visitors are held in an intimate
relationship with each environment.
At the same time, they see the
gardens as a contraction of nature
superimposed upon the urban
environment. The installations on
different scales, set to different
rhythms – seasonal (Field of Crops)
and permanent (the tree-lined park) –
constantly introduce new landscapes,
and hence new potential for
interpretation and appreciation.

1 The Field of Crops presents an artistic interpretation of agriculture in the Bordeaux countryside, and in the Botanical Gardens represents one of the most captivating landscape spaces.
2 View of the Environment Gallery where, in the north, five gardens represent typical landscapes on the right bank of the Garonne. The six gardens in the south represent landscapes on the left bank.
3 View of the south gate. The doors, designed in collaboration with artist Pascal Convert, represent freely drawn lines from the drawings of small children.
4 A monumental fence of oak wood incorporates branches and trunks that fell in the storm of 1999.

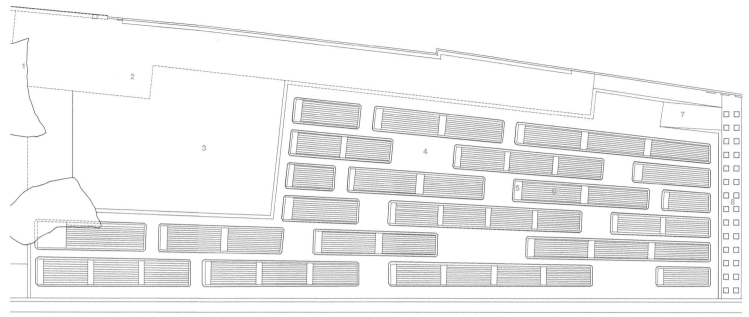

0   10   20m

0   30   60ft

20.01
**Field of Crops Plan
1:1000**
1 Water basin
  for irrigation
2 Allée of climbing
  plants
3 Grassed recreation
  area

4 Small recreation
  areas located
  between the crop
  fields
5 Irrigation pond
6 Typical crop parcel
  representing the
  agriculture of the
  Bordeaux area

7 Ramped access to
  the Field of Crops
8 Allée of Mimosas

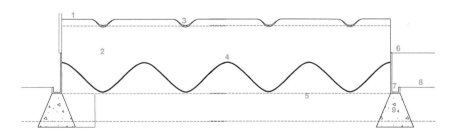

20.02
**Typical Field of Crops
Container Section
1:50**
1 Irrigation pond
2 Stainless steel
  container beyond
3 Overflow channel
4 Ploughed earth

furrows for crop
planting
5 Water line for
  irrigation
6 Stainless steel
  edge strip to
  separate grass
  recreation area
  from crops

7 Stainless steel
  mowing strip
8 Typical grass level
9 Reinforced
  concrete strip
  footing

20.03
Main Entrance Gate
Panel Variations
1:100
The evidence of human presence throughout the ancient history of France is found in the project in the form of the superimposed contours of the handprints of children projected in the design of the gates. These hand contours are reminiscent of the ancient Lascaux caves, and especially the hands drawn in the late Paleolithic era in the Gargas cave in the Pyrenees which remind us of our earliest human origins. The abstracted contours of the tangled hands framed by the gate is also reminiscent of the foliage of trees moving with the wind. The idea of 'moving towards' – the idea of the growth of a child and the growth of the branches of a tree, is thus at the centre of the design. The gates were designed in collaboration with artist Pascal Convert.

20.04
Main Entrance
Gate Detail
1:10
Each individual gate panel, entirely constructed from polished stainless steel, is approximately 2.8 metres (9 feet) wide and 4 metres (13 feet) in height, with each gate made up of three panels so that overall, that gate is nearly 9 metres (29 feet) wide. The choice of the superimposed prints of the hands of children is designed so that the density of the pattern decreases as it rises, leading the eye from the density of the life bearing earth towards the sky.

The interlacing of tightly entangled lines evokes plants in the low part of the gate, and becomes thread-like and slim in the upper part, more akin to the spread fingers of the human hand.

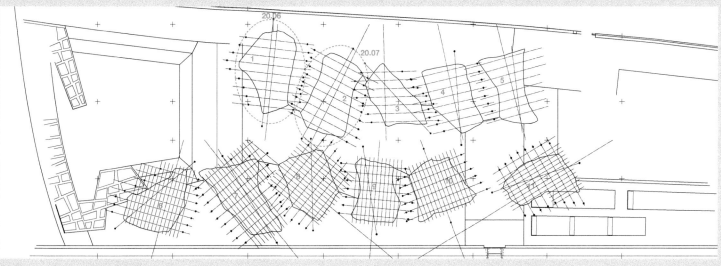

**20.05
Environment Gallery
Plan**

1 Wet meadow
2 Forest of young oak
3 Dry meadow
4 Grassed lawn

5 Limestone cliffs
6 Sand dunes
7 Forest
8 Forest and dunes
9 Lagoons
10 Moorland
11 Wet moorland

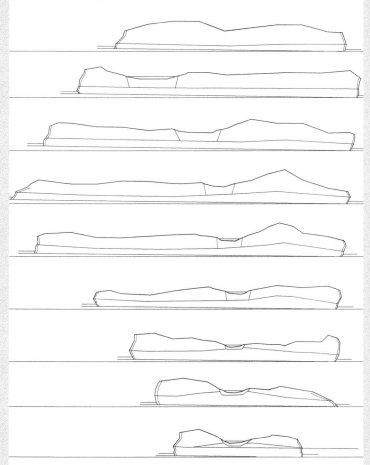

**20.06
Wet Meadow (Prarie
Humide) Sections
1:200**
The vast wetlands of
the estuary of the
Garonne River, which
were artificially drained

centuries ago, now
accommodate
meadows bordered by
alders, poplars and
ash, while in the
wettest area of the
meadow, reeds,
Scirpes and *Carex*

dominate the
landscape.

**20.07
Forest of Young Oak
(Fôret de Chênes)
Sections
1:200**
On the exposed, south
facing limestone
slopes throughout the

Garonne estuary,
thickets of young oaks
have been planted in
the humus-rich soil.
They exist as thin
groves, or are
maintained as
coppiced woods.

In both cases a layer of
shrubs is present and
includes privet, horned
blood, *genévrier* and
boxwood.

21
Nikken Sekkei

Osaka City University Media Centre Plaza
Osaka, Japan

Client
Osaka City

Area
0.32 hectares (0.8 acres)

Project Team
David Buck, Zazuo Ohno, Kenji Yawata, Osamu Nishida, Yasuhiko Tashiro, Tsuneharu Yamada, Takamichi Matsuda, Keishiro Shibata, Masaaki Yoshida, Yukuo Kamiguchi

Landscape Architect
Makoto Noborisaka and David Buck

Structural Engineer
Osamu Nishida, Yasuhiko Tashiro

Lighting Designer
Yukio Oka

The Osaka City University Media Centre and the surrounding plaza represent the first phase of a campus-wide regeneration. The traditional pattern of universities in Japan as enclosed, hallowed grounds of learning gives way to an open plaza, creating what the university considers to be a memorial gift from the university to the citizens. The challenge for the designers was to create a space that would be a gift to the students and residents, and to form a relationship between the people, the library and the landscape. Words were employed to forge this link, taken from the pages of library texts and scattered around the space. Landscape emotions and ecology were chosen as the themes for a series of cast aluminium name-plates.

Arranged on a grid in the paving, grouped around benches, and flowing through the pool and planting, the name-plates are indented into the surfaces of the space. The first group of 52 words are evocative of human interaction with nature, drawing out memories from earlier, more primitive times. Another 39 plates introduce concepts of landscape ecology. The last group of 28 words are the names of key people who have contributed to the discipline of landscape design. No list can ever be fully comprehensive, so blank nameplates are included for future discoveries.

1 The bulk of the aluminium-clad media centre overlooks the calm environment of the plaza below.
2 A pool with angular edges forms the centrepiece to the design, with timber gangplanks projecting over the southern edge, allowing people to get closer to the water.
3 In contrast to the movement of the water and the tactility of the timber surfaces, the aluminium cubes and inlaid ground surfaces act as the formal organizing element of the design.
4 Throughout the scheme, aluminium makes subtle intrusions into the more prosaic materials of the scheme.
5 Detail view of some of the nameplates that are scattered throughout the scheme, representing the themes and personalities of landscape ecology.

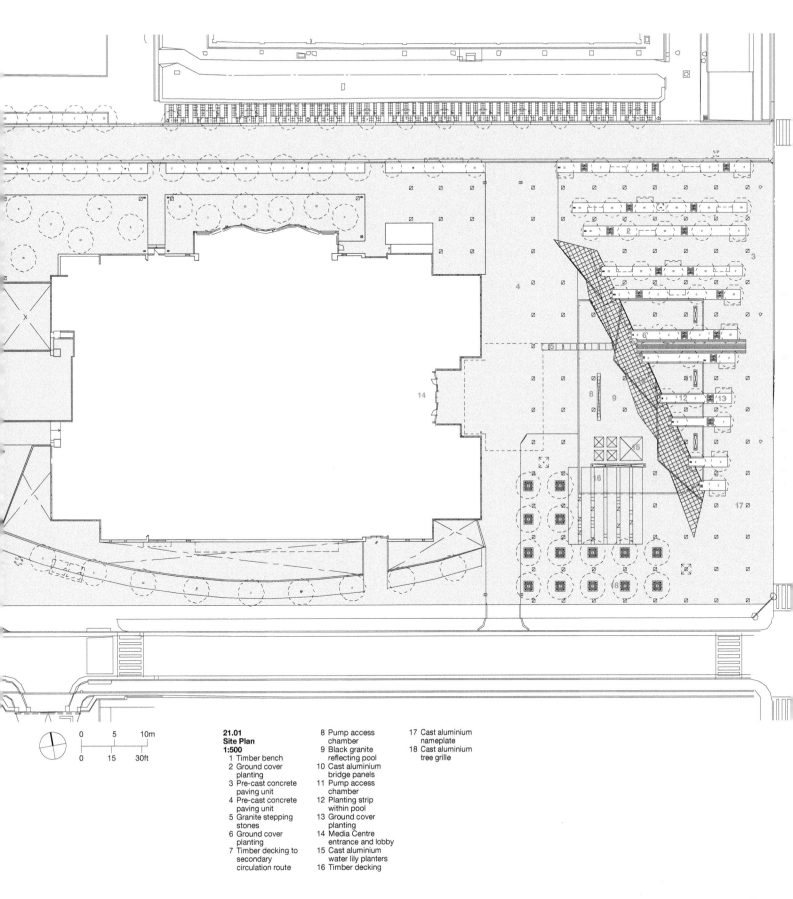

21.01
Site Plan
1:500

1 Timber bench
2 Ground cover planting
3 Pre-cast concrete paving unit
4 Pre-cast concrete paving unit
5 Granite stepping stones
6 Ground cover planting
7 Timber decking to secondary circulation route
8 Pump access chamber
9 Black granite reflecting pool
10 Cast aluminium bridge panels
11 Pump access chamber
12 Planting strip within pool
13 Ground cover planting
14 Media Centre entrance and lobby
15 Cast aluminium water lily planters
16 Timber decking
17 Cast aluminium nameplate
18 Cast aluminium tree grille

0 5 10m
0 15 30ft

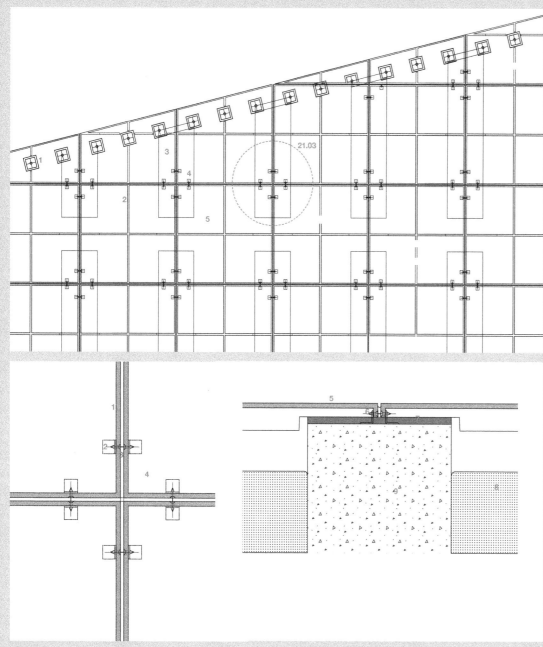

21.03

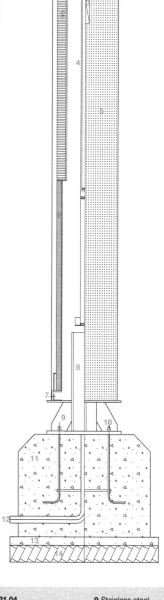

21.02
Aluminium Bridge
Detail Plan
1:20
1 Light-emitting
diode (LED) edge
lighting recess
2 Junction between
cast aluminium
bridge panels
3 Concrete pillar
supporting bridge
4 Stainless steel
angle connection to
foundation pillar
5 595 mm (23²/5 inch)
cast aluminium plate

21.03
Aluminium Bridge
Panel Plan and Cross
Section Detail
1:5
1 Edge of cast
aluminium plate
2 20 x 20 mm
(³/4 x ³/4 inch)
stainless steel angle
connection
3 Aluminium self
tapping screws
4 595 mm (23²/5 inch)
cast aluminium plate
5 595 mm (23²/5 inch)
cast aluminium plate
6 20 x 20 mm
(³/4 x ³/4 inch)
stainless steel angle
7 Mortar filler
8 Pool water
9 Reinforced
concrete column

21.04
Light Pole Detail
1:20
1 13 mm (1/2 inch)
thick stainless steel
top plate with buff
finish
2 50 mm (2 inch)
thick sheet glass
3 Cast aluminium
light reflector with
silver acrylic paint
finish
4 30 mm (1¹/5 inch)
diameter fluorescent
tube light
5 Banner flag
6 Cast aluminium
side panel
7 Self-tapping screw
attachment for
aluminium panel
8 Stainless steel
vertical cross plate

9 Stainless steel
bracing supports
10 Anchor bolts (x 4)
11 Reinforced
concrete base
12 40 mm (1³/5 inch)
diameter electric input
conduit
13 Cinder concrete
14 Brick sub-base

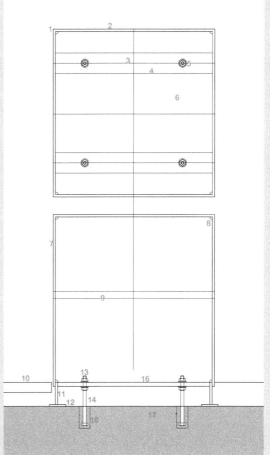

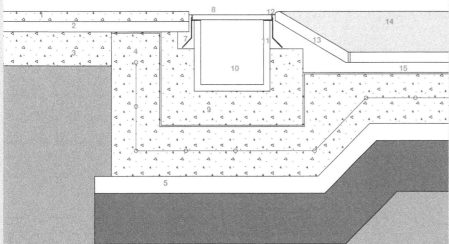

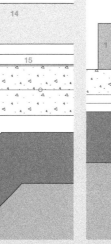

21.05
Light Bollard Plan and Section / Elevation Detail
1:10
1 Cast aluminium light casing with weather finish
2 Cast aluminium foundation pin
3 Stainless steel liner sleeve
4 Cast aluminium light casing with weather finish
5 Aluminium plug
6 Stainless steel support for light fitting
7 Waterproof light socket
8 Cast aluminium casing with acrylic paint finish
9 Energy saving light bulb
10 Horizontal indent to bollard surface
11 Mastic sealant
12 Cast aluminium with acrylic paint finish
13 Dye-cast aluminium with paint finish
14 Stainless steel liner sleeve
15 Void
16 Pre-cast concrete paving slab
17 Cast aluminium foundation pin
18 Incoming electric supply
19 Reinforced concrete base
20 Cinder concrete
21 Rubble sub-base

21.06
Aluminium Bench Plan and Section Detail
1:10
1 Cast aluminium bench feet below
2 Cast textured aluminium panel with silver finish
3 Cast aluminium bracing strips
4 Cast aluminium bracing strips
5 Bolts
6 Void
7 Cast textured aluminium panel with silver acrylic paint finish
8 Inner corner weld
9 Cross brace
10 Pre-cast concrete paving slab
11 Cast aluminium bench feet – vertical element
12 Cast aluminium bench feet – horizontal element
13 M10 aluminium nut
14 M10 aluminium bolt
15 M10 aluminium bolt head set in chemical anchor into foundation
16 Cast aluminium bracing strips
17 Cast in-situ concrete foundation

21.07
Pool Overflow Detail
1:10
1 Precast concrete paver
2 Mortar layer
3 Reinforced concrete slab on ground
4 150 mm (6 inch) thick reinforced concrete base with 6 mm (1/4 inch) diameter weld mesh reinforcing at 150 mm (6 inch) centres
5 Mortar bed
6 Rubble sub-base
7 Mastic joint
8 Stainless steel grate
9 Cast in-situ concrete foundation
10 Overflow channel
11 Pre-cast concrete channel
12 Mastic joint
13 Granite slab
14 Water surface
15 Mortar bed over waterproof membrane

21.08
Hard Wood Timber Deck Detail
1:5
1 45 x 90 mm (1³/4 x 3³/5 inch) preservative treated timber with grey stain finish
2 60 x 90 mm (2¹/3 x 3³/5 inch) timber bearer
3 45 x 145 mm (1³/4 x 5³/4 inch) preservative treated timber decking with grey stain finish
4 9 mm (1/3 inch) diameter anchor bolts at 900 mm (35²/5 inch) centres
5 Levelling mortar
6 Reinforced concrete slab
7 5 mm (1/5 inch) diameter weld mesh reinforcing at 150 mm (6 inch) centres
8 Drainage channel
9 Mortar bed
10 Weld-mesh reinforcing
11 Rubble sub-base

22
Office of Dan Kiley

Cudahy Gardens, Milwaukee Art Museum
Milwaukee, Wisconsin, USA

Client
Milwaukee Art Museum

Area
4.8 hectares (12 acres)

Project Team
Dan Kiley, Patrick Kressin,
Peter Meyer, Nanda Patel,
Rebecca Sherman

Civil and Structural Engineer
Graef, Anhalt, Schloemer &
Associates

Main Contractor
C. G. Schmidt

Water Feature Consultant
Dan Euser Waterarchitecture

Situated between the shore of Lake Michigan and the downtown district, this new museum and garden (a former landfill site), reunite the city and the lake. The design of the arrival plaza garden is inspired by the articulated purity of the architecture. The primary garden is a large rectangle located between the museum and the city, where a series of tall hedges separate the garden into five lawn panels, with paved plazas at each end. Monumental fountains anchor the centre of each plaza. These plazas are connected by a water channel that bisects the entire length of the garden. Jets within the channel create a transparent water curtain which is illuminated to create a shimmering band at the museum's most public face.

Each lawn panel breaks diagonally across its width, with the inner half descending towards the canal. The outer level lawns at street level are a very fine-textured grass while the inner inclined lawns are a rougher grass species – the contrast setting up a subtle diagonal rhythm. Plant and paving palettes within the garden are minimal: there are no trees, no flowerbeds or other elements to relieve the purity of the composition, balancing the delicate impression on the land with the monumentality of the architecture. The museum and gardens have effectively transformed a once derelict site into a seamless integration of architecture, land, water and light.

1 The museum addition, designed by Santiago Calatrava and completed in 2001, provides a majestic inspiration for the gardens. The fluid dialogue between building and landscape synchronizes the cultural qualities of the city and the beauty of the lake.
2 At night, the channel with its illuminated jets of water highlight the steel and glass of the museum.
3 On its east side, the museum faces Lake Michigan and includes a broad, paved pedestrian bike path that links a series of sculpted lawns and terraces.
4 View of the main garden where a series of hedges separates the garden into panels of lawn, the whole bisected by the water channel.
5 A view along the length of the water channel reveals the sloped profile of the lawn panels in the main garden.

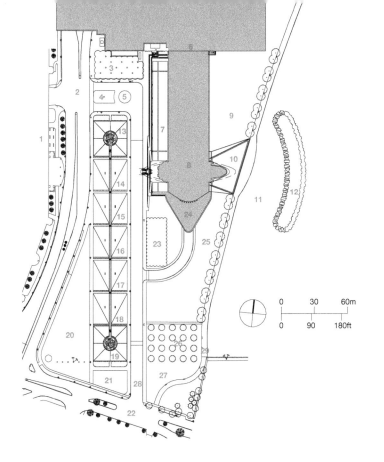

22.01
Site Plan
1:3000
1 O'Donnell Park and parking structure
2 Lincoln Memorial Drive
3 Linden Bosque
4 Flag poles
5 Lawn rotunda
6 Milwaukee Art Museum
7 West plaza
8 Milwaukee Art Museum addition
9 North lawn
10 Prow plaza
11 Lake Michigan
12 Stone breakwater
13 Fountain plaza
14 Lawn
15 Lawn
16 Lawn
17 Lawn
18 Lawn
19 Fountain plaza
20 West lawn
21 Lawn
22 East Michigan Street
23 Sargent Crabapple Bosque
24 South terrace
25 South lawn
26 Future Nikko fir grove
27 Lawn
28 Art Museum Drive
29 Lake Walk

22.02
Central Garden Plan
1:1000
1 Fountain pool
2 Fountain plaza
3 Sloped Lawn
4 Sloped lawn
5 Lawn
6 Lawn
7 Raised walkway
8 Yew hedge
9 Sloped lawn
10 Sloped lawn
11 Lawn
12 Lawn
13 Raised walkway
14 Yew hedge
15 Sloped lawn
16 Sloped lawn
17 Lawn
18 Lawn
19 Raised walkway
20 Yew hedge
21 Sloped lawn
22 Sloped lawn
23 Lawn
24 Lawn
25 Raised walkway
26 Yew hedge
27 Sloped lawn
28 Sloped lawn
29 Lawn
30 Lawn
31 Water channel
32 Fountain canal
33 Fountain pool
34 Existing footpath
35 Existing footpath
36 Fountain plaza

22.03
Fountain and Lawn Panel Plan
1:500
1 Granite cobble paving
2 Fountain pool sump
3 Granite banding to fountain edge
4 Stepping stone
5 Guardrail
6 Concrete wall and walkway
7 Stepping stone
8 Yew hedge planting bed
9 Bench
10 Lawn panel
11 Sloped lawn panel
12 Water channel
13 Sloped lawn panel
14 Sloped lawn panel

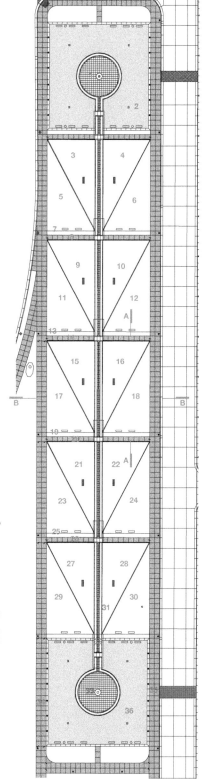

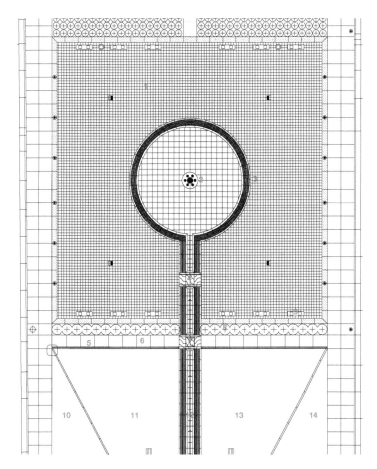

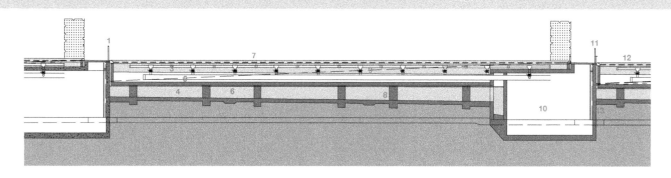

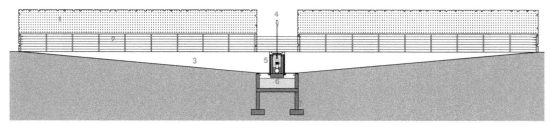

22.04
Fountain Section A–A
1:200
  1 Stainless steel
    cable rail
  2 Jet canal support
    pier inside
    reservoir
  3 100 mm (4 inch)

stainless steel jet
manifold
  4 Concrete canal
    basin
  5 254 mm (10 inch)
    main supply pipe
  6 Reservoir water
  7 Granite weir at
    canal

  8 Concrete reservoir
  9 Pool bed
 10 Pump room
 11 Stainless steel
    cable rail
 12 Jet canal
 13 Pump room wall
    and reservoir slab

22.05
Fountain Section B–B
1:200
  1 Yew hedge beyond
  2 Stainless steel rail
    beyond
  3 Granite-clad haha
    wall beyond
  4 1.5 m (5 foot) high

water sprays from
self equalizing jets
at 63 mm (2½
inch) spacings
  5 Granite-clad
    concrete jet canal
  6 Continuous
    reservoir below
    jet canal

  7 Concrete reservoir
    footing

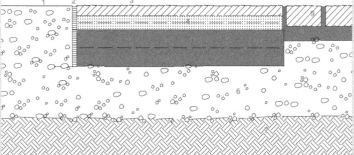

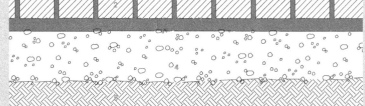

22.06
Granite Perimeter
Banding Detail
1:10
  1 Concrete walkway
    with pavers set flush
    with adjacent surfaces
  2 6 mm (¼ inch)
    expansion joint with
    filler, backer rod and

sealant
  3 Academy black
    granite paver with
    thermal finish
  4 38 mm (1½ inch)
    mortar bed with 50 x
    50 x 405 mm (2 x 2 x
    16 inch) galvanized
    wire mesh
    reinforcement

  5 100 mm (4 inch)
    concrete slab with wire
    mesh reinforcement
  6 150 mm (6 inch)
    compacted aggregate
    base course
  7 Compacted back fill
  8 38 mm (1½ inch)
    torpedo sand setting
    bed

  9 100 x 100 x 76 mm
    (4 x 4 x 3 inch)
    Carnelian granite
    cobble with split sides
    and thermal finish

22.07
Granite Cobble Detail
1:10
  1 12 mm (½ inch)
    polymetric sand joint
  2 100 x 100 x
    76 mm (4 x 4 x 3 inch)
    Carnelian granite
    cobble paver with
    split sides and

thermal finish
  3 38 mm (1½ inch)
    torpedo sand
    setting bed
  4 19 mm (¾ inch)
    crushed gravel
  5 Compacted
    subgrade

22.08
Granite Stepping
Stone at Vault
Hatch Detail
1:20
  1 30 mm (1¼ inch)
    thick Academy black
    granite with polished
    finish
  2 Academy black
    granite weir with
    polished finish
  3 Epoxy grout setting
    bed
  4 Concrete jet canal
    basin

  5 Fibre optic cable at
    south pool stepping
    stone
  6 50 mm (2 inch)
    thick granite stepping
    stone with thermal
    finish
  7 Concrete pump
    room wall
  8 Pump room hatch
    pneumatic balancing
    opener
  9 19 mm (¾ inch)
    thick Academy black
    granite stepping stone
    with thermal finish

applied to vault hatch
cover with thin set
setting bed
 10 Vault hatch
 11 50 mm (2 inch)
    thick granite stepping
    stone with thermal
    finish
 12 Concrete pump
    room wall
 13 Academy black
    granite with
    polished finish
 14 Concrete jet canal
    basin

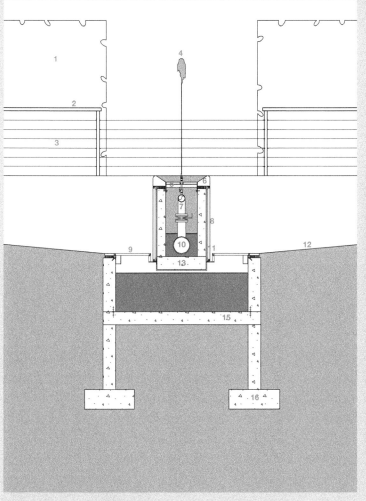

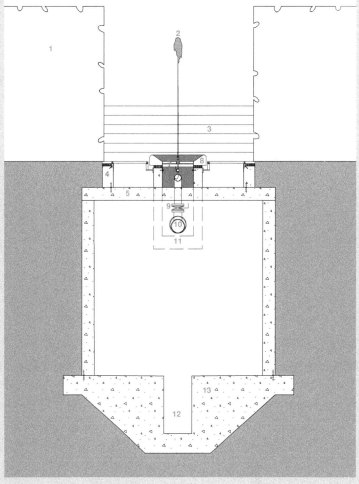

22.09
Section Detail
at Canal
1:50
  1 Yew Hedge
  2 Stainless steel rail
  3 Cable railing
  4 1.5 m (5 foot) high
water sprays from self-
equalizing jets at 63
mm (2½ inch)
spacings
  5 Removable granite
paver
  6 Granite weir
  7 100 mm (4 inch)

stainless steel jet
manifold
  8 Granite cladding
  9 Removable
stainless steel grate
  10 254 mm (10 inch)
main supply header
  11 12 mm (½ inch)
gap
  12 Grass slope
  13 Concrete jet canal
basin
  14 Reservoir water
  15 Concrete
waterproof reservoir
  16 Concrete footing

22.10
Section Detail at
Pump Room
1:50
  1 Yew hedge
  2 1.5 m (5 foot) high
water sprays from self-
equalizing jets at
63 mm (2½ inch)
spacings
  3 Cable railing
  4 Reservoir wall
  5 Pump room roof
and reservoir floor
  6 Water
  7 Removable granite

paver
  8 Granite weir
  9 100 mm (4 inch)
balancing valve at
every manifold section
  10 254 mm (10 inch)
main supply header
  11 Concrete jet
canal beyond
  12 Pump room sump
  13 Concrete pump
room floor

22.11
Fountain End Sump
Section Detail
1:20
  1 Submersible lights
on strap hangers with
hole cut in stone to
receive lights
  2 Submersible
junction box on 25 mm
(1 inch) red brass stub
  3 19 mm (¾ inch)
orifice clear stream jet
spray with 38 mm (1½
inch) connection and
50 mm (2 inch)
threaded valve
and reducer
  4 Custom octagonal
distributor box of 6
mm (¼ inch) plate
with internal
reinforcement, with
300 x 50 mm (12 x 2
inch) jet feeds and
vanstone flanged 200
mm (8 inch) inlet
secured with stainless
steel anchor bolts and

gaskets to floor at
corners
  5 Vanstone flags
  6 50 mm (2 inch) plug
drain pipes to reservoir

23
PWP Landscape Architecture

Nasher Sculpture Center Garden
Dallas, Texas, USA

Client
The Nasher Foundation

Area
1.25 hectares (3 acres)

Project Team
Peter Walker, Douglas Findlay, Tony Sinkosky, Jennifer Brooke, Gisela Steber, Jim Grimes, Gabriel Meil, Adam Greenspan

Architect
Renzo Piano Building Workshop

Structural Engineer
Datum Engineers

PWP Landscape Architecture were selected as the landscape architects for a sculpture garden and small museum that houses one of the most important private collections of modern sculpture in the world. The Nasher family decided to build the garden and museum as a home for the collection and as a gift to the citizens of Dallas. The Sculpture Garden is designed as an outdoor gallery that can accommodate between 20 and 30 sculptures. Because of the great weight of some of the sculptures and the necessity for moving pieces in and out, a special soil was developed that drains without catch basins, is strong enough to support heavy loads, and can support the growth of a specially resilient grass as well as many large trees.

A series of stone plinths distribute a flexible system of lighting, sound, security and irrigation, while serving as bases for smaller sculptures and providing casual seating. The museum was conceived as a parallel series of 'archaeological' walls directing sight and movement through the lightly glazed building. The garden walls extend this concept and are opened up by a series of transparent gates and windows allowing glimpses of the garden and the collection from adjacent streets. The planting too has been designed to form a series of continuous linear spaces with oak alleés, cedar elms, hedges, and the stone plinths situated along the axis of the garden. A broadstone terrace and steps connect the museum with the garden and street in a continuous flowing movement.

1 Aerial view of the Nasher Sculpture Center where the building, designed by Renzo Piano, opens up to the garden via a series of glazed walls.
2 An ipe wood board-walk separates reflecting pools from the terraced west end of the garden and the James Turrell installation, 'Tending (Blue)'.
3 Monumental sculptures including 'Tom's' by Alexander Calder (left), are presented in a calming landscaped context, in sharp contrast to the towers of downtown Dallas.
4 A window in the exterior wall of the garden provides a view of the reflecting pools and Henry Moore's working model for 'Three Piece No. 3: Vertebrae'.
5 The turf surface, which at first looks like a simple garden component, had to be tough enough to allow forklifts to move sculptures and to survive a high volume of pedestrian traffic.

100

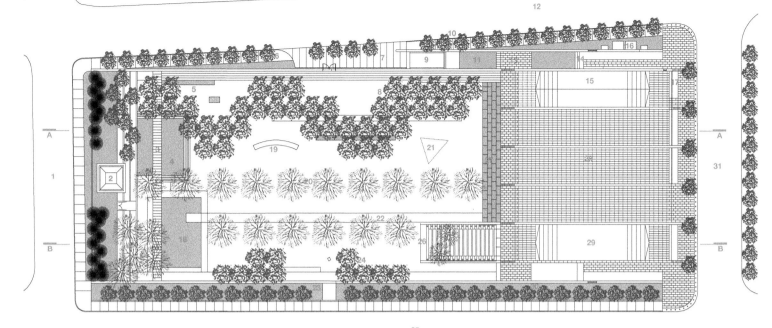

0 | 10 | 20m
0 | 30 | 60ft

23.01
Site Plan
1:1000
1 McKinney Avenue
2 James Turrell
  sculpture
  'Tending (Blue)'
3 Timber boardwalk
4 Reflecting pool
5 Cedar Elm
  sculpture room
6 Magnolia trees to
  garden edge
7 Truck ramp

8 Cedar Elm
  sculpture room
9 Loading dock
10 Magnolia trees to
  garden edge
11 Reflecting pool
12 Olive Street
13 Terrace and
  café seating
14 Bamboo terrace
15 Museum stair
16 Mechanical plant
17 Museum entrance
18 Reflecting pool

19 Richard Serra
  sculpture 'My
  Curves Are
  Not Mad'
20 Live Oak Allée
21 Mark Di Suvero
  sculpture 'Eviva
  Amor'
22 Stone walk
23 Magnolia trees at
  garden edge
24 Cedar Elm
  sculpture room
25 North Harwood

Street
26 Amphitheatre
27 Terrace and café
  seating
28 Nasher Sculpture
  Museum roof
29 Museum stair
30 Magnolia trees at
  garden edge
31 Flora Street

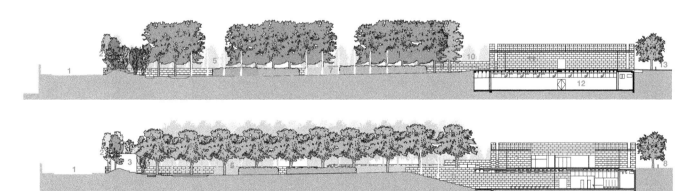

23.02
Section A–A
1:1000
1 McKinney Avenue
2 Magnolia trees at
  garden edge
3 Timber boardwalk
4 Cedar Elm
  sculpture room
5 Magnolia trees at
  garden edge
6 Cedar Elm
  sculpture room
7 Hedge

8 Cedar Elm
  sculpture room
9 Exterior wall
10 Terrace and café
  seating
11 Museum
12 Lower level
  of museum
13 Magnolia trees at
  garden edge

23.03
Section B–B
1:1000
1 McKinney Avenue
2 Magnolia trees at
  garden edge
3 James Turrell
  sculpture
  'Tending (Blue)'
4 Live Oak Allée
5 Outdoor sculpture
  room
6 Amphitheatre
7 Museum

8 Magnolia trees at
  garden edge

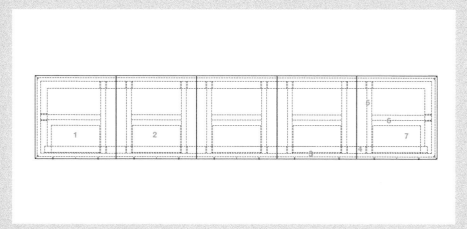

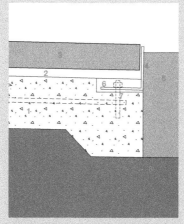

23.04
Stone Plinth Plan
1:50
1 1219 x 1219 mm
(4 x 4 foot) granite
end capping stone
2 1219 x 1219 mm
(4 x 4 foot) granite end
capping stone
3 Blockwork footing
below
4 Line of concrete
sub-wall below

5 76 x 76 mm (3 x 3
inch) rectangular steel
support tubes below
6 75 x 75 mm (3 x 3
inch) rectangular steel
support tubes below
7 1219 x 1219 mm
(4 x 4 foot) granite
end capping stone

23.05
Paving Edge To
Lawn Detail
1:10
1 150 mm (6 inch)
thick reinforced
concrete slab
2 25 mm (1 inch)
thick sand-cement
setting bed
3 Stone paver
4 127 x 127 mm (5 x
5 inch) galvanized steel

retention angle
5 Lawn soil mix
6 Grout bed
7 Anchor rod
8 Structural planting
soil mix

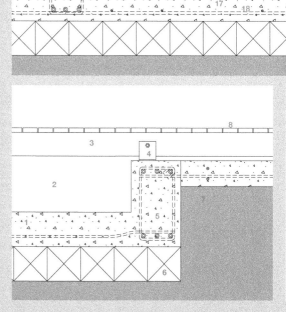

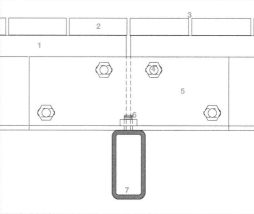

23.06
Boardwalk and
Reservoir Between
Water Feature Pool
Detail
1:20
1 Reinforced
concrete wall
to reservoir
2 Reinforcing stirrup
bar beyond
3 Flashing
4 Reservoir space
5 Void
6 Steel anchor
angles
7 Screw fixing
between deck and
joist
8 Steel anchor
angles
9 Timber beam
10 Timber joists at
550 mm (21 3/5 inch)
intervals
11 Timber decking
boards
12 Deck board support
angle
13 Beam support
angle
14 Reinforced
concrete wall to
reservoir
15 Water stop
16 Concrete fill
17 Reinforced
concrete reservoir
bottom
18 Steel reinforcing
19 Void boxes
20 Sub-grade soil

23.07
Boardwalk
Connection to
Reservoir Detail
1:20
1 Reinforced
concrete reservoir
bottom
2 Void
3 Timber joist
4 Steel anchor
angle
5 Reinforced
concrete wall to
reservoir
6 Void boxes
7 Subgrade soil
8 Timber decking
boards

23.08
Boardwalk Beam
Support at End
Joint Detail
1:5
1 Timber joist
2 Timber decking
boards
3 5 mm (3/16 inch)
gap between boards
4 Slotted bolt hole
edge in angle
5 Anchor splice angle
6 Threaded stud and
nut assembly
connection
7 Rectangular hollow
section joist

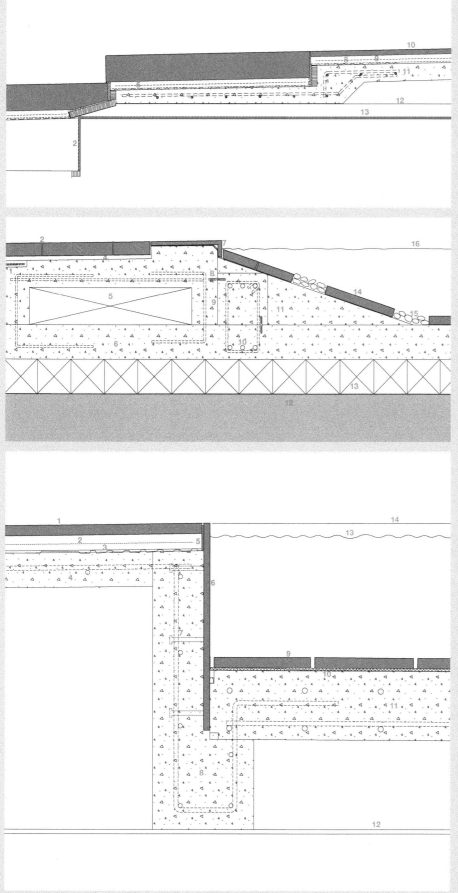

23.09
Stone Terrace Paving Edge to Stone Stairs Detail
1:20
1 150 mm (6 inch) thick stone step slab
2 Water proofing system
3 Drain mat
4 Expansion joint fill material
5 Top of drain mat beyond
6 150 mm (6 inch) thick stone step slab
7 Drain mat
8 Top of drain mat beyond
9 Welded wire fabric mesh in 50 mm (2 inch) thick mortar setting bed
10 30 mm ($^{13}/_{16}$ inch)

stone paver
11 100 mm (4 inch) thick reinforced concrete slab
12 Rigid insulation
13 Top of water proofing system

23.10
Water Feature Edge Paving Detail
1:20
1 Steel anchor angle
2 5 mm ($^3/_{16}$ inch) stabilized sand joint
3 75 mm (3 inch) thick stone paver
4 Sand-cement setting bed
5 Light weight fill block
6 Reinforced concrete slab
7 25 mm (1 inch) thick stone paver with adhesive joint at mitred corner
8 Waterstop
9 Cold joint
10 Reinforced concrete pool wall beam
11 Concrete fill

12 Subgrade soil
13 Void boxes
14 50 mm (2 inch) thick stone slabs to pool bottom
15 Stone aggregate
16 Water level

23.11
Water Feature Pool Edge and Stone Paving Detail
1:10
1 30 mm ($^3/_{16}$ inch) thick stone paver
2 Welded wire fabric in mortar setting bed
3 Drain mat beyond
4 Reinforced concrete slab
5 Expansion joint fill material
6 19 mm ($^3/_4$ inch) thick stainless steel wall plate
7 12 mm ($^1/_2$ inch) diameter), 100 mm (4 inch) long stainless steel headed stud welded to pool wall plate
8 Reinforced concrete pool wall
9 30 mm ($^3/_{16}$ inch) thick stone slab to pool bottom
10 Waterproof membrane and drain mat
11 Reinforced concrete slab to pool bottom
12 Rigid insulation over waterproofing membrane
13 Water level
14 Top of pool wall beyond

Garden of Australian Dreams, The National Museum of Australia, Canberra, ACT, Australia

Client
The National Museum of Australia

Area
10 hectares (24.7 acres)

Project Team
Vladimir Sitta, Richard Weller, Elizabeth Burt, Kioshi Furuno, Luca Ginoulhiac, Scott Hawken, Silvia Krizova, Pavol Moravcik, Maren Parry, Daniel Firns, Karl Kullmann

Architect
Ashton Raggatt McDougall

The National Museum of Australia is charged with documenting Australia's popular culture through the themes of 'Land', 'People' and 'Nation'. The museum building is tentatively connected to the Gallery of First Australians, Australia's premier collection of indigenous culture. The design concept consists of tangled lines that carve voids into the architecture to create landscape spaces. The tangled conditions also operate as a metaphor for the nation's interwoven pluralist destiny. The Garden of Australian Dreams recognizes emergent senses of place, writing, mapping, imaging, reading and singing the Australian landscape. The garden is based on a layered series of maps imprinted in concrete.

The two main maps are a standard English language map of Australia and Horton's map of the tribal boundaries of indigenous Australia. The names and lines on these maps interweave, erase and overlay one another, forming a complex weave. Adding to the mosaic is the word 'home' translated into the various languages spoken in contemporary Australia and written across the surface of the whole map. The map provides a continuous ground sheet but it is not always flat. The concrete map surface folds and rises like a sand dune or a ridge to form a tunnel under the map so that visitors can, in one brief passage, pass under the layers of information. The Garden of Australian Dreams is richly woven with the light and shadow of contemporary Australia and aspects of the aesthetic concerns of contemporary global landscape design.

1 View into the Garden of Australian Dreams flanked by the National Museum of Australia and the Gallery of First Australians. The 'garden' is a large concrete rendition of various maps of Australia. The yellow cursive writing appears half in and out of the waterbody and is a direct copy of the word 'Australian' copied from Australia's national currency.
2 Extending the Boolean geometry of the architecture, the end of the Uluru axis curls toward the landscape beyond.
3 View across the 'Backyard'. The red X is based on the fact that many illiterate indigenous Australians often signed documents with an X.
4 An amphitheatre links the museum to Lake Burley Griffin.
5 Entrance into 'Place Under the Map' which is conceived as a future soundscape featuring the voices of Australia.

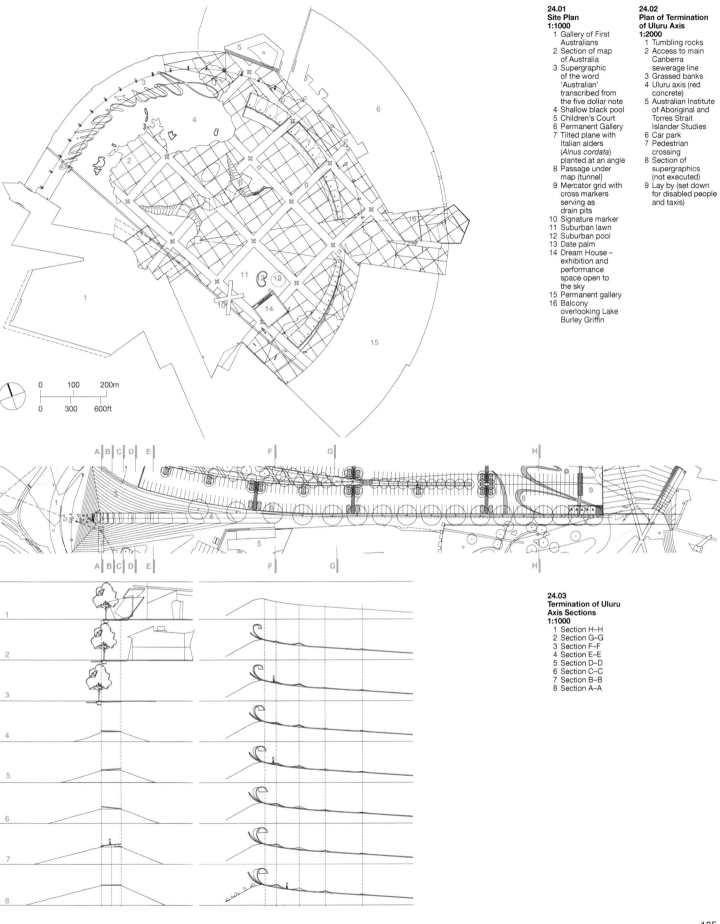

24.01
Site Plan
1:1000

1 Gallery of First Australians
2 Section of map of Australia
3 Supergraphic of the word 'Australian' transcribed from the five dollar note
4 Shallow black pool
5 Children's Court
6 Permanent Gallery
7 Tilted plane with Italian alders (*Alnus cordata*) planted at an angle
8 Passage under map (tunnel)
9 Mercator grid with cross markers serving as drain pits
10 Signature marker
11 Suburban lawn
12 Suburban pool
13 Date palm
14 Dream House – exhibition and performance space open to the sky
15 Permanent gallery
16 Balcony overlooking Lake Burley Griffin

24.02
Plan of Termination of Uluru Axis
1:2000

1 Tumbling rocks
2 Access to main Canberra sewerage line
3 Grassed banks
4 Uluru axis (red concrete)
5 Australian Institute of Aboriginal and Torres Strait Islander Studies
6 Car park
7 Pedestrian crossing
8 Section of supergraphics (not executed)
9 Lay by (set down for disabled people and taxis)

24.03
Termination of Uluru Axis Sections
1:1000

1 Section H–H
2 Section G–G
3 Section F–F
4 Section E–E
5 Section D–D
6 Section C–C
7 Section B–B
8 Section A–A

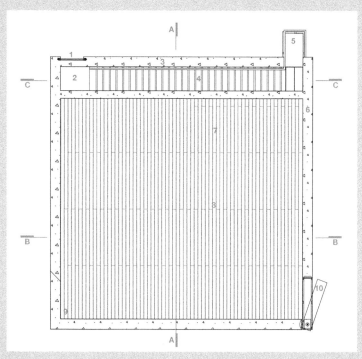

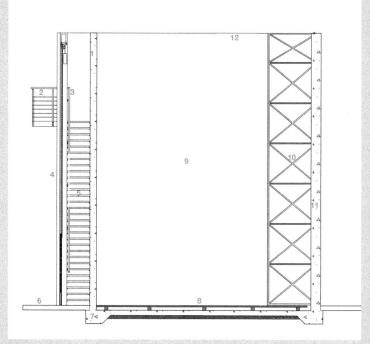

24.04
The Living Room Plan
1:100
1 Balcony access via guillotine door
2 Landing
3 Concrete walls
4 Steel staircase
5 Balcony with a statue of the 'Antipodean'
6 Concrete walls
7 Timber decking
8 Cables to ceiling
9 Sliding corner (alternative access)
10 Large door of steel frame and fiber cement sheeting to open entire section of wall

24.05
The Living Room
Section A–A
1:100
1 Partition wall
2 Steel balcony
3 Steel railings
4 White painted walls
for projections
5 Steel access stairs
6 Paving
7 Concrete footing
8 Timber decking to floor
9 White painted walls
10 Door frame
11 Concrete wall
12 Cables to ceiling

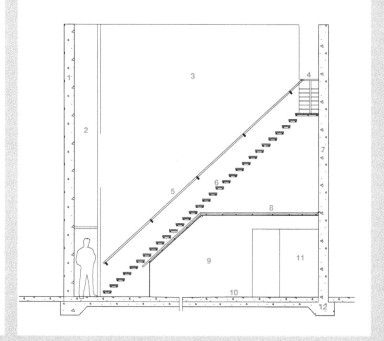

24.06
The Living Room
Section B–B
1:100
1 Concrete walls
2 White painted walls
3 Concrete footing
4 Timber decking
5 Drainage pipe
6 Concrete floor slab
7 Access to plant room via pivoting wall

24.07
The Living Room
Section C–C
1:100
1 Concrete walls
2 Access via guillotine door
3 White painted wall
4 Balcony
5 Steel railing
6 Access stairs
7 Concrete wall
8 Plant room ceiling
9 Pump and switchboard area
10 Concrete floor
11 Pivoting door
12 Concrete footing

24.08
Map Surface at Pool Edge Detail
1:200
1 Colonnade
2 Roof outline
3 Supergraphic of the word 'Australian'
4 Shallow black pool
5 Map of Australia
6 Construction joints
7 Construction joints
8 Embankments at sides of tunnel

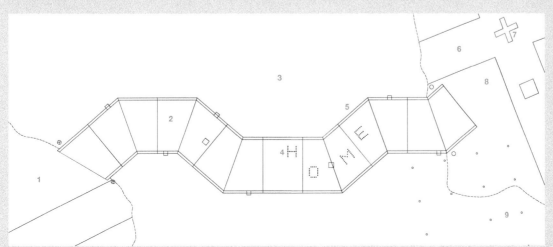

24.09
Tunnel Floor Plan
1:200
1 Rubber surface
2 Planned soundscape
3 Map surface
4 Word 'HOME' in red stainless glass in tunnel ceiling (not executed)
5 Pre-cast concrete culvert
6 Mercator grid
7 Cross marking-drain
8 Rubber surface
9 Surveyor poles

Copia: The American Center for Wine, Food and the Arts Napa, California, USA

Client
Copia

Area
4.6 hectares (11.5 acres)

Project Team
Peter Walker, Doug Findlay, Tony Sinkosky, Paul Sieron, Jim Grimes, James A. Lord, Dorothee Imbert, Tom Leader, Carol Souza

Architect
Polshek Partnership Architects

Structural Engineer
Rutherford & Chekene

Copia is a non-profit institution that features the food, wine and arts of the Napa Valley in California's wine country. In conjunction with a museum, the client asked PWP Landscape Architecture to design demonstration gardens, an outdoor dining terrace, and an amphitheatre overlooking along an oxbow of the Napa River. Through the use of 15 metre (50 foot) planted squares set on a grid separated by walkways and surrounded by stone seat walls, the geometry of the museum is extended across the 4.6 hectare (11.5 acre) site. The squares are accessed from a central decomposed granite path that runs at an angle, separating the gardens from the parking areas to the west. This path is flanked by poplars, which run from the museum entrance to the southern tip of the site – some 250 metres (820 feet).

Within this angled poplar alleé is a shallow 4.5 metre (15 foot) concrete fountain, which slopes away from the museum. The fountain is composed of three pools in a row, one cascading and two still, the bottom of each covered in black river rocks. Located closest to the museum entrance, the cascading pool is divided into 11 sections, each separated by a stainless steel weir turned to align with the garden grid. The walls of the fountain act as seats, providing a comfortable place to rest, dip a hand into the cooling water and listen to the soothing splash of the weirs.

1 The 76 metre (250 feet) long weir is the central feature of the design and provides a distinctive boundary between the car park to the west and the gardens to the east.
2 The Copia Museum, designed by Polshek Partnership Architects, provides a focus for an appreciation and understanding of the food and wine of the Napa region.
3 The planted squares are defined by seat-height rubble stone walls.
4 Detail view of one of the garden squares which provide fruit and vegetables for the restaurant.
5 Detail view of a section of the weir which is flanked by an alleé of poplars.

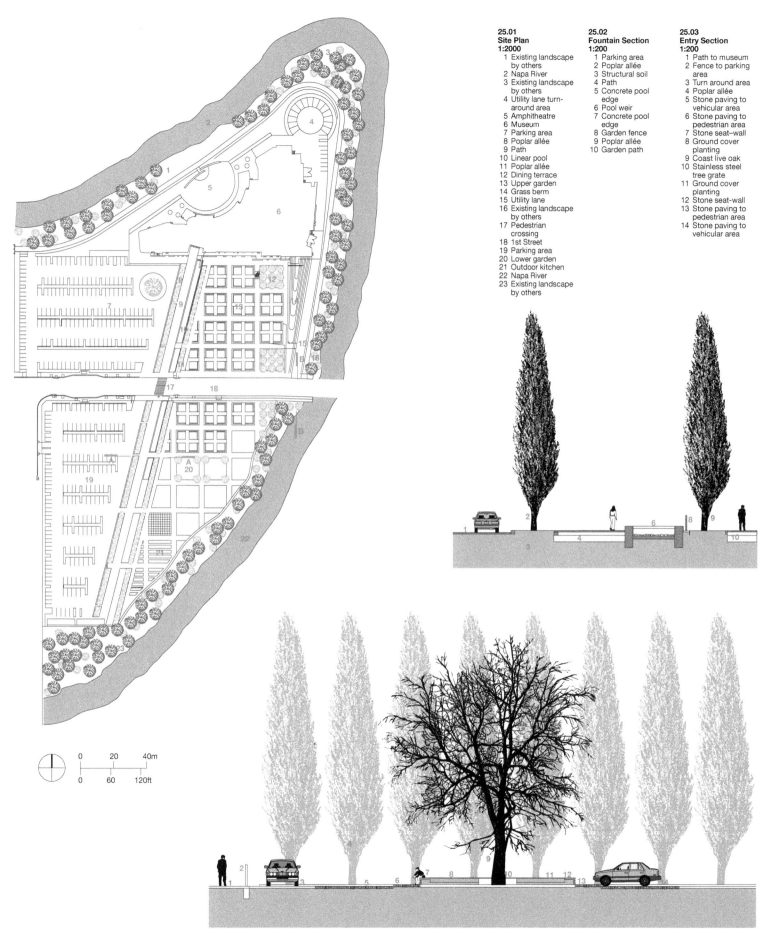

25.01
Site Plan
1:2000
1 Existing landscape by others
2 Napa River
3 Existing landscape by others
4 Utility lane turn-around area
5 Amphitheatre
6 Museum
7 Parking area
8 Poplar allée
9 Path
10 Linear pool
11 Poplar allée
12 Dining terrace
13 Upper garden
14 Grass berm
15 Utility lane
16 Existing landscape by others
17 Pedestrian crossing
18 1st Street
19 Parking area
20 Lower garden
21 Outdoor kitchen
22 Napa River
23 Existing landscape by others

25.02
Fountain Section
1:200
1 Parking area
2 Poplar allée
3 Structural soil
4 Path
5 Concrete pool edge
6 Pool weir
7 Concrete pool edge
8 Garden fence
9 Poplar allée
10 Garden path

25.03
Entry Section
1:200
1 Path to museum
2 Fence to parking area
3 Turn around area
4 Poplar allée
5 Stone paving to vehicular area
6 Stone paving to pedestrian area
7 Stone seat–wall
8 Ground cover planting
9 Coast live oak
10 Stainless steel tree grate
11 Ground cover planting
12 Stone seat-wall
13 Stone paving to pedestrian area
14 Stone paving to vehicular area

0 20 40m
0 60 120ft

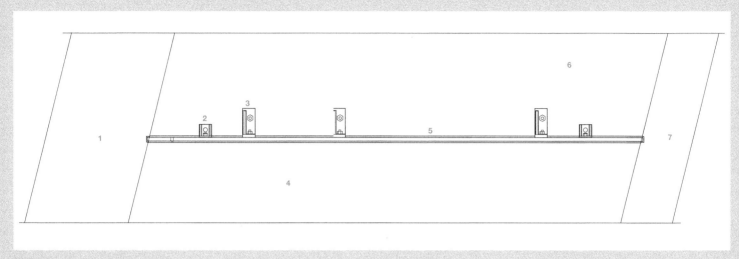

25.04
Northern Water
Feature Weir Plan
Detail
1:20
  1 Pool seat wall
  2 Steel levelling
angle

3 Steel gusset
4 Bottom of pool
5 Weir
6 Bottom of pool
7 Pool side wall

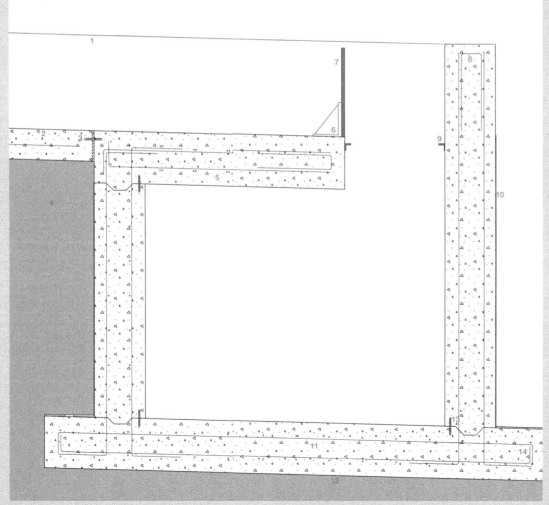

25.05
Northern Water
Feature Reservoir
Detail
1:20
  1 Top of pool side
wall
  2 Reinforced
concrete slab to pool
bottom
  3 Steel dowel
  4 Sub-grade soil
  5 Reinforced
concrete bottom to
pool and ceiling
to reservoir below
  6 Steel gusset
  7 Stainless steel weir
plate
  8 Steel reinforcing at
200 mm (8 inch)
centres in 300 mm
(12 inch) thick concrete
reservoir wall
  9 Steel grate
10 Concrete pool end
wall with damp proof
lining
11 Concrete floor slab
to pool bottom
12 Sub-grade soil
13 Waterstop
14 Reinforcing hook
bars at ends of slab

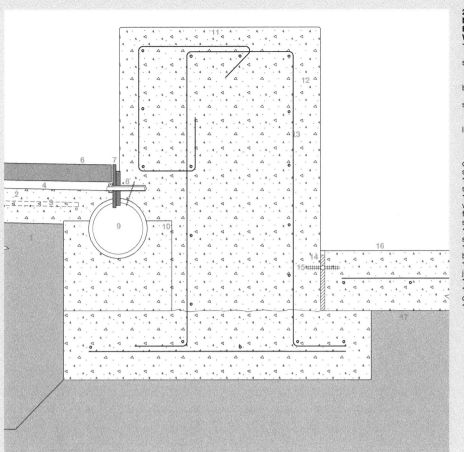

25.06
Northern Water
Feature Pool Seat
Wall Detail
1:10
 1 Structural planting
soil mix
 2 Concrete sub-slab
 3 Steel reinforcing
bar beyond
 4 Cement stabilized
sand setting bed
 5 Stone paver
 6 Finished ground
level
 7 Steel plate
 8 Steel anchor pin
 9 150 mm (6 inch)
diameter corrugated
slot drain pipe
 10 Concrete pipe
support
 11 Finished pool seat
with medium sandblast
finish to all exposed
surfaces
 12 Concrete pool
seat wall
 13 Steel reinforcing
bar
 14 Expansion
joint material
 15 Waterstop
 16 Finished surface to
concrete pool bottom
 17 Sub-grade soil

25.07
Pool Weir Anchor
Detail
1:2.5
 1 19 mm (³/₄ inch)
thick steel weir plate
 2 19 mm (³/₄ inch)
thick steel weir
anchor plate
 3 Serrated nut
washer
 4 Steel nut
 5 Stainless steel
threaded rod anchor
stud
 6 Steel nut
 7 19 mm (³/₄ inch)
thick steel weir
anchor plate
 8 Serrated
lockwasher
 9 12 mm (¹/₂ inch)
wide by 25 mm (1 inch)
high slot void
 10 Stainless steel nut
 11 12 mm (¹/₂ inch)
diameter by 63 mm
(2¹/₂ inch) long
stainless steel
threaded stud
 12 Typical weld
 13 Waterproof,
non-shrink grout
 14 8.5 mm (³/₈ inch)
thick sealant
 15 Backer rod
 16 Steel anchor plate
parallel with pool
bottom slope
 17 Serrated nut
washer
 18 Steel nut
 19 12 mm (¹/₂ inch)
wide by 25 mm (1 inch)
high slot void
 20 Stainless steel
threaded rod anchor
stud
 21 Epoxy grout
 22 Concrete pool
bottom
 23 Rebar beyond

25.08
Weir Levelling
Bracket Detail
1:2.5
 1 19 mm (³/₄ inch)
thick steel weir plate
 2 Upper part of
76 x 76 mm (3 x 3 inch)
stainless steel angle
 3 Heavy duty,
stainless steel hex nut
 4 8.5 mm (³/₈ inch)
thick stainless steel
gusset plate
 5 19 mm (³/₄ inch)
diameter stainless
steel threaded rod
stud
 6 76 x 76 mm (3 x 3
inch) stainless steel
angle
 7 Heavy duty,
stainless steel levelling
hex nut
 8 25 mm (1 inch)
diameter, 125 mm
(5 inch) long stainless
steel threaded rod
 9 Grout
 10 9.5 mm (³/₈ inch)
thick sealant
 11 Backer rod
 12 Adhesive
 13 Concrete pool
bottom slab

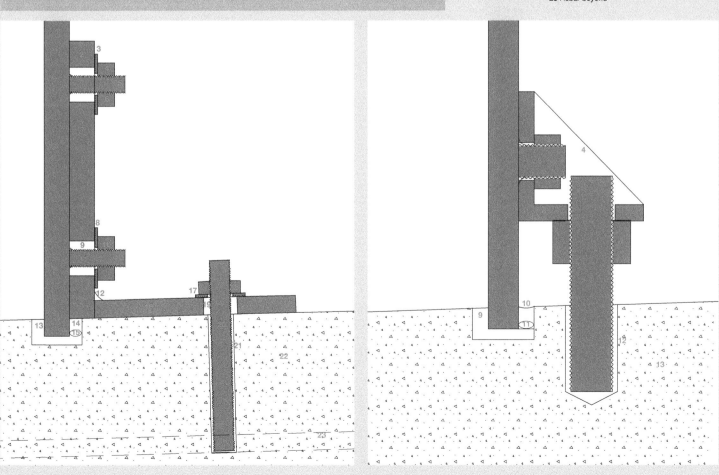

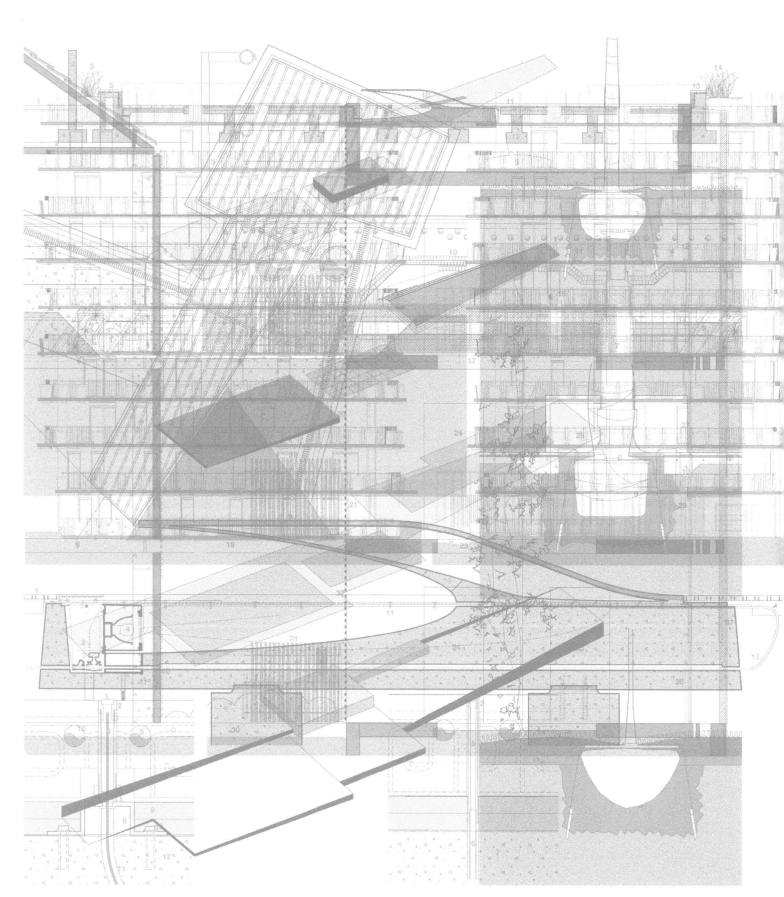

112

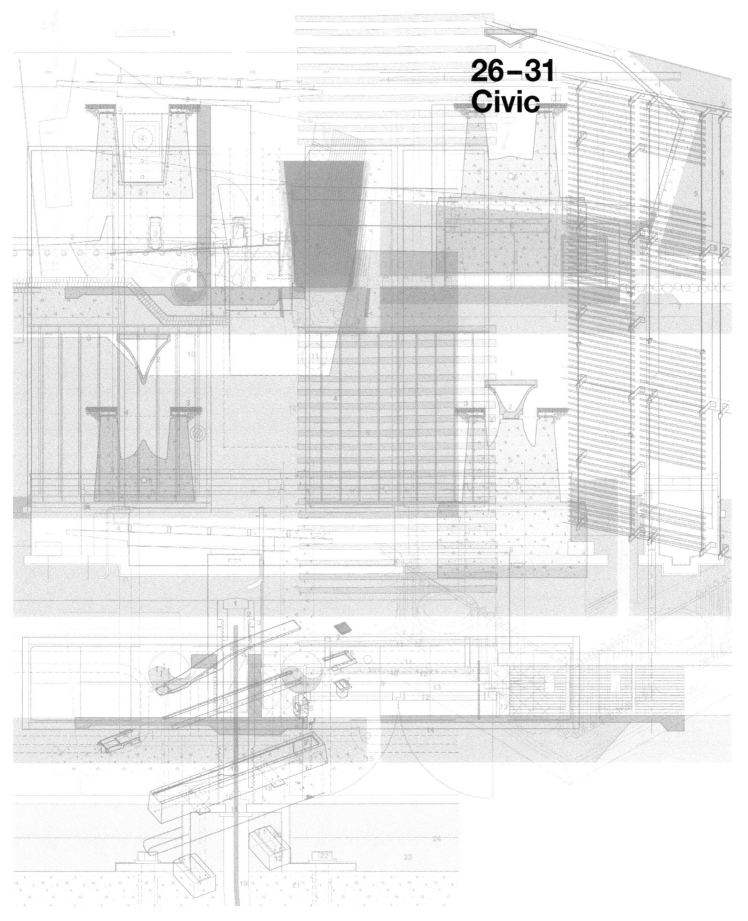

26-31
Civic

Flower Tower
Paris, France

Client
OPAC de Paris

Area
0.26 hectares (0.64 acres)

Project Team
Edouard François, Marika Lemper,
José Reis de Matos

Structural Engineer
Beaulieu Ingènierie, Verdier

Structural Concrete Consultant
Ductal, Lafarge

This playful, in fact outright witty building is, in fact, a simple inner-city apartment block, called, for obvious reasons, 'Flower Tower'. In this off-beat solution to a ten-storey high concrete structure with apartments gathered around a central lift core, a diaphanous screen of vegetation sheathes the block in a corona of lush greenery. Almost cartoon-like white flower pots are planted with bamboo, which grows quickly, providing natural sunshades for the apartments and screens from prying neighbours. The bamboo plants are fed and watered automatically through artificial stems running inside the metal balustrades of each storey. This ensures that when tenants are away, the bamboo will thrive.

The result is a modest, urban home that fits comfortably into its city while offering the illusion of being by the sea. What the block shows is that it is possible to build thoughtful, practical, low-cost housing in city centres, getting nature to do a significant part of the work of turning these places into visual, and even sensual, delights. There was a rush to live in the Flower Tower, for not only does each apartment enjoy a more or less enclosed timber balcony, but residents knew that sooner or later, the wall would bloom, as indeed it has. François has taken no chances on the vagaries of nature however. By planting bamboo in pots, he has ensured that the building looked as he planned it to from day one.

1 It is apparent from this view of the Flower Tower that its underlying structure has much in common with its neighbours. The confronting and yet humourous bamboo screen, however, make it an apartment building like no other. **2** The massive white-painted concrete pots are structurally attached to the concrete frame. The plants are fed and watered automatically so that the bamboo is kept healthy and so that all four façades are uniform in appearance. **3** The bamboo plants provide perfect sun and privacy screens for the residents of Flower Tower.

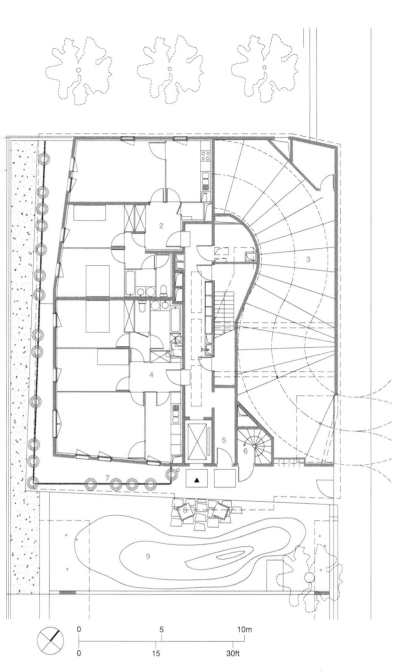

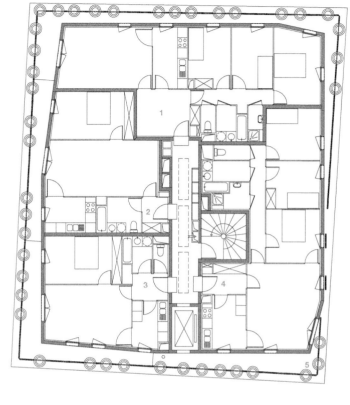

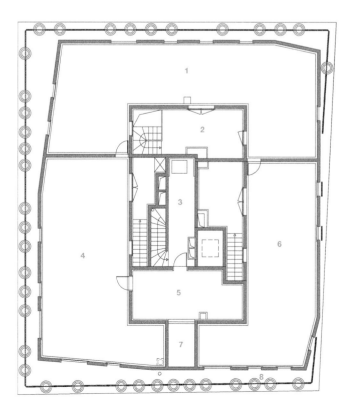

0 5 10m

0 15 30ft

26.01
Ground Floor Plan
1:200
1 Gravel path
2 Apartment lobby
3 Driveway from street to underground parking garage
4 Apartment lobby
5 Main entrance
6 Emergency stair exit
7 Perimeter steel balustrade incorporating white-painted concrete pots planted with bamboo
8 Stone paving
9 Grass mound

26.02
Fifth Floor Plan
1:200
1 Entrance lobby to three bedroom apartment
2 Entrance lobby to one bedroom apartment
3 Entrance lobby to one bedroom apartment
4 Entrance lobby to three bedroom apartment
5 Perimeter steel balustrade incorporating white-painted concrete pots planted with bamboo

26.03
Ninth Floor Plan
1:200
1 Terrace
2 Attic
3 Technical installation
4 Terrace
5 Gas boiler room
6 Terrace
7 Lift shelter
8 Perimeter steel balustrade incorporating white-painted concrete pots planted with bamboo

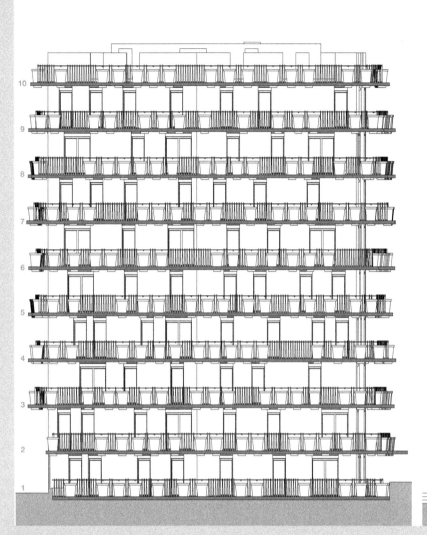

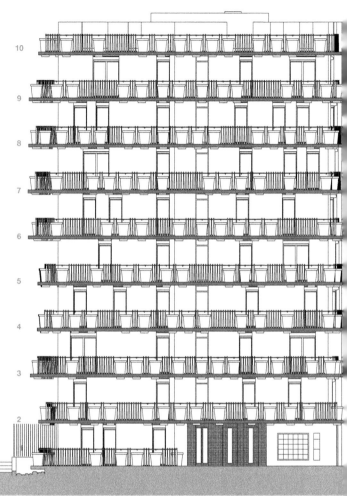

26.04
South-West Elevation
1:200
1 Ground floor
2 First floor
3 Second floor
4 Third floor
5 Fourth floor
6 Fifth floor
7 Sixth floor
8 Seventh floor
9 Eighth floor
10 Ninth floor

26.05
South-East Elevation
1:200
1 Ground floor
2 First floor
3 Second floor
4 Third floor
5 Fourth floor
6 Fifth floor
7 Sixth floor
8 Seventh floor
9 Eighth floor
10 Ninth floor

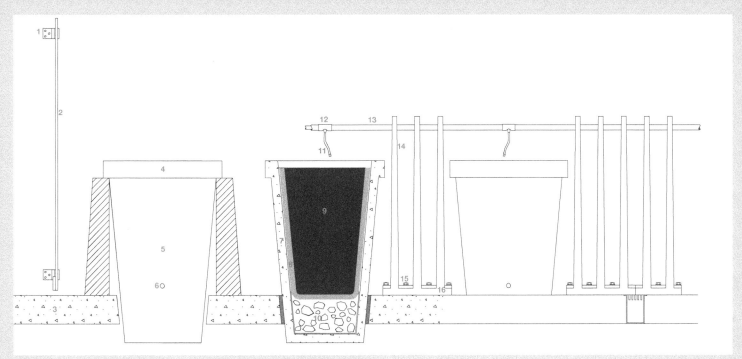

26.06
Typical Balustrade
Sectional Detail 1
1:20
  1 Stainless steel
hinge
  2 Hinged toughened
coloured glass balcony
divider to allow for
maintenance access
  3 Cantilevered

reinforced concrete
blacony slab
  4 Top edge of
concrete bamboo pot
  5 'Ductal' ultra-high-
performance concrete
with chemical and
environmental
resistance bamboo pot
  6 Drainage hole
  7 Sectional view of

'Ductal' ultra-high-
performance concrete
bamboo pot
  8 Felt cloth
insulation layer
  9 Steppe black soil
  10 Lava stone or clay
rubble layer
  11 Irrigation pipe
  12 Stainless steel
reinforcement sheath

  13 Stainless steel
irrigation pipe to allow
for automatic watering
  14 Pre-cast 'Ductal'
balustrade post
  15 Stainless steel
screw to balustrade
fixing
  16 Pre-cast 'Ductal'
balustrade post

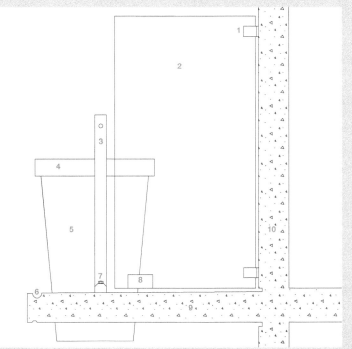

26.07
Typical Balustrade
Sectional Detail 2
1:20
  1 Stainless steel
hinge
  2 Hinged toughened
coloured glass balcony
divider to allow for
maintenance access
  3 Pre-cast 'Ductal'

balustrade post
  4 Top edge of
concrete bamboo pot
  5 'Ductal' ultra-high-
performance concrete
with chemical and
environmental
resistance bamboo pot
  6 Drainage channel to
edge of reinforced
concrete balcony slab

  7 Stainless steel
screw to balustrade
fixing
  8 Stainless steel
lock to glass balcony
divider
  9 Cantilevered
reinforced concrete
blacony slab
  10 Reinforced
concrete structure

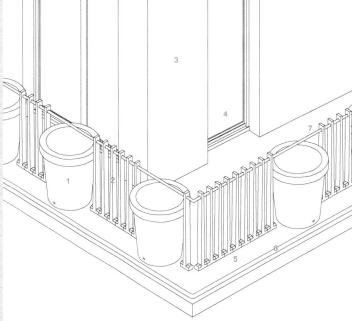

26.08
Typical Balustrade
Axonometric Detail
  1 'Ductal' ultra-high-
performance concrete
with chemical and
environmental
resistance bamboo pot
  2 Pre-cast 'Ductal'
balustrade post
  3 Reinforced

concrete structure
  4 Clear glazing with
PVC frames to
apartment windows
  5 Cantilevered
reinforced concrete
balcony slab
  6 Drainage channel to
edge of reinforced
concrete balcony slab
  7 Stainless steel

irrigation pipe to allow
for automatic watering

Ecliptic
Grand Rapids, Michigan, USA

Client
The Frey Foundation and the City of Grand Rapids

Area
1.4 hectares (3.5 acres)

Project Team
Maya Lin, Nicole Pellogré, Sarah Wayland-Smith, Sherry Shiehl, Stas Zakrzewski

Landscape Architect
Quennell Rothschild and Partners

Structural Engineer
Moore & Bruggink

The design concept for this park and fountain embraces the use of water in its three states – liquid, solid and vapour. Two circular fountains mark the northern and southern entrances. One is a raised granite circle with water flowing from one half of the circle and gently cascading over the front of the fountain. The second is a sunken granite circle surrounded by a low stone ring that holds hidden mist fountains, creating a circular room of mist that one can sit around or step into. The walkway connecting the two fountains is landscaped into gentle rolling waves of grass, expressive of water in its liquid state.

At the heart of the park is the amphitheatre, with curved seating terraces that suggest the concentric rings formed by a drop of water. In the winter the amphitheatre becomes an ice skating rink, representing water in its solid state. Although water must freeze on a flat level plane, the seating surrounding the rink is deliberately sloped so that when one stands upon this elliptical plane there is an illusion that the surface is tilted. Embedded into the concrete floor of the amphitheatre are fibre optic points of light that map out the location of the stars overhead on January 1, 2000, marking the parks' place in time. The lights are visible year round, with their light refracting and magnifying under the ice in the winter months. The artwork incorporates an interest in natural phenomena and the passage of time as well as exploring ways to change ones perception with subtle shifts in the ground plane.

1 The heart of the scheme is a skating rink that converts into an amphitheatre in the warmer months and is lit by tiny fibre-optic lights embedded in its surface.
2 The park includes a small service building in steel and concrete and wandering paths through landscaped mounds of grass that rise and fall in waves.
3 Water is featured in all three states: in the ice-skating rink, a vapour fountain and here in a water fountain.
4 Fibre-optic lights beneath the ice, created in collabora-tion with lighting designer Linnaea Tillett, match the pattern of the constella-tions on January 1, 2000, the year the park was created.
5 During the warmer months, the ice rink serves as an amphitheatre for public performances.

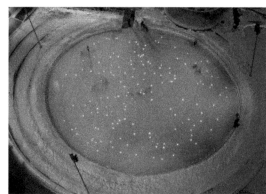

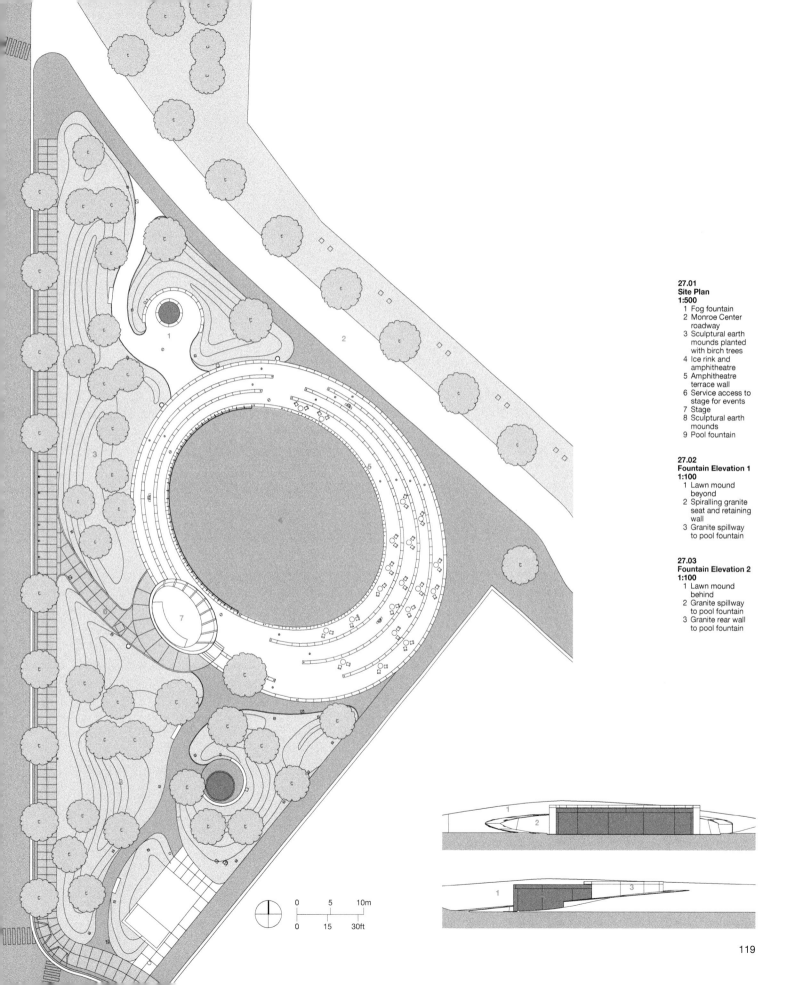

27.01
Site Plan
1:500
1 Fog fountain
2 Monroe Center
  roadway
3 Sculptural earth
  mounds planted
  with birch trees
4 Ice rink and
  amphitheatre
5 Amphitheatre
  terrace wall
6 Service access to
  stage for events
7 Stage
8 Sculptural earth
  mounds
9 Pool fountain

27.02
Fountain Elevation 1
1:100
1 Lawn mound
  beyond
2 Spiralling granite
  seat and retaining
  wall
3 Granite spillway
  to pool fountain

27.03
Fountain Elevation 2
1:100
1 Lawn mound
  behind
2 Granite spillway
  to pool fountain
3 Granite rear wall
  to pool fountain

0   5   10m

0   15   30ft

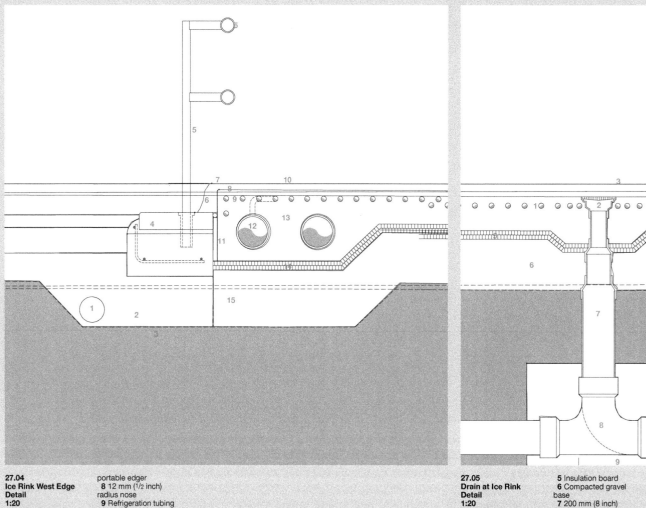

27.04
Ice Rink West Edge
Detail
1:20
1 150 mm (6 inch) perforated pipe
2 Crushed stone sub-base
3 Filter fabric
4 Flush cast stone curb on reinforced concrete base
5 Removeable aluminium railing set in anchor sleeves
6 Ungroomed ice at vertical face
7 Ice sheet under railing groomed using

portable edger
8 12 mm (1/2 inch) radius nose
9 Refrigeration tubing
10 Top of ice sheet
11 25 mm (1 inch) expansion joint
12 200 mm (8 inch) diameter supply header pipes
13 Reinforced concrete
14 Insulation board
15 Compacted gravel base with filter fabric underlay

27.05
Drain at Ice Rink
Detail
1:20
1 Refrigeration tubing with layout deformed around drain
2 Drain with nickel bronze top and nickel bronze vandal-proof tractor gate, covered with plastic during the ice season and 100 mm (4 inch) cast iron outlet pipe with slip connection
3 Ice surface
4 Reinforced concrete

5 Insulation board
6 Compacted gravel base
7 200 mm (8 inch) cast iron soil pipe
8 200 mm (8 inch) cast iron T-bend
9 Concrete encasement
10 200 mm (8 inch) PVC pipe

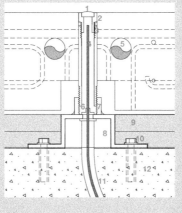

27.06
Fibre Optic Light to
Ice Rink Detail
1:5
1 Glass lens bonded within ferrule
2 Fibre optic lens ferrule threaded and screwed into place after concrete pour
3 Sealant
4 Fibre optic cable
5 Refrigeration tubing
6 Lock-nut
7 Threaded collar welded to stabilizing bracket
8 Stabilizing bracket
9 Two layers of 25 mm (1 inch) rigid insulation
10 Expansion bolt

11 19 mm (3/4 inch) conduit
12 Concrete footing

27.07
Tent Guy Anchor to
Ice Rink Detail
1:5
1 Stainless steel plug
2 15 mm (3/5 inch) stainless steel receptacle
3 Refrigeration tubing
4 Steel reinforcement to concrete slab
5 Threaded stainless steel support threaded on anchor bolt with threaded adaptors as necessary
6 Stainless steel anchor bolt embedded 100 mm (4 inches) into concrete base
7 Concrete footing

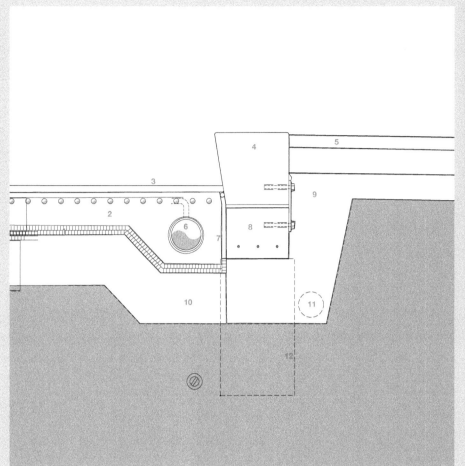

27.08
Ice Rink East Edge
Detail
1:20
  1 Insulation board
  2 Reinforced
concrete slab with
refrigeration tubing
  3 Ice surface
  4 Cast stone kerb
wall
  5 Stabilized gravel
pavement
  6 200 mm (8 inch)
diameter refrigerator
return header pipe
  7 25 mm (1 inch)
expansion joint
  8 Poured in place
concrete grade beam
continuous with inside
face aligned with
bottom of cast stone
for clean vertical
expansion joint at
rink slab
  9 Compacted
crushed stone
sub-base
  10 Gravel base
under ice rink slab
  11 150 mm (6 inch)
perforated pipe
  12 457 mm (18 inch)
reinforced concrete
pier

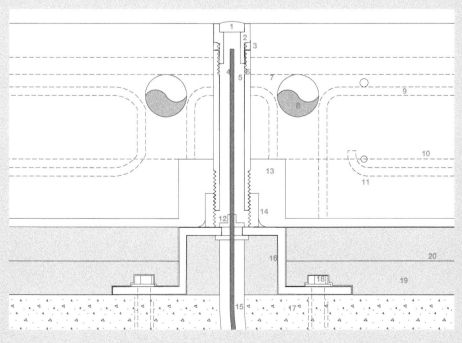

27.09
Ice Rink Slab
Refrigeration Piping
System Detail
1:10
  1 Glass lens bonded
with ferrule
  2 Fibre optic lens
ferrule threaded and
screwed in place after
concrete pour
  3 Sealant
  4 Fibre optic cable
  5 Concrete slab with
integral colourant and
surface colour
hardener
  6 Threaded sleeve
  7 Fibre optic star with
stainless steel bracket
  8 Refrigeration tubing
  9 Reinfocing bars at
300 mm (12 inch)
centres
  10 Two layers of
25 mm (1 inch) rigid
insulation
  11 Compacted gravel
base
  12 Lock nut
  13 150 x 300 mm
(6 x 14 inch) concrete
footing poured in
sonotube
  14 Threaded collar
welded to stabilizing
bracket

  15 19 mm (³/4 inch)
conduit
  16 Stabilizing bracket
  17 Concrete footing
  18 Expansion bolt
  19 Compacted
sub-grade
  20 Filter fabric

**Bus Stop and Station Square
Enschede, The Netherlands**

Client
City of Enschede

Area
13 hectares (32 acres)

Project Team
Martin Knuijt, Christ-Jan Van Rooy,
Wim Voogt

Architect
VanderTak Architecten

The city of Enschede is located on the German border, where the abolition of European frontiers shifted the city from its peripheral location to the heart of an economic region. A decisive element of the city's transformation is the redevelopment of a 13 hectare (32 acre) area round the station. The strategy was to create public space that would act as a motor for urban development. The landscape design expresses confidence in the site, helping to convince investors to erect buildings of high architectural quality. The inclined topography of the site inspired the design of three squares facing the city centre, with an elongated pool registering the varying heights as a 'spirit level'.

The squares serve as transfer points from one means of public transport to another, becoming lively spaces where buses, taxis, park-and-ride stations, cyclists and pedestrians intermingle, and where car traffic is limited or moved to the ring roads. The bus terminal, the largest of the three squares, is the most prominent, notable for its displays on columns announcing departures. Passengers can also wait in the third square, known as the 'outdoor waiting room' with its canopy of foliage filtering the light. From the curving benches people have a view of the terminal and can see departure information on the displays. On the other side of the station, a small green park forms a counterpart to the squares – a 'green gem' in the immediate vicinity of the inner city.

1 The station square is a lively gateway to the city. What was a chaotic area has been transformed with comprehensive but simple interventions into a public square.
2 From the curving benches passengers have a view of the terminal and can see departure information on the displays.
3 Even at night when there is little going on, lingering in the squares is a pleasure. A fairy-tale atmosphere is created by special lighting effects, such as the square of illuminated stones lighting up the tops of the trees from below at night.
4 The materials reflect a deliberate modernity. The squares have three different stone surfaces framed with neutral clinker paving which picks up the materials and colours of downtown.
5 A black granite pool – a table of water – emphasizes the changes in level across the site.

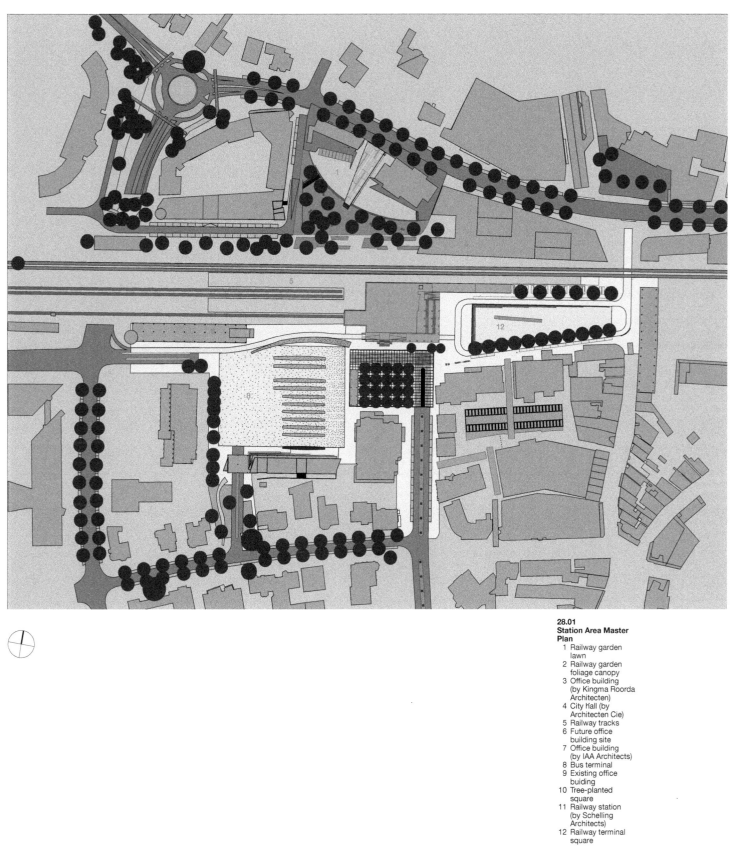

28.01
Station Area Master Plan
1 Railway garden lawn
2 Railway garden foliage canopy
3 Office building (by Kingma Roorda Architecten)
4 City Hall (by Architecten Cie)
5 Railway tracks
6 Future office building site
7 Office building (by IAA Architects)
8 Bus terminal
9 Existing office building
10 Tree-planted square
11 Railway station (by Schelling Architects)
12 Railway terminal square

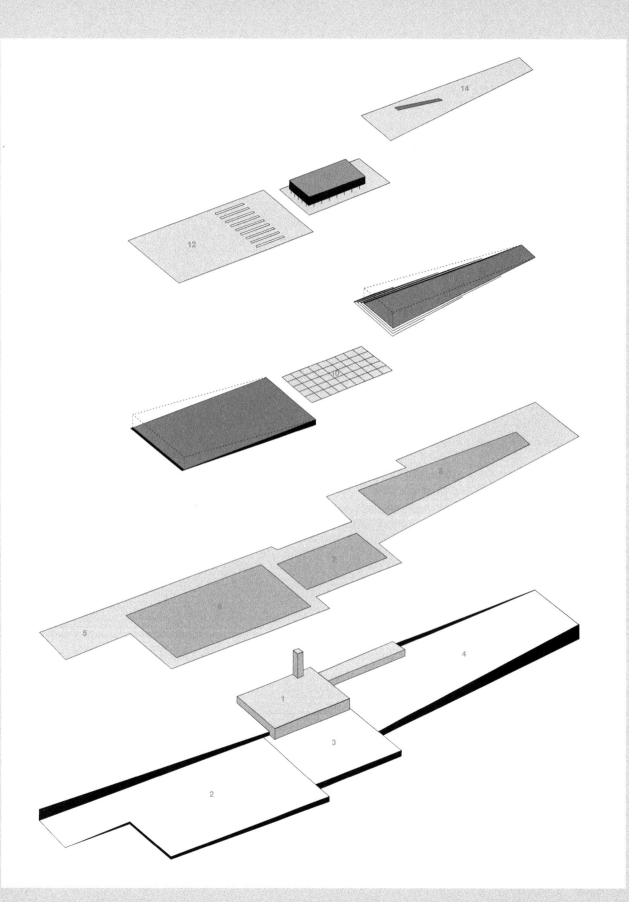

**28.02
Exploded
Axonometric of the
Three Squares
Facing the City**

Landscape:
 1 Railway station
 2 Sloped area
 3 Flat area
 4 Sloped area

The Three Squares:
 5 Three squares with
   clinker paving
 6 Bus terminal
 7 Outdoor waiting
   area
 8 Front square

Character:
 9 Bus terminal as
   monolithic element
10 Grid structure of the
   railway station
   reflected in the
   tree-planted square
11 Front square as a
   monolithic element

Special Features:
12 Train platforms
13 Canopy of foliage
14 Reflection pool

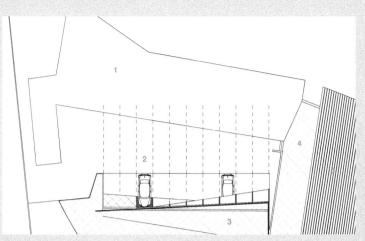

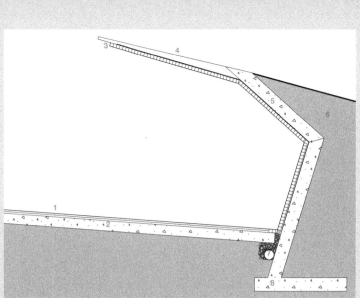

28.03
**Railway Garden Lawn
and Green Roof Plan
Detail**
1:500
1 Existing building
2 Asphalt pavement
3 Lawn-covered roof
4 Lawn at ground
level
5 Corsican quartzite
paving

28.04
**Green Roof Section
Detail**
1:50
1 Asphalt paving
2 Gravel bed to
asphalt paving
3 Pressed steel grids
to underside of roof
4 Lawn-covered roof
5 Reinforced
cantilevered concrete
roof and walls
6 Topsoil and lawn

7 Gravel-filled
drainage
8 Reinforced
concrete foundation

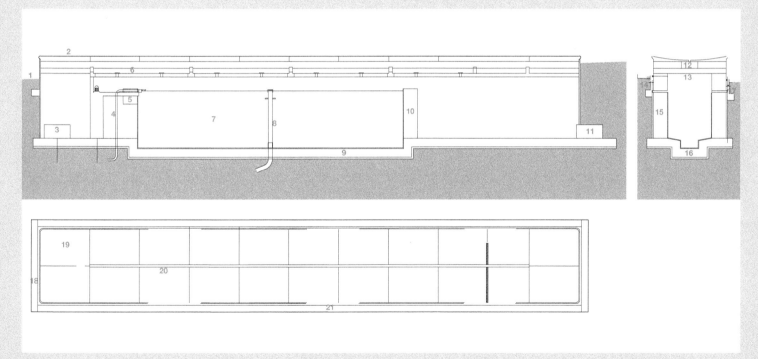

28.05
**Water Table
Sections and Plan to
Front Square**
1:100
1 Ground level of
square
2 Polished black
granite slab
3 Fibreoptic light
generator
4 Water pump
5 Siphon shutter
6 Prefabricated
concrete tiles forming

the upper water
reservoir
7 Lower water
reservoir
8 Excess water outlet
9 Basement floor
level
10 Lower reservoir wall
11 Fibre optic light
generator and
electrical switch box
12 Water reservoir
13 Prefabricated
concrete tiles forming
the upper water

reservoir
14 Drainage gutter
15 Reinforced
concrete basement
wall
16 Reinforced
concrete basement
foundation
17 Drainage gutter
18 Pressed steel
drainage grid
19 Polished black
granite slab
20 Water outlet
between two slabs of

granite
21 Pressed steel
drainage grid

La Closeraie
Louviers, France

Client
SA HLM La Plaine Normande

Area
0.25 hectares (0.6 acre)

Project Team
Edouard François, Isabelle Gaspard,
Randa Kamel, Caroline Stahl

Landscape Architect
Société Forestière

Main Contractor
Plaine Normande, ICADE G3A

This design for 18 dwellings in Louviers, Normandy, takes the most ordinary design (four walls and a red-tiled pitched roof), and imbues it with a spark of imagination, respect for the environment and a generosity of spirit. Achieved within the tightest of budgets, François fulfils a brief that is able to satisfy the expectations of any tenant. Set in a small park and surrounded by trees, the three buildings are laid out running north–south so that the long façades take advantage of eastern and western sun. Between each block is a triangular shaped services building which includes covered outdoor space, a barbecue, cellar, and storage for bicycles and prams. A covered walkway leads to each of the apartments (two per floor), each of which have triple orientation. Every room receives direct daylight, including the kitchen and the bathroom.

The external walls are constructed from fired-clay which support the untreated concrete floors and ceilings, maximizing the opportunity for open plan interior spaces. The exterior wall is left in its natural state, protected by a water repellent film. Some 200 mm (8 inches) in front of the wall is an eye-catching 'palisade' made from recyclable chestnut wood. Twisted stainless steel wire provides the necessary rigidity, while the palisade, or screen, is fixed to the façades by steel bars. This timber screen gives protection from both rain and sun, as well as mediating between the apartment interiors and heat, noise, ventilation, odours, sun and views.

1 While the primary envelope of these buildings are of the most ordinary, even banal character, the timber screen elevates these apartments from the ordinary to the unique.
2 Each of the three apartment buildings (left) is linked to a small services building (right) for the benefit of all residents, via elevated walkways.
3 Detail view of the chestnut wood screen. The timber is left in a virtually raw state, contrasting with the pristine white walls beneath, whilst still providing a unfied aesthetic for the entire development.

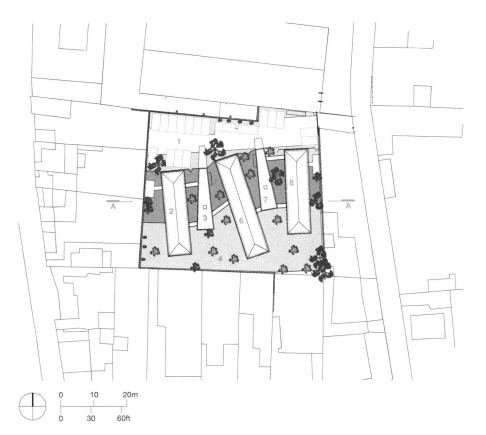

29.01
Site Plan
1:1000
1 Carpark
2 Apartment
buildiing
3 Covered loggia to
service building
4 Flower meadow
5 Garden of spiny
plants
6 Apartment building
7 Covered loggia to
service building
8 Apartment building

0   10   20m
0   30   60ft

29.02
Typical Floor Plan
1:500
1 68.7 square metre
(740 square foot)
two bedroom
apartment
2 68.7 square metre
(740 square foot)
two bedroom
apartment
3 Walkway 1
4 Walkway 2
5 Entrance
6 Foyer
7 Private undercover
loggia space
8 Private undercover
loggia space
9 Walkway
10 84.6 square metre
(910 square foot)
three bedroom
apartment
11 84.6 square metre
(910 square foot)
three bedroom
apartment
12 Timber screen to
exterior façades

13 Communal social
space
14 Private undercover
loggia space
15 Private undercover
loggia space
16 Walkway 1
17 Walkway 2
18 68.7 square metre
(740 square foot)
two bedroom
apartment
19 68.7 square metre
(740 square foot)
two bedroom
apartment

29.03
Section A–A
1:500
1 Red clay-tiled roof
2 Concrete walkway
3 Roof terrace
4 Concrete walkway
5 Red clay-tiled roof
6 Concrete walkway
7 Roof terrace
8 Concrete walkway
9 Red clay-tiled roof

127

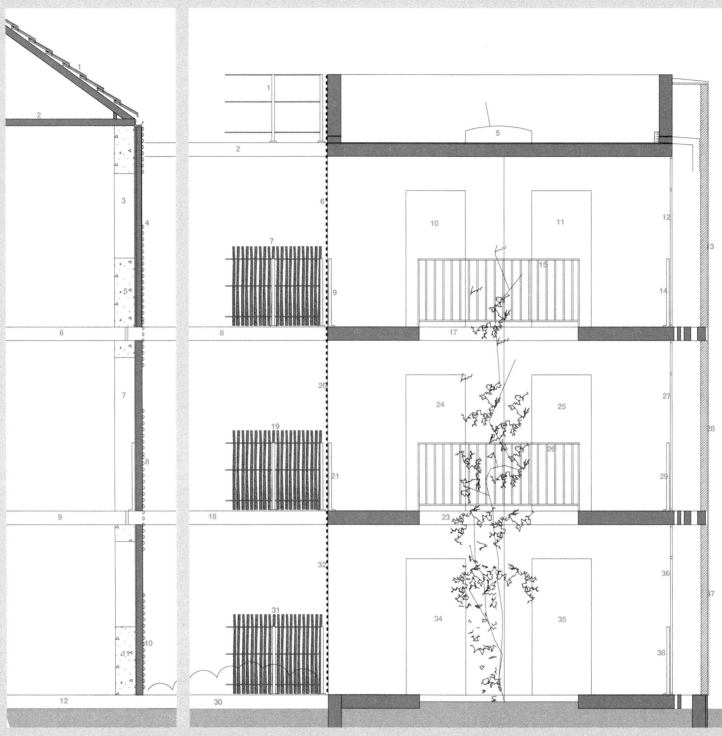

29.04
Sectional Detail 1
1:50
  1 Red clay roof tiles
  2 Lower chord of timber roof truss
  3 'Biobrick' hollow core technology exterior wall for thermal efficiency
  4 Timber screen to exterior façades
  5 'Biobrick' hollow core technology exterior wall for thermal efficiency

6 Reinforced concrete floor slab
  7 'Biobrick' hollow core technology exterior wall
  8 Timber screen to exterior façades
  9 Reinforced concrete floor slab
  10 Timber screen to exterior façades
  11 'Biobrick' hollow

core technology exterior wall
  12 Reinforced concrete slab on ground

29.05
Sectional Detail 2
1:50
  1 Steel balustrade to roof terrace
  2 Reinforced concrete floor slab
  3 Reinforced

concrete upstand to roof terrace
  4 Reinforced concrete roof slab
  5 Rigid polythene skylight
  6 Timber screen to exterior façade
  7 Timber screen balustrade
  8 Reinforced concrete floor slab
  9 Steel balustrade
  10 Timber door to

private loggia space
  11 Timber door to private loggia space
  12 Timber screen
  13 Zinc rainwater down pipe
  14 Steel balustrade
  15 Steel balustrade to central void
  16 Reinforced concrete floor slab
  17 Edge of floor slab to void
  18 Reinforced

concrete floor slab
  19 Timber screen balustrade
  20 Timber screen to exterior façade
  21 Steel balustrade
  22 Reinforced concrete floor slab
  23 Edge of floor slab to void
  24 Timber door to private loggia space
  25 Timber door to private loggia space

26 Steel balustrade to central void
  27 Timber screen
  28 Zinc rainwater down pipe
  29 Steel balustrade
  30 Reinforced concrete floor slab
  31 Timber screen balustrade
  32 Timber screen to exterior façade
  33 Reinforced concrete floor slab

34 Timber door to private loggia space
  35 Timber door to private loggia space
  36 Timber screen
  37 Zinc rainwater down pipe
  38 Steel balustrade

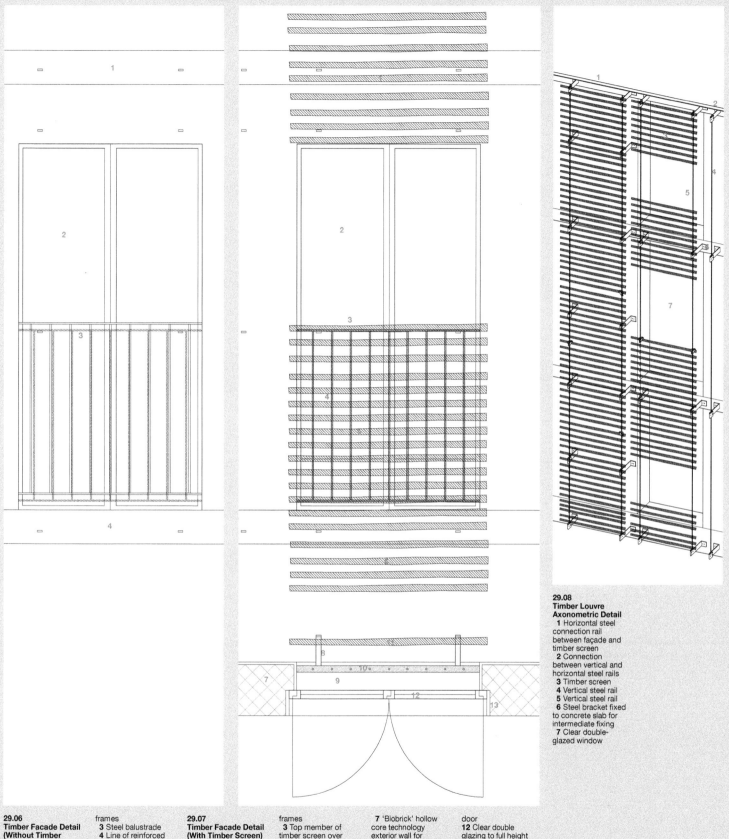

29.08
Timber Louvre
Axonometric Detail
  1 Horizontal steel
connection rail
between façade and
timber screen
  2 Connection
between vertical and
horizontal steel rails
  3 Timber screen
  4 Vertical steel rail
  5 Vertical steel rail
  6 Steel bracket fixed
to concrete slab for
intermediate fixing
  7 Clear double-
glazed window

29.06
Timber Facade Detail
(Without Timber
Screen)
1:20
  1 Line of reinforced
concrete floor slab
  2 Clear double
glazing to full height
double doors with PVC

frames
  3 Steel balustrade
  4 Line of reinforced
concrete floor slab

29.07
Timber Facade Detail
(With Timber Screen)
Elevation and Plan
1:20
  1 Chestnut wood
timber screen
  2 Clear double
glazing to full height
double doors with PVC

frames
  3 Top member of
timber screen over
glass doors
  4 Steel balustrade
behind
  5 Timber screen over
door
  6 Timber screen over
façade

  7 'Biobrick' hollow
core technology
exterior wall for
thermal efficiency
  8 Timber connection
between façade and
screen
  9 Concrete sill
  10 Steel balustrade
  11 Timber screen over

door
  12 Clear double
glazing to full height
double doors with PVC
frames
  13 Timber door reveal

129

KBAS: Keith Kaseman and Julie Beckman

The Pentagon Memorial
Arlington, Virginia, USA

Client
The Pentagon Memorial Fund

Area
0.7 hectares (1.7 acres)

Structural Engineer
Buro Happold (Memorial Unit)
Alpha Corporation (Memorial Park)

Main Contractor
Centex Lee

The Pentagon Memorial is located on the West Lawn of the Pentagon, adjacent to the point of impact of American Airlines Flight 77 which crashed there on the 11th of September 2001. Both individual and collective in nature, the Memorial records the sheer magnitude of that tragic day. Organized by a timeline based on the ages of the victims, 184 Memorial Units are placed along Age Lines parallel with the trajectory of Flight 77, each marking a birth-year, from 1998 to 1930. The Memorial Unit is the heart of the project, with each Unit marking a special place dedicated to each individual. The orientation of each cantilevered Unit indicates whether an individual was aboard the plane or in the Pentagon at the time of impact. Each person's name is engraved at the end of the cantilever, hovering above a pool of water that glows with light at night.

The Units are dispersed throughout a tactile, sensory driven environment. Porous, stabilized gravel will not only allow visitors to hear their own footsteps and those of others, but also allows a grove of trees to thrive and grow directly through the gravel without protective grates. Shading the Memorial Units, brilliant foliage creates a dynamic canopy of light and colour throughout the day and seasons, while elegantly exfoliating bark will register change into the future. The Park is surrounded by a continuous perimeter bench which is backed by a soft border of ornamental grasses. Designed by three dimensional computer modelling, the Memorial Units will be produced through Computer Numerically Controlled technologies and cast in a highly specialized stainless steel.

1 Located on the West Lawn of the Pentagon, the Memorial Units are set in a grove of trees. **2** At night, integrated lighting is directed from a small pool and reflected off the smooth underside of the stainless steel units, highlighting the names of the victims. **3** A full scale, working prototype reveals the fluid geometry between the cast stainless steel and the pre-cast concrete basins. A reveal joint at the connection allows the water to slip in, making the stainless steel seemingly float on the water's surface.

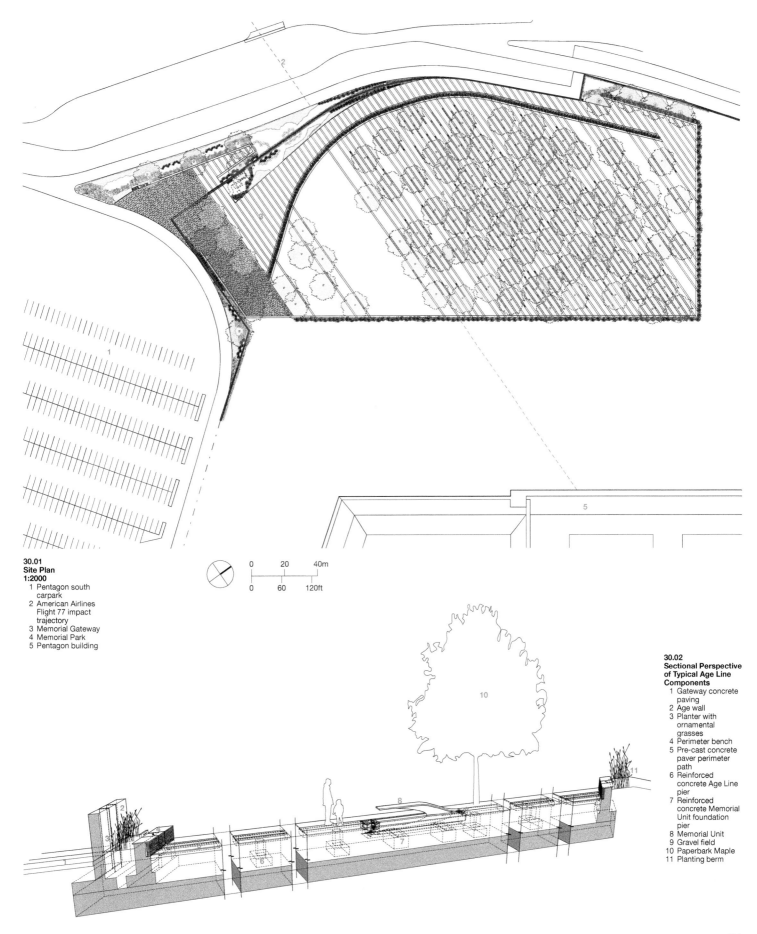

30.01
Site Plan
1:2000
1 Pentagon south carpark
2 American Airlines Flight 77 impact trajectory
3 Memorial Gateway
4 Memorial Park
5 Pentagon building

30.02
Sectional Perspective of Typical Age Line Components
1 Gateway concrete paving
2 Age wall
3 Planter with ornamental grasses
4 Perimeter bench
5 Pre-cast concrete paver perimeter path
6 Reinforced concrete Age Line pier
7 Reinforced concrete Memorial Unit foundation pier
8 Memorial Unit
9 Gravel field
10 Paperbark Maple
11 Planting berm

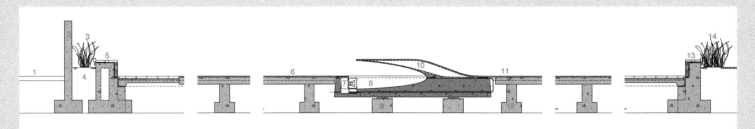

**30.03
Memorial Park
Section Along Age
Line 1956**
1:100
1 Concrete paving
in Memorial Gateway
2 Age wall
3 Ornamental

grasses
4 Planter
5 Perimeter bench
6 Gravel field
7 Light house utility
box
8 Memorial Unit
fountain
9 Reinforced

concrete Memorial
Unit foundation pier
10 Memorial Unit
11 Gravel field
12 Reinforced
concrete Age Line pier
13 Perimeter bench
14 Planting berm

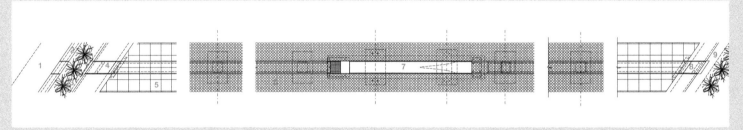

**30.04
Memorial Park Plan
Along Age Line 1956**
1:100
1 Concrete paving in
Memorial Gateway
2 Age Wall
3 Ornamental
grasses

4 Perimeter bench
5 Perimeter path of
pre-cast concrete
pavers
6 Gravel field
7 Memorial Unit
8 Birth year text
9 Planting berm

**30.05
Memorial Unit
Sectional Detail**
1:20
1 Gravel containment
mat system
2 Fountain filter
basket
3 Fountain display
and check valves

4 Induction lamp
5 Name plate
6 Reinforced
concrete foundation
piers
7 Stainless steel
mounting plate
8 Foundation
mounting bolts
9 Epoxy polymer

concrete seating
surface
10 Stainless steel top
cast
11 Fountain display
jets
12 Pre-cast concrete
pool basin
13 Custom fabricated
water supply pipe

30.06
Memorial Unit
Section Detail 1
1:20
 1 Name plate
 2 Gravel containment
mat system
 3 Stainless steel age
line
 4 Light housing unit
 5 Pre-cast concrete
basin

30.07
Memorial Unit
Section Detail 2
1:20
 1 Epoxy Polymer
concrete seating
surface
 2 Stainless steel top
cast
 3 Gravel containment
mat system
 4 Stainless steel age
line
 5 Pre-cast concrete
basin
 6 Water supply pipe
and sleeve
 7 Foundation
mounting bolts
 8 Reinforced
concrete foundation
pier

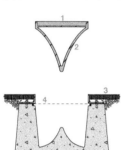

30.08
Memorial Unit
Section Detail 3
1:20
 1 Epoxy polymer
concrete seating
surface
 2 Stainless steel top
cast
 3 Gravel containment
mat system
 4 Stainless steel age
line
 5 Pre-cast concrete
basin
 6 Water supply pipe
and sleeve

30.09
Memorial Unit
Section Detail 4
1:20
 1 Epoxy Polymer
concrete seating
surface
 2 Stainless steel top
cast
 3 Gravel containment
mat system
 4 Stainless steel age
line
 5 Pre-cast concrete
basin
 6 Water supply pipe
and sleeve
 7 Foundation
mounting bolts
 8 Reinforced
concrete foundation
pier

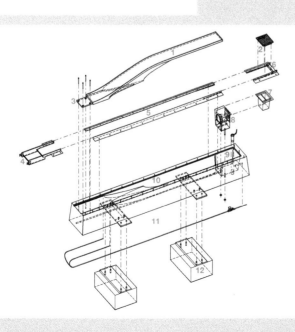

30.10
Memorial Unit
Components Detail
 1 Memorial Unit
stainless steel top cast
 2 Light house utility
box access panel
 3 Mounting bolts
 4 Age line coupling
bracket
 5 Age line angles
 6 Age line assembly
and panel track
 7 Pool filter basket
 8 Light housing and
pool weir
 9 Pool basin drain
pipe
10 Pre-cast concrete
basin
11 Custom fabricated
water supply pipe and
valve assembly
12 Reinforced
concrete foundation
piers

31
Tract Consultants with Cox Rayner Architects

Cairns Esplanade
Cairns, Queensland, Australia

Client
Cairns City Council

Area
11 hectares (27 acres)

Project Team
Stephen White, Steve Calhoun, Helen Balffe

Structural Engineer
Patterson Britton in association with McPherson Maclean

Cairns is known internationally as Australia's gateway to the Great Barrier Reef. Tourism has become its prime industry, with three million visitors arriving every year. However in the late 1990s Cairns was suffering economic decline through its inability to get visitors to stay, mostly due to the unattractiveness of its town centre and foreshore and the impact of a new regional shopping centre. The foreshore, while an internationally recognized bird watching habitat, was unappealing due to the lack of beaches with mud flats that extended 800 metres (2,625 feet) out to sea at low tide.

A competition was held to provide a leisure and recreation focus to the foreshore and to revitalize the city. Tract Consultants created a simple concept that linked the city to the water via legible pedestrian boulevards and promenades. The swimming lagoon's elongated shape acts as a visual link, bringing water into the city. The lagoon's elevation above the mud flats and infinity edge design allows an uninterrupted water view even when the tide is fully out. The boardwalk, with its enlarged nodes has protected the bird feeding sites with minimal impact and provides a comfortable place for bird watchers, while the lagoon provides a safe swimming environment, away from marine stingers. The regeneration has been a major success for Cairns and together with the boardwalk, interpretive centres and additional parkland achieved through reclamation, the design has resoundingly revitalized the heart and soul of the city.

1 Cairns was historically a rural service town with sugar refining mills and deep water port used for exporting agricultural produce. The Esplanade has since made Cairns one of Australia's most popular tourist destinations.
2 Located on the banks of the Barron River, on a site that was originally mangrove-lined swamp land, Cairns has been transformed into a cosmopolitan centre.
3 Through the Interpretive Centres the design clearly defines the cultural, environmental and historical features of Cairns and the Far North Queensland region.
4 The elongated, triangular form of the lagoon brings water right into the heart of the city and creates a popular place for swimming and sun bathing.

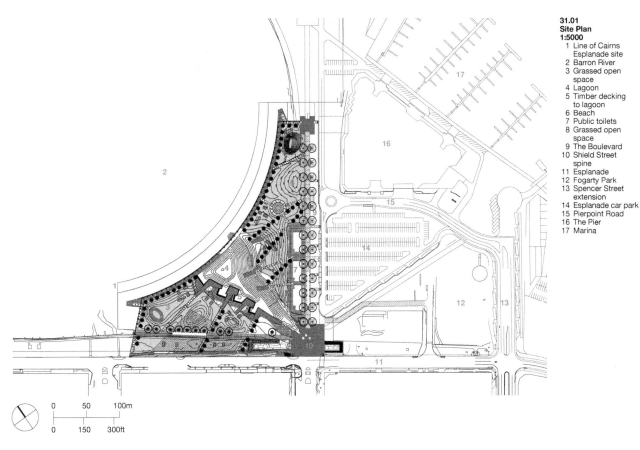

31.01
Site Plan
1:5000
1 Line of Cairns
  Esplanade site
2 Barron River
3 Grassed open
  space
4 Lagoon
5 Timber decking
  to lagoon
6 Beach
7 Public toilets
8 Grassed open
  space
9 The Boulevard
10 Shield Street
  spine
11 Esplanade
12 Fogarty Park
13 Spencer Street
  extension
14 Esplanade car park
15 Pierpoint Road
16 The Pier
17 Marina

0   50   100m
0   150   300ft

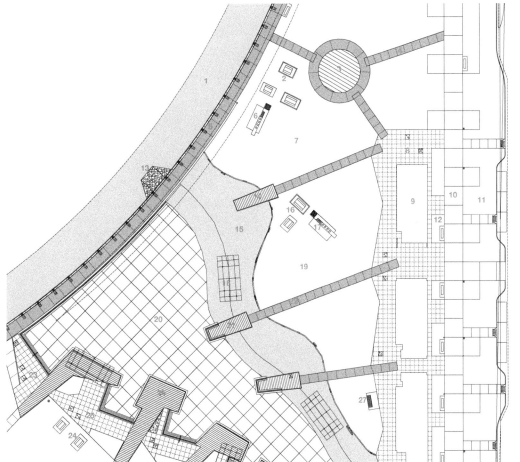

31.02
Lagoon Area Surface
Treatment Plan
1:1000
1 Extent of
  Esplanade
2 Timber tables
  and seats
3 Feature tree and
  planting
4 Broom-finished
  concrete path
5 Esplanade and
  lagoon revetment
  wall
6 Public BBQ
7 Grassed open
  space
8 Courtyard with
  unit paving
9 Public facilities
  including toilets
10 Shield Street spine
11 Grassed open
  space
12 Seating
13 Culvert outlet with
  scour protectioin
14 Lagoon deck
15 Beach
16 Timber tables
  and seats
17 Public BBQ
18 Shade structure
19 Grassed open
  space
20 Lagoon
21 Lagoon deck
22 Broom finished
  concrete path
23 Broom-finished
  concrete to lagoon
  edge
24 Timber tables and
  seats
25 Broom-finished
  concrete to
  lagoon edge
26 Lagoon decking
27 Outdoor shower

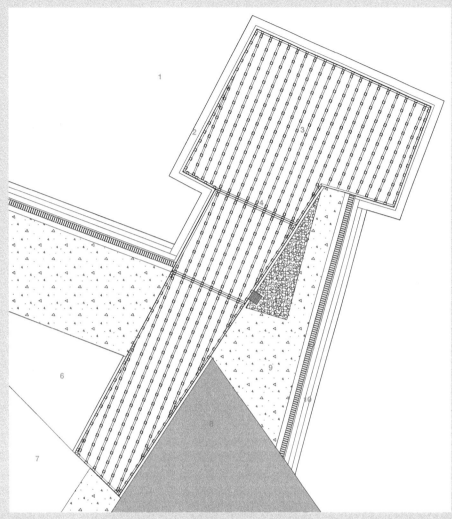

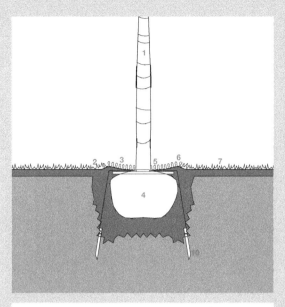

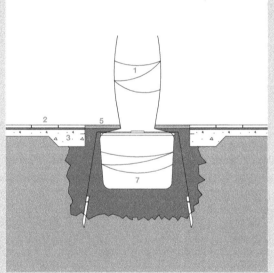

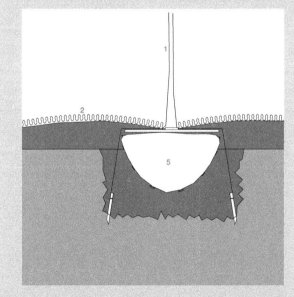

31.03
Deck Framing
Plan Detail
1:200
1 Lagoon
2 Timber decking
edge trim
3 100 x 75 mm (4 x 3
inch) hardwood
bearers at 600 mm
(23³/5 inch) centres
4 Movement joints to
engineers details
5 Decomposed
granite
6 Grass
7 Planting bed
8 Exposed aggregate
concrete
9 Broom-finished
concrete
10 Steps into lagoon
11 Heel guard drain

31.04
Planting Detail 1:
Ground Trees and
Palms in Turf
1:50
1 Palm tree
2 Spade edge
3 1200 mm (47¹/5
inch) organic mulch to
100 mm (4 inch) depth
4 Root ball
5 Top of root ball at
ground level
6 Topsoil dished
around trunk for
watering
7 Turf
8 Tree pit back-filled
with tree mix topsoil
9 Tree pit excavated
to required size – (200
mm / 8 inch) greater
than root ball in all
directions
10 Root ball guying
system

31.05
Planting Detail 2:
Palm Tree in
Pre-cast Paving
1:50
1 Palm tree
2 Precast concrete
unit pavers
3 Reinforced
concrete slab
on ground
4 130 x 5 mm (5¹/10 x
²/5 inch) galvanized flat
bar to perimeter of
bed, fixed with
anchors at 600 mm
(23²/3 inch) centres
5 50 mm (2 inch)
deep decomposed
granite
6 Root ball
guying system
7 Root ball
8 Tree mix topsoil to
200 mm (7³/4 inch)
depth around root ball

31.06
Planting Detail 3: Fig
Trees in Garden Beds
1:50
1 Fig tree
2 Turf
3 100 mm (4 inch)
deep organic mulch
over 300 mm (11⁴/5
inch) deep topsoil
garden mix
4 Minimum of 400
mm (16 inch) thick tree
mix topsoil around root
ball
5 Root ball
6 50 x 30 mm (2 x
1¹/5 inch) CCA
(chromated copper
arsenate) treated
hardwood battens
7 Root ball guying
system

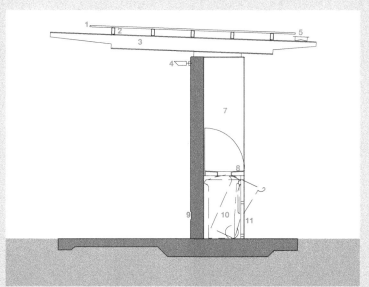

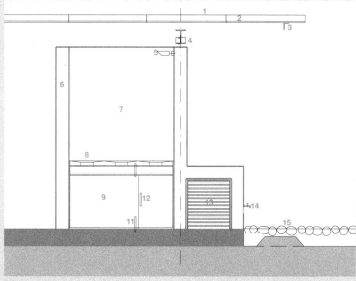

31.07
**BBQ Structure Detail
Section 1**
1:50
 1 Compressed fibre cement roof cladding laid with two degree fall
 2 150 x 50 mm (6 x 2 inch) galvanized rectangular hollow section roof joists
 3 200 mm (8 inch) galvanized and painted universal beam

roof bearer
 4 Wall mounted stainless steel light fitting
 5 300 x 75 mm (11⁴/5 x 3 inch) stainless steel gutter
 6 Rendered block-work wall
 7 Concrete blade wall from class two formwork with cement render finish
 8 Bin enclosure lid from 1.2 mm (1/25 inch) thick stainless steel on 12 mm (1/2 inch)

thick stainless steel on 12 mm (1/2 inch) thick plywood backing fixed to pre-welded steel sub-frame, with top hinges pinned in place with steel bar chained to frame
 9 Tile recess
 10 Removeable plastic rubbish bin
 11 Bin enclosure gates from 1.2 mm (1/25 inch) thick stainless steel on 12 mm (1/2 inch)

thick plywood backing
 12 Reinforced concrete slab on ground

31.08
**BBQ Structure Detail
Section 2**
1:50
 1 Compressed fibre cement roof cladding with backing rods and silicone seal joints to roof and soffitt
 2 150 x 50 mm (6 x 2 inch) galvanized rectangular hollow section roof joists
 3 150 x 75 mm (6 x 3 inch) galvanized

joist trimmer
 4 200 mm (8 inch) galvanized and painted universal beam roof bearer
 5 Wall mounted stainless steel light fitting
 6 Rendered block-work wall
 7 Concrete blade wall from class two formwork with cement render finish
 8 Bin enclosure lid

from 1.2 mm (1/25 inch) thick stainless steel on 12 mm (1/2 inch) thick plywood backing fixed to pre-welded steel sub-frame, with top hinges pinned in place with steel bar chained to frame
 9 Bin enclosure gates from 1.2 mm (1/25 inch) thick stainless steel on 12 mm (1/2 inch) thick plywood backing
 10 Reinforced

concrete slab on ground
 11 Barrel bolt behind
 12 Gate lock and handle
 13 Gate from timber battens on 50 x 50 mm (2 x 2 inch) pre-welded angle frame
 14 Hose cock
 15 Gravel over concrete slab laid to fall

31.09
**BBQ Structure Detail
Section 3**
1:50
 1 Compressed fibre cement roof cladding laid with two degree fall
 2 150 x 50 mm (6 x 2 inch) galvanized rectangular hollow section roof joists
 3 200 mm (8 inch) galvanized and painted universal beam

roof bearer
 4 300 x 75 mm (11⁴/5 x 3 inch) stainless steel gutter
 5 Wall mounted stainless steel light fitting
 6 Galvanized and painted strut flange fixed 20 mm (4/5 inch) from concrete wall
 7 Concrete blade wall from class two formwork with cement render finish

 8 Concrete bench from class two formwork with polished finish
 9 BBQ screen from 50 x 50 mm (2 x 2 inch) thick pre-welded angle frame with vertical support frames
 10 BBQ surface
 11 Tile recess
 12 Reinforced concrete slab on ground

31.10
**BBQ Structure Detail
Section 4**
1:50
 1 Roof structure from compressed fibre cement roof cladding laid with two degree fall, 150 x 50 mm (6 x 2 inch) galvanized rectangular hollow section roof joists and 200 mm (7⁹/10 inch) galvanized and painted universal beam

roof bearer
 2 Concrete blade wall from class two formwork with cement render finish
 3 Wall mounted stainless steel light fitting
 4 Rendered blockwork wall
 5 Fixed spotted gum batten screen with 20 mm (4/5 inch) spacing, with battens in same plane as

battens to BBQ doors
 6 BBQ enclosure door
 7 BBQ enclosure door
 8 Fixed spotted gum batten screen with 20 mm (3/4 inch) spacing, with battens in same plane as battens to BBQ doors
 9 Concrete bench from class two formwork with polished finish

 10 Reinforced concrete slab on ground

32–40
Waterfront

32
Abel Bainnson Butz, LLP

Hudson River Park
New York, New York, USA

Client
Hudson River Park Trust

Area
4.2 hectares (10.3 acres)

Project Team
Howard Abel, John Butz, Terri-Lee
Burger, Christopher Gavlick, William
Johnson, Carla Tiberi, Petra Mager,
Ronan Wilk, Helen Alexoudis, Alison
Duncan, Kathy Morrison

Architect
Sowinski Sullivan Architects

Civil, Structural and
Mechanical Engineer
Afridi Associates

Heralded as the largest public park
project undertaken in New York City
since the opening of Central Park 150
years before, the Hudson River Park
stretches from Battery Park City to
59th Street along the western
Manhattan shoreline. The reclamation
of this part of the waterfront from a
deteriorating former industrial dock,
provides the opportunity for the
creation of a public open space
offering varied recreational
opportunities. The linear park, which
includes a continuous waterfront
esplanade with distinctive granite and
blue-stone pavement, offers spatial
diversity through open lawn areas
against a back drop of lush plantings,
the subtle use of topographic
variations and the creation of plazas
that respond to park entrances, pier
connections and river views.

Other features within the park
include a magnificent granite fountain,
a display garden, a dog run, two
comfort stations and a food
concession. Three piers offer varied
recreational opportunities. The
longest, Pier 45, features a lawn for
passive activities, tensile fabric shade
structures and a water feature
offering relief to sunbathers. Pier 46
features a synthetic turf playing field,
seating beneath the shade of a
tree bosque and a picnic grove. Pier
51 features water features, a ship's
prow jutting out over the edge of the
pier, play structures and a shade
canopy.

1 Aerial view of Pier 46 where a synthetic turf playing field offers a multitude of recreational opportunities for space-starved New Yorkers.
2 Aerial view of Pier 45 where white tensile fabric shade structures and an interactive water feature offer relief from the sun.
3 A magnificent granite fountain takes pride of place on the land-side portion of the new park.
4 View of Pier 45 looking towards the city. Popular with walkers and sun bathers, various textures including granite paving, timber boardwalks and grass offer a multitude of recreational options.

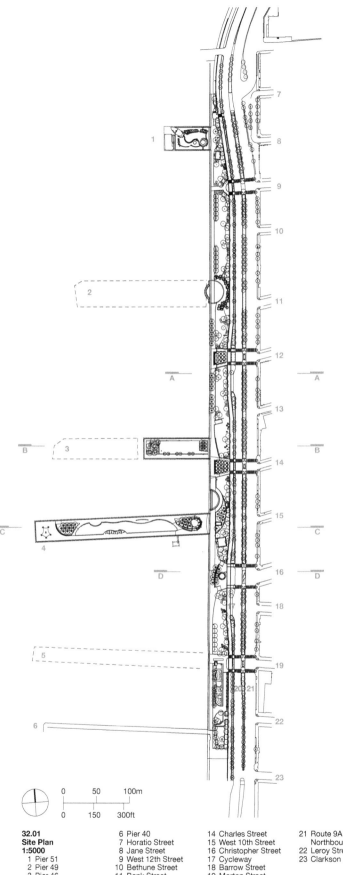

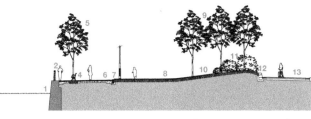

32.02
Section A–A,
Esplanade Bulkhead
Seating
1:500
1 Hudson River
2 Bulkhead railing
3 Bulkhead

4 Timber and
  metal bench
5 Major tree
6 Esplanade
7 Granite curb
8 Lawn
9 Major trees
10 Upland park

11 Shrub mass
12 Existing stone wall
13 Existing cycleway

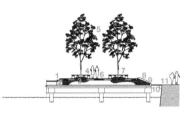

32.03
Section B–B at
Pier 46
1:500
1 Seating steps
2 Synthetic field turf
3 Continuous topsoil
  for tree

planting
4 Circular bench
  around tree pit
5 Major trees
6 Stabilized gravel to
  seating area
7 Circular bench
  around tree pit

8 Shrubs and
  ground cover
9 Concrete curb
10 Steel grate
11 Esplanade

32.04
Section C–C at
Pier 45
1:500
1 Typical pier rail
2 Existing pier
  structure
3 Timber deck

4 Backless bench
5 Concrete curb
6 Planting
7 Flush stone band
8 Major trees
9 Table and chairs
10 Stabilized gravel
11 Continuous top

soil for tree
  planting
12 Concrete
  pavement
13 Curb wall
14 Timber deck
15 Typical pier rail

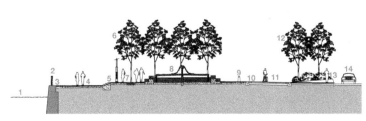

32.05
Section D–D at
Christopher Street
1:500
1 Hudson River
2 Bulkhead railing
3 Bulkhead
4 Esplanade

5 Steps – three risers
  150 mm (6 inches)
  high
6 Major trees
7 Granite-paved
  entrance plaza
8 Fountain
9 Bollard

10 Flush curb
11 Existing cycleway
12 Existing trees
13 Existing pedestrian
  crossing
14 Route 9A

32.01
Site Plan
1:5000
1 Pier 51
2 Pier 49
3 Pier 46
4 Pier 45
5 Pier 42

6 Pier 40
7 Horatio Street
8 Jane Street
9 West 12th Street
10 Bethune Street
11 Bank Street
12 West 11th Street
13 Perry Street

14 Charles Street
15 West 10th Street
16 Christopher Street
17 Cycleway
18 Barrow Street
19 Morton Street
20 Route 9A
  Southbound

21 Route 9A
  Northbound
22 Leroy Street
23 Clarkson Street

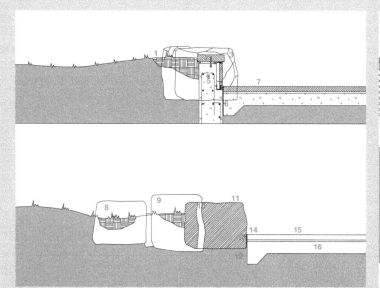

32.06
Pier 45 Shade
Structure Section
and Plan Detail
1:500
1 Tensile cable
2 Tensile shade fabric
3 Curved steel pipe
fabric support
4 Steel pipe structure
5 Light fixture
6 Tapered steel
column
7 Tensile fabric roof
8 Line of curved

steel pipe
9 Tapered steel
column
10 Tensile cables
11 Horizontal steel
members

32.07
Christopher Street
Fountain Plan and
Section Detail
1:200
1 Granite slab
2 Basin
3 Granite seating
steps
4 Bluestone border
5 Wall drain with cap
and waterstop
6 Floor drain with
strainer and waterstop
7 Operating water

level sensor with
housing
8 Static water level
sensor with housing
9 Overflow standpipe
drain with waterstop
10 Anti-vortex plate
11 Jet pod with geyser
nozzles
12 Adjustable diverter
inlet with waterstop
13 Anti-vortex plate
14 Fountain light
15 Jet pod with geyser
nozzles

16 Adjustable operator
inlet with waterstop
17 Floor drain with
strainer and waterstop
18 Upper sump drain
outlet
19 Operating water
level sensor with
housing
20 Static water level
sensor with housing
21 Anti-vortex plate
22 Overflow standpipe
drain with waterstop
23 Granite veneer

24 Fountain wall and
basin
25 Wall-mounted
overflow
26 Granite seating
steps and bluestone
border

32.08
Upland Informal
Seating Sections and
Plan Detail
1:50
1 Finished grade
planting
2 Granite seat top
fixed to concrete wall
with high-tension
anchor bolts
3 Informal seating
block
4 Granite veneer wall
5 Reinforced

concrete wall
6 Pre-moulded filler
with bond breaker
and sealant
7 Granite or asphalt
block pavement
8 Informal seating
stone beyond
9 Informal seating
stone beyond
10 All joints and gaps
between adjacent
stones filled to retain
soil at wall line
11 Informal seating

block from selected
granite quarry's grout
pile with smooth
face up
12 Compacted
subgrade
13 Joint filler with
bond breaker and
sealant
14 Field-cut paver
adjacent to stone
15 Granite or asphalt
block pavement
16 Reinforced
concrete slab

32.09
Pier 51 Timber
Footbridge Section
and Plan Detail
1:50
1 Ipe timber slats
to bridge walkway
2 Concrete water
channel
3 Ipe timber slats
to bridge walkway
4 Ipe timber slats
secured to steel straps
with wood screws, on
steel angle bridge

frame with through
bolts countersunk with
nut washers and wood
plugs
5 Concrete water
channel
6 Mortar setting
bed for levelling
7 Fixing bolts with nut
and washer fixing
8 Non-slip safety
surface
9 Ipe timber slats
secured to steel straps
with wood screws, on

steel angle bridge
frame with through
bolts countersunk with
nut washers and wood
plugs
10 Steel base plate
11 Steel angle bridge
frame
12 Steel strap deck
support, eight per
section, fastened to
decking with wood
screws
13 Steel flat bar
bracing

14 Pre-drilled holes for
wood screws
15 Pre-drilled bolt
holes
16 Expansion bolt with
nut and washer

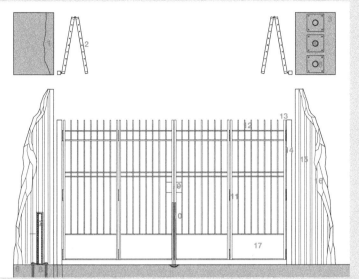

32.10
Pier 51 Steel Gate Plan and Elevation Detail
1:50
 1 Stone pier
 2 Folding steel bar gate
 3 Steel base plate welded to steel pipe upright
 4 Steel pipe filled with concrete
 5 Stainless steel anchor bolts secured

with epoxy adhesive
 6 Pier curb
 7 Steel pipe
 8 Stainless steel anchor bolts and grout leveling course
 9 Gate latch with lock and key
 10 Plunger rod
 11 Gate hinge, three per gate
 12 Steel bar gate assembly
 13 Solid steel end picket

 14 Solid steel post
 15 Stone pillar with drill-marked finish
 16 Split face finish to stone pillar
 17 Solid steel plate

32.11
Pier 51 Boat Balcony Railing Section and Elevation Detail
1:50
 1 Steel top rail
 2 Steel plate rail support
 3 Timber cap
 4 Clapboard secured to steel channel with countersunk lag screws
 5 Steel sheet hull bolted to steel channel

 6 Recessed light fitting
 7 Machine bolts with washer fastened to existing inserts
 8 Timber ledge with anchor bolts and expansion shield nut
 9 Steel I-beam primary structure
 10 Brace secured to existing anchor bolt
 11 Steel brace
 12 Steel top rail
 13 Steel plate rail

support
 14 Timber cap
 15 Steel sheet hull bolted to steel channel
 16 Recessed light fitting

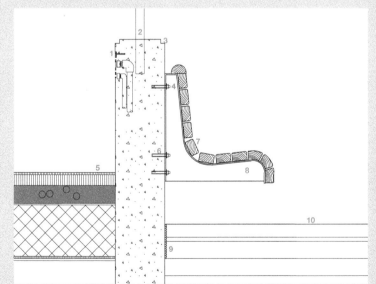

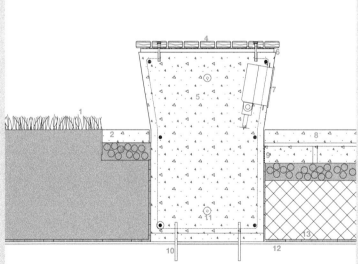

32.12
Pier 51 Wall-Mounted Bench Section Detail
1:20
 1 Spray nozzle on play wall
 2 Concrete wall with steel fence
 3 Continuous shadow line
 4 Steel expansion bolt
 5 Finished grade
 6 Galvanized steel anchor bolts with

expansion shield
 7 Timber slat bench
 8 Steel wall-mounted bench support
 9 Expansion joint filler with bond breaker and sealant
 10 Precast concrete pavement

32.13
Timber and Concrete Seat Wall Section Detail
1:20
 1 Lawn over topsoil to finished grade
 2 Pre-cast concrete pavement strip with steel edge strip
 3 Crushed stone
 4 Ipe timber slats secured to steel channel with vandal-resistant screws

 5 Concrete bench with light sandblast finish to colour-conditioned concrete
 6 Steel channel
 7 Light fixture
 8 Pre-cast concrete pavement
 9 Expansion joint with bond breaker and sealant
 10 Steel bar embedded in concrete, installed with adhesive anchor system

 11 Epoxy-coated smooth dowel greased at one end
 12 Cast in place concrete topping to pier structure
 13 Expanded polystyrene foam fill

33
Camlin Lonsdale Landscape Architects

Donegal Quay
Belfast, Northern Ireland, UK

Client
Laganside Corporation

Area
0.8 hectares (2 acres)

Structural, Civil and Services Engineer
Kirk McClure Morton

Quantity Surveyor
Simon Fenton Partnership

Donegal Quay and the Custom House epitomize the cultural identity of Belfast as a city of trade. The fabric of the city has undergone very significant changes in the recent past. A once tight knit composition of streets, quaysides, squares, and dignified buildings has degenerated to the extent that the existence of a continuous and viable public realm connecting the city centre with the river has been lost. The regeneration of Donegal and Queens Quays represents the vision for a place of civic grandeur, spectacle and interchange with its architectural roots in a celebration of the culture of the city. The language of the elements which make up the composition is elegant, robust, unambiguous and legible. 'The Big Fish', by artist John Kindness, gives a compelling kaleidoscopic account of the history of Belfast and celebrates the return of the salmon to the Lagan River.

The public square formed between the Custom House and the quayside extends over the river itself utilizing a redundant concrete 'dolphin', formerly part of the embarkation ramp for a RoRo (Roll on–Roll off) ferry. The ramp terminates with a stone paved platform that effectively hovers above the tidal water below. Glass balustrades around the platform edge provide for safety but also allow the slenderness of the platform's horizontal plane to be visible. Belfast's Millennium Beacon, constructed with marine grade stainless steel and etched glass, also resides here. The beacon contains a gas-fired brazier which, when lit, provides further animation to the quayside, now reclaimed for public use.

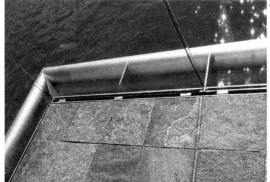

1 The toughened glass parapets around the platform greatly enhance the experience of being out over the Lagan, taking in views of the river and the city.
2 The 30 metre (98 foot) long ramp joins the quayside where an underlit glass floor plate bridges the gap between the two structures.
3 The Belfast Millennium Beacon was comissioned, designed, fabricated and installed in the eight weeks before December 31, 1999.
4 The edge of platform detail includes a spaced gap for surface drainage, clamp plates to secure the glass and a steel brace to absorb the impact of colliding vessels.
5 'The Big Fish' by artist John Kindness is covered with irregular ceramic tiles decorated with images exploring the history of Belfast, Donegal Quay and the Lagan.

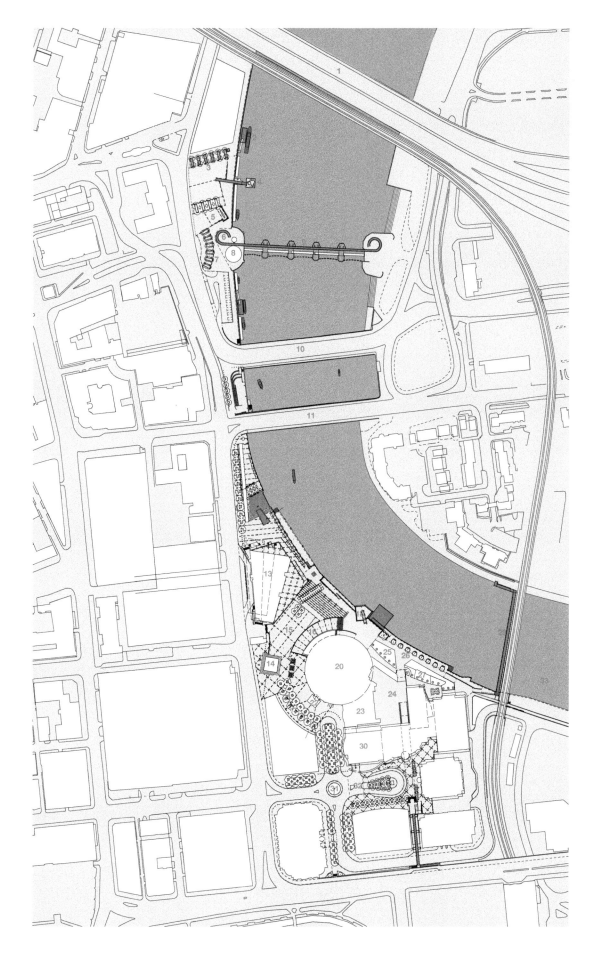

33.01
**Laganbank and
Donegal Quay
Masterplan**
1 Dargan Bridge
2 Mooring pontoon
3 Custom House
  Square
4 Dolphin platform
5 'The Big Fish' by
  John Kindness
6 Ramp up to Lagan
  Weir walkway
7 Crescent of
  Lombardy poplar
8 Lagan Lookout
9 Lagan Weir
10 Queen Elizabeth
  Bridge
11 Queens Bridge
12 Hardwood deck
  over Sand Quay
13 No. 1 Lanyon Quay
14 Raised lawn and
  tree boxes
15 Civic procession
16 Café terrace
17 River terraces
18 Bastion
19 Laganbank
  pontoon
20 Waterfront Hall
21 Concourse
22 Entrance canopy
23 Waterfront Hall,
  Studio and
  other facilities
24 Service yard
25 Lawn
26 Riverside gardens
27 Conifer Crescent
28 Lagan Viaduct
  Footbridge
29 North Boulevard
30 Hilton car park
31 Roundabout
32 City Square
33 River Lagan

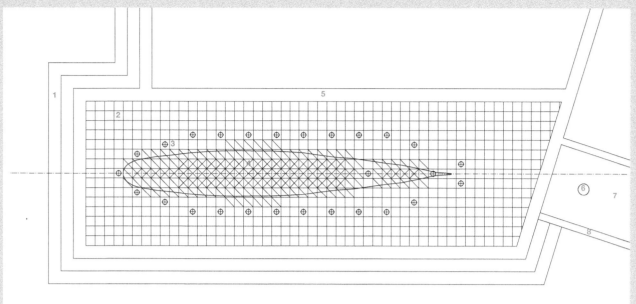

33.02
The Big Fish Paving and Lighting Detail 1:100
1 375 x 320 mm (14 3/4 x 12 3/5 inch) section Mondariz granite terrace steps
2 275 x 275 x 75 mm (10 4/5 x 10 4/5 x 3 inch) 'Black Satin' schniess granite flags with split top face
3 Uplighters, asymetrical towards fish
4 'Black Satin' flags with coarser texture towards centre
5 375 x 100 mm (14 3/4 x 4 inch) section Mondariz granite with flush trim
6 Aesculus hippocastanum (horse chestnut) planted semi mature
7 Crushed granite unbound surface
8 200 x 600 mm (7 9/10 x 23 3/4 inch) section Mondariz granite raised tree pit

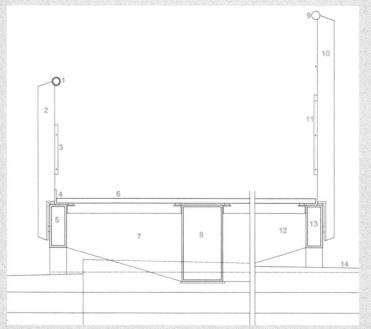

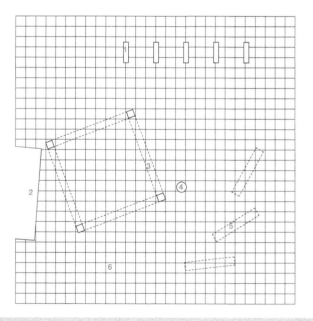

33.03
Ramp Typical Section 1:20
1 57 mm (2 1/4 inch) diameter stainless steel circular hollow section welded to verticals
2 Bracing fins profiled from 10 mm (2/5 inch) thick stainless steel plate
3 12 mm (1/2 inch) thick toughened glass panel
4 5 x 75 mm (1/5 x 3 inch) stainless steel closing plate

5 80 x 40 x 4.5 mm (3 1/5 x 1 3/5 x 1/5 inch) thick rectangular hollow section
6 28 x 44 mm (1 1/10 x 1 3/4 inch) balau hardwood boards with ribbed top surface
7 Fully welded structural fins from 12 mm (1/2 inch) steel plate
8 250 x 450 x 12.5 mm (9 7/8 x 17 3/4 x 1/2 inch) rectangular hollow section
9 57 mm (2 1/4 inch) diameter stainless

steel circular hollow section welded to verticals
10 Bracing fins profiled from 10 mm (2/5 inch) thick stainless steel plate
11 12 mm (1/2 inch) thick toughened glass panel
12 Fully welded structural fins from 12 mm (1/2 inch) steel plate
13 80 x 40 x 4.5 mm (3 1/5 x 1 3/5 x 1/5 inch) thick rectangular hollow section

14 Agregate and epoxy surface dressed asphalt

33.04
Platform Paving 1:100
1 Stone bench from Ballyalton limestone blocks
2 Asymetrical recess for ramp
3 'Cube' from fully welded 200 x 200 mm (8 x 8 inch) rectangular hollow section
4 Nominal 200 mm (8 inch) diameter collar around CCTV column
5 Hardwood seats from large sections of laminated balau timber

6 275 x 275 x 75 mm (10 4/5 x 10 4/5 x 3 inch) 'Black Satin' granite flags with split top face

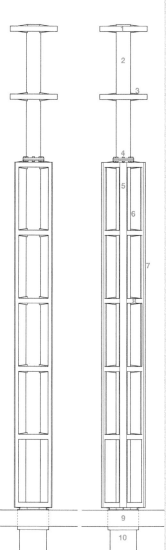

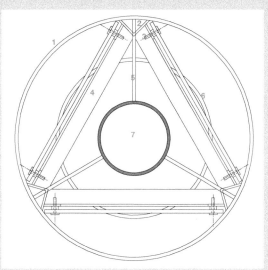

33.06
Millennium Beacon
Section 1
1:10
  1 720 mm (28$^{1}/_{3}$ inch) diameter, 10 mm ($^{2}/_{5}$ inch) thick, 80 mm (3$^{1}/_{5}$ inch) high steel ring
  2 75 x 75 x 5 mm (3 x 3 x $^{1}/_{5}$ inch) thick steel corner angle
  3 Tamper-proof fixings
  4 50 x 5 mm (2 x $^{1}/_{5}$ inch) plate behind 75 x 5 mm (2 x $^{1}/_{5}$ inch) horizontal
  5 10 mm ($^{2}/_{5}$ inch) thick plate radial arms, tapering from 125 mm to 75 mm (5 to 3 inches)
  6 Top edge of 472 mm (18$^{3}/_{5}$ inch) diameter platform level sleeve from 10 mm ($^{2}/_{5}$ inch) thick rolled plate

  7 219 mm (8$^{3}/_{5}$ inch) diameter central circular hollow section

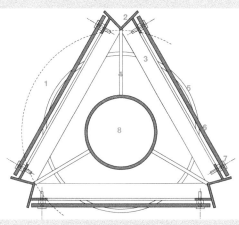

33.07
Millennium Beacon
Section 2
1:10
  1 Back of 75 x 75 mm (3 x 3 inch) angles set on 300 mm (11$^{1}/_{5}$ inch) radius
  2 75 x 75 x 5 mm (3 x 3 x $^{1}/_{5}$ inch) thick steel corner angle
  3 50 x 5 mm (2 x $^{1}/_{5}$ inch) plate behind 75 x 5 mm (2 x $^{1}/_{5}$ inch) horizontal
  4 10 mm ($^{2}/_{5}$ inch) thick plate radial arms, tapering from 125 mm to 75 mm (5 x 3 inches)
  5 50 x 5 mm (2 x $^{1}/_{5}$ inch) plate behind 75 x 5 mm (2 x $^{1}/_{5}$ inch) horizontal

  6 Top edge of 472 mm (18$^{3}/_{5}$ inch) diameter platform level sleeve from 10 mm ($^{2}/_{5}$ inch) thick rolled plate
  7 Tamper-proof fixings
  8 219 mm (8$^{3}/_{5}$ inch) diameter central circular hollow section

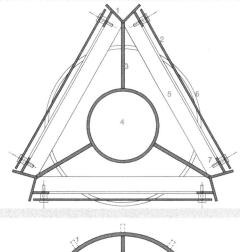

33.08
Millennium Beacon
Section 3
1:10
  1 75 x 75 x 5 mm (3 x 3 x $^{1}/_{5}$ inch) thick steel corner angle
  2 5 mm ($^{1}/_{5}$ inch) thick stainless steel perforated plate panel
  3 10 mm ($^{2}/_{5}$ inch) thick plate radial arms, tapering from 125 mm to 75 mm (5 to 3 inches)
  4 219 mm (8$^{3}/_{5}$ inch) diameter central circular hollow section
  5 50 x 5 mm (2 x $^{1}/_{5}$ inch) plate behind 75 x 5 mm (2 x $^{1}/_{5}$ inch) horizontal
  6 Top edge of

472 mm (18x$^{3}/_{5}$ inch) diameter platform level sleeve from 10 mm ($^{2}/_{5}$ inch) thick rolled plate
  7 Tamper-proof fixings

33.09
Millennium Beacon
Section 4
1:10
  1 25 mm (1 inch) long, 12 mm ($^{1}/_{2}$ inch) diameter dowell studs to key into concrete platform
  2 Continuous 10 mm ($^{2}/_{5}$ inch) thick radial steel plates
  3 219 mm (8$^{3}/_{5}$ inch) diameter central circular hollow section

  4 Top edge of 472 mm (18$^{3}/_{5}$ inch) thick platform level sleeve from 10 mm ($^{2}/_{5}$ inch) thick rolled plate

33.10
Millennium Beacon
Section 5
1:10
  1 Continuous 10 mm ($^{2}/_{5}$ inch) thick radial steel plates
  2 219 mm (8$^{3}/_{5}$ inch) diameter central circular hollow section

33.05
Millennium Beacon
Elevation
1:50
  1 720 mm (28$^{1}/_{3}$ inch) diameter, 10 mm ($^{2}/_{5}$ inch) thick, 80 mm (3$^{1}/_{5}$ inch) high steel ring
  2 219 mm (8$^{3}/_{5}$ inch) diameter central circular hollow section
  3 720 mm (28$^{1}/_{3}$ inch) diameter, 10 mm ($^{2}/_{5}$ inch) thick, 80 mm (3$^{1}/_{5}$ inch) high steel ring
  4 Lighting brackets
  5 75 x 75 x 5 mm (3 x 3 x $^{1}/_{5}$ inch) thick steel corner angle
  6 12 mm ($^{1}/_{2}$ inch) thick frosted toughened glass panel
  7 75 x 75 x 5 mm (3 x 3 x $^{1}/_{5}$ inch) thick steel corner angle

  8 10 mm ($^{2}/_{5}$ inch) thick plate radial arms, tapering from 125 mm to 75 mm (5 x 3 inches)
  9 Hole cored through completed reinforced concrete platform and paving, 472 mm (18$^{3}/_{5}$ inch) diameter, 10 mm ($^{2}/_{5}$ inch) thick rolled plate sleeve
  10 Continuous 10 mm ($^{2}/_{5}$ inch) thick radial steel plates

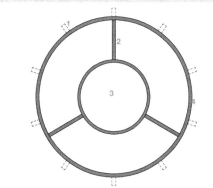

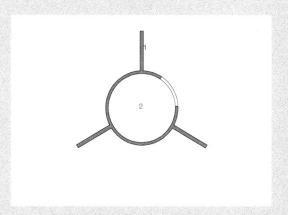

34
Foreign Office Architects (FOA)

**South-East Coastal Park,
Diagonal Mar
Barcelona, Spain**

Client
City of Barcelona

Area
5 hectares (12 acres)

Project Team
Farshid Moussavi, Alejandro Zaera-Polo, Lluís Viú Rebes, Juanjo Gonzalez, Marco Guarnieri, Sergio López-Piñeiro, Daniel Valle, Pablo Ros

Landscape Architect
Teresa Galí

This project is part of the infrastructure that the City of Barcelona planned as the host city for the International Forum of Cultures in 2004. The design is an alternative to geometries that attempt to reproduce the picturesque qualities of nature. Instead, this scheme explores strategies that produce complex landscapes through artificially generated topographies via mediated integration of rigorously modelled spaces. The organization proposed for the park is borrowed from a frequent model in coastal areas – sand dunes. The dunes have little internal structure and are made merely of sand, shaped by the wind.

The programme for the park is based on the analysis of the different sport and leisure activities that the park hosts, as well as the harsh environmental conditions of this exposed location. The topography provides open-air auditoria and spaces for events and activities, protection from the prevailing south-westerly wind, suitable habitats for vegetation and determines zones for a variety of different activities. The park allows and encourages sports and leisure activities, from walking to running, biking, skateboarding and a series of performance and relaxation areas through a network of paths or activity zones. The topography is also designed to control views and sight-lines. Views are deliberately controlled by the demarcation of activity zones – narrow, focused views within the park broaden to take in open views of the Mediterranean.

1 Aerial view. The park can be considered as a dune topography that protects vegetation from the salt and contamination contained in the sea breeze, and as a connection of ramps between the artificial beach and the city.
2+3 Internal view of the park's streets, where vegetation grows between the natural dunes, protected by the artificial dunes.
4+5 Outdoor concerts in front of the sea are an important part of the programme for the park. Auditoria are integrated into the geometry of the dunes to contain a total of 12,000 seats in the large auditorium and 4,000 in the smaller one.

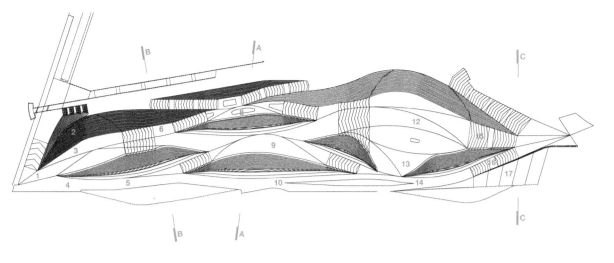

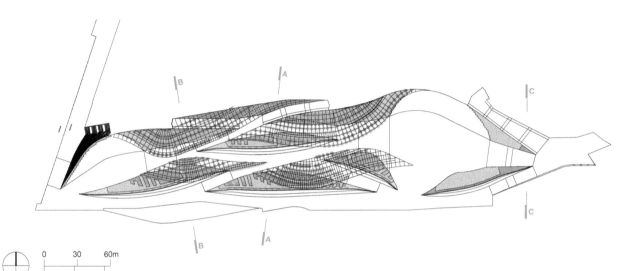

0 30 60m
0 90 180ft

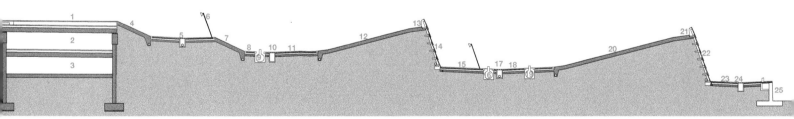

34.04
Section B–B
1:500
1 Pedestrian esplanade of coloured asphalt with structural resistance for vehicles
2 Concrete parking structure and retaining wall between water treatment plant

and the park
3 Concrete parking structure
4 Ramp connection for pedestrian and maintenance vehicles between esplanade and small auditorium
5 Ramp connection for pedestrian and maintenance vehicle use between

esplanade and small auditorium
6 Excavation for parking structure
7 Small auditorium arena
8 Prepared hole for tree
9 Prepared hole for tree
10 Hydroponic *Festuca Arundinacea*, Ray grass and

Poa pratense grasses
11 Concrete under-dune structure, mechanical room and WC
12 Concrete retaining wall and border between park and artificial beach

34.05
Section C–C
1:500
1 Pedestrian esplanade of coloured asphalt with structural resistance for vehicles
2 Balustrade from conveyor belt pieces
3 Ventilation to garage

4 Tile pavement system of pre-cast concrete conveyor belt pieces on mortar and concrete base
5 Hydroponic *Stipa tenufolia* grass
6 Tile pavement system of pre-cast concrete conveyor belt pieces
7 Balustrade from

conveyor belt pieces
8 Prepared hole for tree
9 Concrete retaining wall with surface of conveyor belt pieces on mortar bed
10 Tile pavement system of pre-cast concrete conveyor belt pieces
11 Concrete retaining

wall and border between park and artificial beach

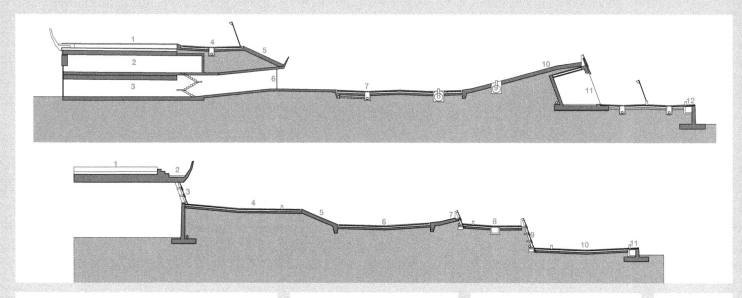

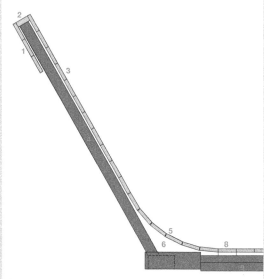
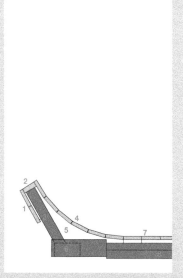

34.06
Wall System Detail 1
1:100
1 Conveyor-belt tiling
2 Flush wall capping on mortar bed
3 Flush wall capping from 550 mm (21³/₅ inch) diameter pre-cast and coloured conveyor belt pieces on 60° incline
4 Reinforced concrete base wall

5 Conveyor belt tiling system adapted to the 3 metre (9³/₄ foot) radius transition between wall and paving
6 Concrete fill
7 Reinforced concrete foundation
8 Conveyor-belt tiling
9 Reinforced concrete foundation

34.07
Wall System Detail 2
1:100
1 Conveyor-belt tiling
2 Flush wall capping on mortar bed
3 Reinforced concrete base wall
4 Conveyor belt tiling system adapted to the 3 metre (9³/₄ foot) radius transition between wall and paving

5 Concrete fill
6 Reinforced concrete foundation
7 Conveyor-belt tiling
8 Reinforced concrete foundation

34.08
Wall System Detail 3
1:100
1 Conveyor-belt tiling
2 Flush wall capping on mortar bed
3 Conveyor belt tiling system adapted to the 3 metre (9³/₄ foot) radius transition between wall and paving
4 Concrete fill
5 Reinforced

concrete foundation
6 Conveyor-belt tiling
7 Reinforced concrete foundation

34.09
Wall System Detail 4
1:100
1 Double thickness end piece from conveyor belt pieces
2 Concrete fill adapted to 3 metre (9⁴/₅ foot) radius geometry
3 Conveyor-belt tiling

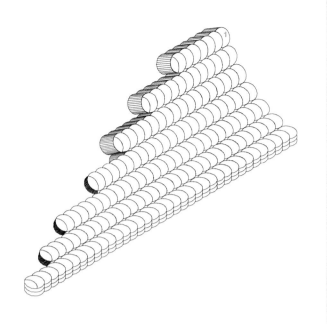

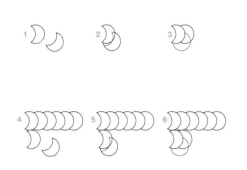

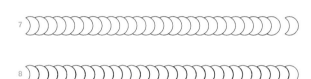

34.10
Pavement Layout
Axonometric
1 Conveyor belt tiling system adapted to the 3 metre (9³/₄ foot) radius transition between wall and paving

34.11
Pavement Placement Detail
1:100
1 The geometry of the conveyor belt pieces is obtained by intersecting two 550 mm (21³/₅ inch) diameter pieces. The result is a custom designed but modular shape in which the centre of the piece cointains a 550 mm (21³/₅ inch) arc.
2 The previous rule of compostion of the tiles allows connection and fit in any position of two conveyor belt pieces.
3 Building a row (see 7 and 8). The second piece is rotated so that the centre of rotation coincides with the centre of the previous piece. The process starts again with the next piece of the row.
4–6 The second row relies on the first for positioning, then configurations 5 and 6 are automatic as the previous row prevents rotation.
7–8 Finished rows. Small gaps between pieces are considered only in special cases as connection between rows.

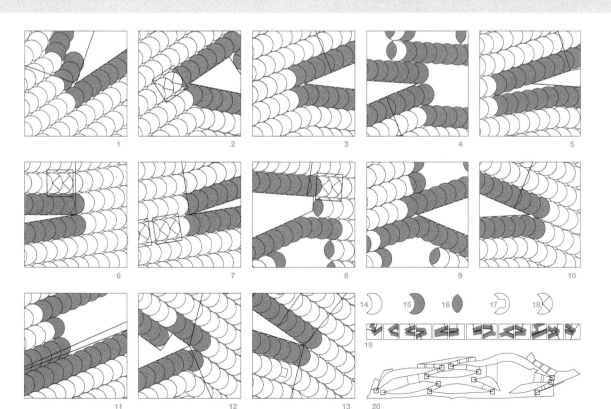

34.12
Pavement Details
1–13 Examples of possible bifurcations of conveyor belt pieces in the park. These situations appear when a dune is placed between two rows. Then each row is placed on one side of the dune, either the retaining wall side or the soft, earthy side. In some cases special double-width pieces broach the complex geometry.
14 Typical conveyor belt piece
15 Double thickness conveyor belt piece
16 Double thickness edge completion tile
17 Special fire hydrant tile
18 Special manhole cover tile
19 Diagrammatic representation of tile bifurcation situations across the park
20 Park diagram

35
Groupe Signes, Patel Taylor

Thames Barrier Park
London, England, UK

Client
London Development Agency

Area
14 hectares (34.6 acres)

Structural Engineer
Arup

Main Contractor
May Gurney

The site of Thames Barrier Park was formerly an industrial complex housing a chemical works, dyeworks and an armaments factory. These industries declined in the early twentieth century, leaving the site derelict and the soils and groundwater contaminated. A decision was taken to create a publicity-funded park which would act as a catalyst for private development. The design strategy was to create a clear urban and park framework containing contrasting spaces for different uses, and to create something more than another 'green lung' salvaged from the leftover spaces between buildings. Instead, the designers aimed for a special place of cultural significance.

The resultant park fronts the River Thames next to the northern end of the stainless steel-clad Thames Barrier. The design comprises settings for different activities including the plateau, which consists of mown grassland but features contrasting open and closed views of the Thames through copses of birch trees. A green trench running through the park is a reminder of the area's former industrial heritage. Cutting through the plateau, this 'dry dock', with its high concrete walls, depicts the scale of former docks, providing a sheltered microclimate for the 'rainbow garden', a series of parallel strips of plantings and paths. Overhead views of the rainbow garden are available from pedestrian bridges, with a water plaza forming a dramatic entrance to the north. The floodlit water feature comprises 32 choreographed jets of water. At the river end of the dock is the Pavilion of Remembrance, consisting of 23 irregularly spaced steel columns supporting a slatted timber roof with a large circular hole.

1 The Pavilion of Remembrance is a focal point on the river, framing views of the iconic Thames Barrier. It acts as a place for sheltered contemplation, reading and relaxing.
2 A river promenade terminates the park at the river's edge, providing opportunities for contemplating the river.
3 The Green Dock cut through the plateau recalling the scale and depth of the old dock structures and providing a microclimate for the 'rainbow garden', narrow strips of variously coloured and textured planting.
4+5 A simple visitor centre and café, also designed by Patel Taylor, feature a frame of green oak and a shaded verandah.

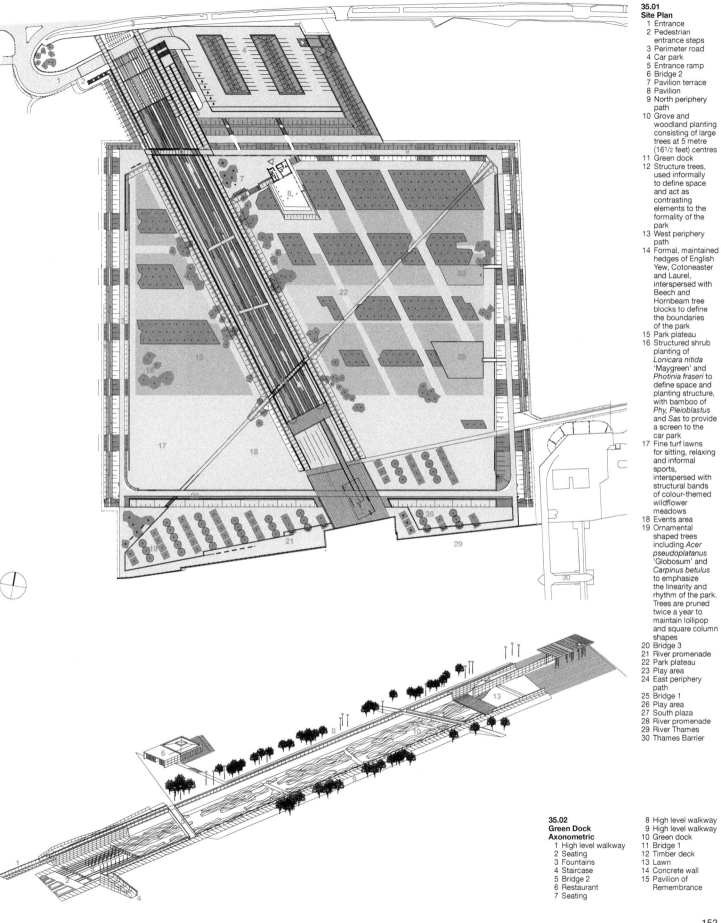

35.01
Site Plan

1 Entrance
2 Pedestrian entrance steps
3 Perimeter road
4 Car park
5 Entrance ramp
6 Bridge 2
7 Pavilion terrace
8 Pavilion
9 North periphery path
10 Grove and woodland planting consisting of large trees at 5 metre (16 1/2 feet) centres
11 Green dock
12 Structure trees, used informally to define space and act as contrasting elements to the formality of the park
13 West periphery path
14 Formal, maintained hedges of English Yew, Cotoneaster and Laurel, interspersed with Beech and Hornbeam tree blocks to define the boundaries of the park
15 Park plateau
16 Structured shrub planting of *Lonicara nitida* 'Maygreen' and *Photinia fraseri* to define space and planting structure, with bamboo of *Phy, Pleioblastus* and *Sas* to provide a screen to the car park
17 Fine turf lawns for sitting, relaxing and informal sports, interspersed with structural bands of colour-themed wildflower meadows
18 Events area
19 Ornamental shaped trees including *Acer pseudoplatanus* 'Globosum' and *Carpinus betulus* to emphasize the linearity and rhythm of the park. Trees are pruned twice a year to maintain lollipop and square column shapes
20 Bridge 3
21 River promenade
22 Park plateau
23 Play area
24 East periphery path
25 Bridge 1
26 Play area
27 South plaza
28 River promenade
29 River Thames
30 Thames Barrier

35.02
Green Dock
Axonometric

1 High level walkway
2 Seating
3 Fountains
4 Staircase
5 Bridge 2
6 Restaurant
7 Seating
8 High level walkway
9 High level walkway
10 Green dock
11 Bridge 1
12 Timber deck
13 Lawn
14 Concrete wall
15 Pavilion of Remembrance

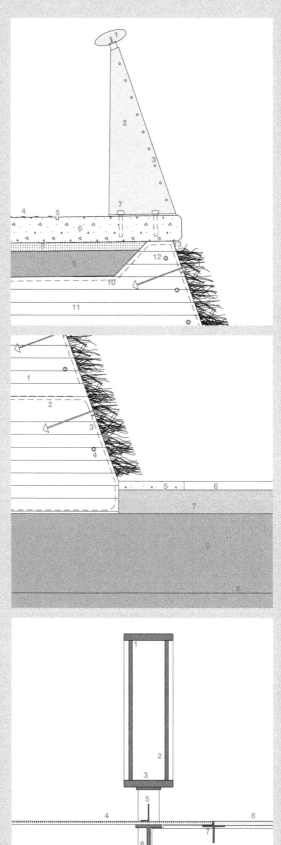

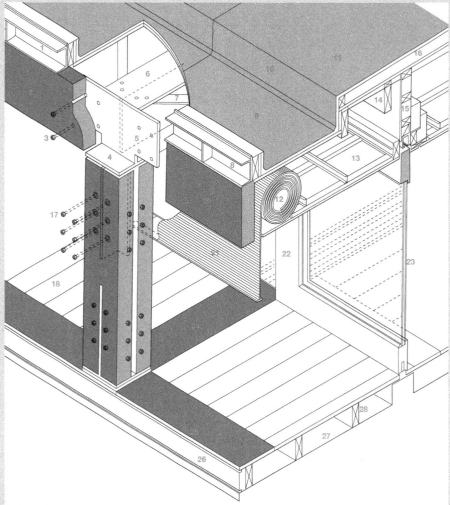

35.03
Top of Green Wall Detail
1:20
1 200 x 80 mm
(8 x 3¹/₅ inch) elliptical
hardwood handrail
with concealed fixings
to balustrade upright
at 2.4 metre (7⁴/₅ foot)
centres
2 Cast iron upright
at 2.4 metre (7⁴/₅ foot)
centres
3 Horizontal
tensioned 5 mm
(1/₅ inch) diameter
stainless steel cables
at 100 mm (4 inch)
vertical centres
sleeved through
isolators through cast
iron upright
4 Sandblasted
walkway
5 15 mm (2/₃ inch)
saw cut
6 150 mm (6 inch)
precast concrete
paving
7 Bolt fixing cast iron
upright to slab
8 50 mm (2 inch)
sand layer
9 150 mm (6 inch)
crushed concrete
10 Geotextile matting
to contain topsoil
11 Soil

12 Irrigation pipes
13 Steel mesh with
100 x 100 mm
(4 x 4 inch) openings
anchored with
brackets to retain
soil where geotextile
matting is cut to
accept planting

35.04
Green Wall Base Detail
1:20
1 Topsoil
2 Geotextile matting
to contain topsoil
3 Steel mesh with
100 x 100 mm
(4 x 4 inch) openings
anchored with
brackets to retain soil
where geotextile
matting is cut to
accept planting
4 Irrigation pipes
5 400 x 400 x 50 mm
(15³/₄ x 15³/₄ x 2 inch)
concrete flag pavers
6 60 mm (2²/₅ inch)
dry bonded macadam
7 140 mm (5¹/₂ inch)
thick layer of granular
material
8 Soil
9 Geotextile layer to
prevent contaminants
rising from soil below

35.05
Bridge Section
1:20
1 900 x 300 mm
(35¹/₂ x 11⁴/₅ inch)
fabricated steel girder
to act as structure and
handrail
2 20 mm (³/₄ inch)
thick steel plate
3 40 mm (1³/₅ inch)
thick steel plate
4 25 mm (1 inch)
thick steel grating with
continuous plate
welded to edge
5 100 x 50 mm
(4 x 2 inch) steel angle
6 200 x 160 mm
(8 x 6¹/₃ inch) steel
T-section with 160 x 10
mm (6¹/₃ x ²/₅ inch)
plate welded to base
7 Secondary steel
T-section
8 149 x 25 mm
(5⁴/₅ x 1 inch) timber
decking

35.06
Pavilion Isometric Detail
1 Steel coping
2 Green oak beam
3 Bolted connections
4 Steel connection
plate
5 Steel connection
plate
6 Steel roof beam
7 Steel tie
8 Steel coping
9 Asphalt-lined gutter
10 Asphalt upstand
11 Asphalt roofing
12 Steel roller shutter
13 Plasterboard ceiling
14 Timber roof framing
15 Glazing sub-frame
16 Roof decking
17 Bolted connections
18 Timber decking
19 Green Dock column
20 Green oak beam
21 Metal grille security
shutter
22 Oak-framed glass
sliding door
23 Double glazing unit
24 Oak flooring
25 Oak flooring
26 Timber sub-frame
to decking
27 Reinforced
concrete floor slab
28 Timber sub-frame
to decking

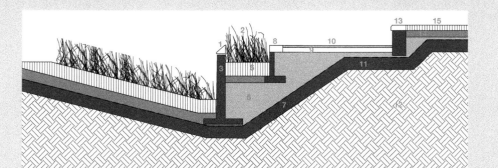

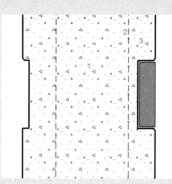

35.07
Ha-Ha Detail
1:100
1 Granite stone coping
2 Planting bed
3 Pre-cast concrete wall
4 200 mm (8 inch) sub soil
5 Fill

6 400 mm (15³/4 inch) layer of top soil
7 350 mm (13³/4 inch) layer of crushed concrete
8 400 x 200 mm (15³/4 x 8 inch) granite stone cap on pre-cast concrete wall
9 140 mm (5¹/2 inch) granular foundation

10 60 mm (2¹/3 inch) dry bonded macadam
11 Geotextile layer to prevent contaminants risiing from below
12 Pre-existing contaminated ground
13 450 x 150 mm (17³/4 x 6 inch) granite stone cap on pre-cast concrete wall

14 200 mm (8 inch) thick layer of sub soil
15 150 mm (6 inch) layer of top soil

35.08
Granite Inlay Detail
1:5
1 200 mm (8 inch) insitu concrete wall
2 Steel concrete reinforcement
3 Minimum 40 mm (1¹/2 inch) cover to reinforcement to allow for granite inlay

4 96 x 23 x 900 mm (3³/4 x 9/10 x 35²/5 inch) granite strip bedded in 3 mm (1/10 inch) grout

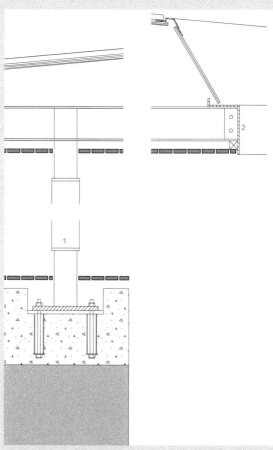

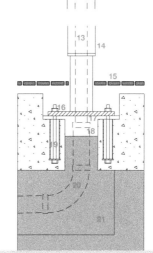

35.09
Pavilion of Remembrance Canopy Details
1:20
1 Structural 169 x 10 mm (6²/3 x ²/5 inch) circular hollow section
2 Roof light lined with fabricated steel
3 203 x 133 mm (8 x 5¹/5 inch) grid frame at 2 metre (6¹/2 foot) centres
4 Z-spacer
5 203 x 133 mm (8 x 5¹/5 inch) grid frame at 2 metre (6¹/2 feet) centres
6 Steel connection

plate
7 200 x 50 mm (8 x 2 inch) timber notched to take rain water pipe
8 75 x 22 mm (3 x 4/5 inch) treated soft wood boards with 10 mm (2/5 inch) gaps screwed to soft wood battens
9 Custom fabricated steel to form gutter and drip detail with localized deeper sections to accommodate rainwater pipe
10 Edge fabricated from steel plate

11 139 mm (5¹/2 inch) diameter circular hollow section
12 169 mm (6²/3 inch) diameter, 10 mm (²/5 inch) thick steel plate
13 75 mm (3 inch) UPVC rainwater pipe
14 169 mm (6²/3 inch) diameter, 10 mm (²/5 inch) thick non load bearing circular hollow section to accommodate rain water pipe
15 75 x 22 mm (3 x 4/5 inch) timber decking on spacers to concrete slab

16 400 x 400 x 25 mm (15³/4 x 15³/4 x 1 inch) steel base plate
17 Grout
18 Cast level
19 60 mm (2¹/3 inch) diameter, 3.2 mm (1/8 inch) thick cast in steel tube welded to plate and bolt
20 100 mm (4 inch) diameter drainage pipe
21 Concrete surround to pipe

36
Hargreaves Associates

Homebush Bay
Sydney, New South Wales, Australia

Client
Olympic Coordination Authority

Area
5.6 hectares (13.8 acres)

Project Team
George Hargreaves, Gavin McMillan,
Glenn Allen, Kirt Rieder

Hargreaves Associates designed the public domain for Homebush Bay in Sydney, site of the Olympic Games in 2000. The programme included stadia, arenas, aquatic and athletic centres, exhibition halls and major infrastructure such as rail and ferry terminals. These buildings are grounded in a well defined urban landscape that gives the public domain its own distinct identity. The creation of coherent public spaces and the establishment of connections to the larger landscape were essential goals of the design. The Olympic Plaza, the most important public space, is an inclined plane that engages the monumental buildings through its bold pattern, which is derived from an overlay of historical alignments and the proposed site grid. The plaza is framed by tree-lined edges and 'forests', and punctuated by a grid of lighting pylons.

Existing rows of mature trees are preserved in Plaza Park at the heart of the site, while 'green fingers' of tree-lined corridors link the urban core to the surrounding parklands, making connections to the wider landscape. Water is introduced to mark the high point of the plaza at Fig Grove Fountain, where ten magnificent mature fig trees salvaged from other development areas are reintroduced, creating an active public space. At the low point of the inclined plaza, where the urban core opens to the mangrove wetlands, the Northern Water Feature Wetland fountain projects arcing rows of 12 metre (39 feet) high jets of water into the wetland and engages the surrounding landscape. The wetland, fountain, terraces and pier allow for public access and interpretation of this remade landscape where public space, remediation and storm water management become legible as an interconnected landscape system.

1 View of the constructed wetland with its planted edge of macrophytes which are active components in the cleansing of storm water.
2 Aerial view of the Northern Water Feature and Olympic Plaza (centre), with key Olympic buildings ranged along its length.
3 At the northern end of Olympic Plaza, the land terraces down to meet a newly created wetland where a pier provides views over the wetland plantings.
4 View of the Northern Water Feature from the pier. The fountain contains 60 water cannons shooting water down the terraces.
5 View of the aerating water jets with the wetland landform in the background.

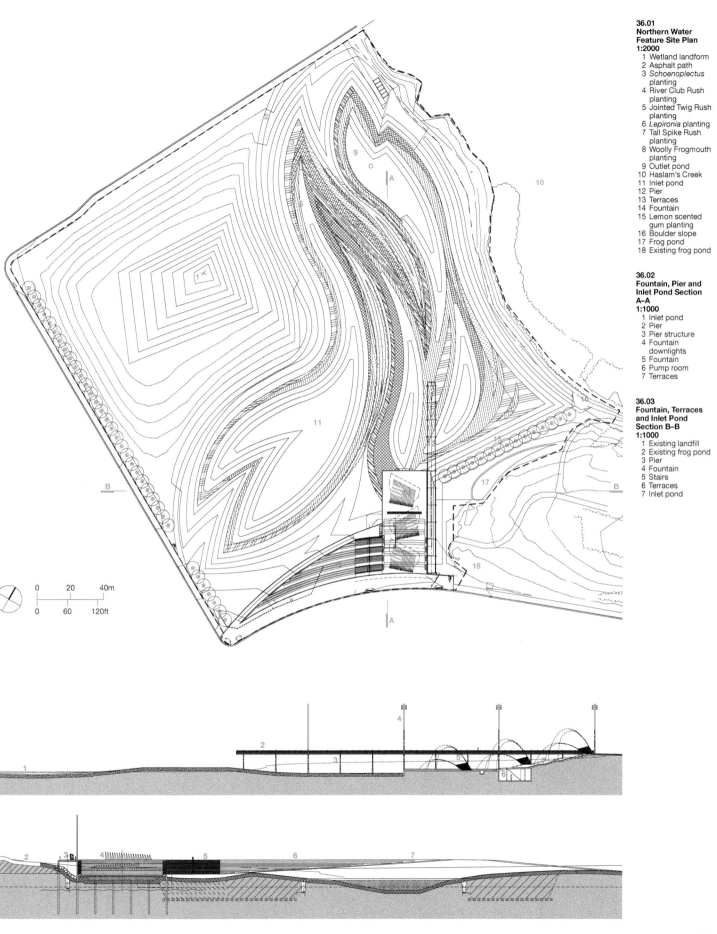

36.01
Northern Water
Feature Site Plan
1:2000
1 Wetland landform
2 Asphalt path
3 *Schoenoplectus*
  planting
4 River Club Rush
  planting
5 Jointed Twig Rush
  planting
6 *Lepironia* planting
7 Tall Spike Rush
  planting
8 Woolly Frogmouth
  planting
9 Outlet pond
10 Haslam's Creek
11 Inlet pond
12 Pier
13 Terraces
14 Fountain
15 Lemon scented
  gum planting
16 Boulder slope
17 Frog pond
18 Existing frog pond

36.02
Fountain, Pier and
Inlet Pond Section
A–A
1:1000
1 Inlet pond
2 Pier
3 Pier structure
4 Fountain
  downlights
5 Fountain
6 Pump room
7 Terraces

36.03
Fountain, Terraces
and Inlet Pond
Section B–B
1:1000
1 Existing landfill
2 Existing frog pond
3 Pier
4 Fountain
5 Stairs
6 Terraces
7 Inlet pond

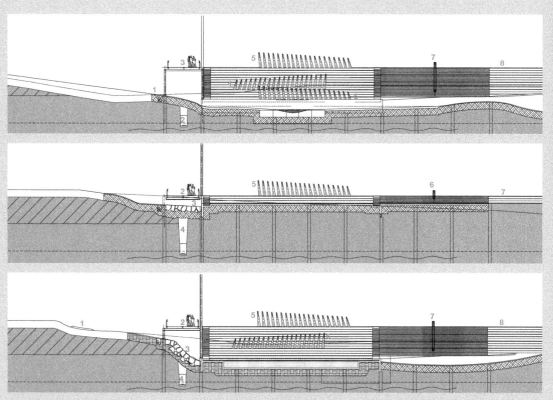

36.04
Section Facing
Fountain
1:500
1 Services corridor
2 Drain
3 Pier
4 Mid-level fountain jets
5 Top level fountain jets
6 Lower level fountain jets
7 Stairs
8 Terraces

36.06
Section Through
Fountain Pool
1:500
1 Existing frog pond
2 Pier
3 Boulder layer for stability
4 Drain
5 Top level fountain jets
6 Mid level fountain jets
7 Stairs
8 Terraces

36.05
Section Through
Fountain Terraces
1:500
1 Services corridor
2 Pier
3 Boulder layer for stability
4 Drain
5 Top level fountain jets
6 Stairs
7 Terraces

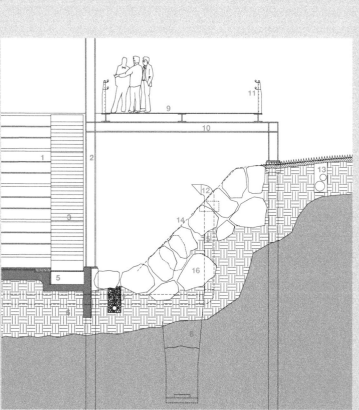

36.07
Pier Section Detail
1:100
1 Stairs
2 Steel pier structure
3 Runnel stair
4 Fountain edge
5 Fountain runnel
6 Clay sub-surface
7 Subsoil drainage
8 Leachate drain
9 Pier
10 Steel pier structure
11 Pier handrail
12 Fountain pump room vents in charcoal oxide concrete collar
13 Services corridor
14 Frog-friendly filter fabric
15 Soil reinforcement
16 Basalt boulder slope with grey flat faces to surface arranged to create honeycomb joints with basalt rubble used to fill larger joints

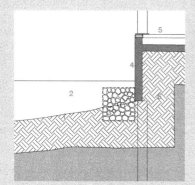

36.08
Pond and Fountain
Pool Interface at
Weir Detail
1:100
1 Top of clay liner
2 Pond
3 Gabions
4 Overflow to trickle down face of concrete pond structure
5 Fountain pool
6 1 metre (39²/5 feet) minimum clay layer

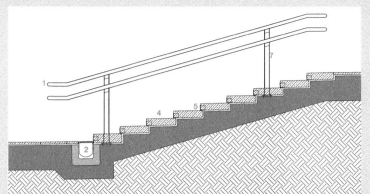

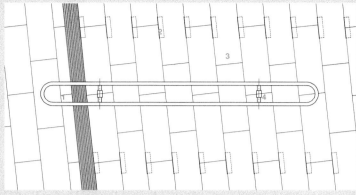

36.09
**Handrail Elevation
Detail**
1:50
 1 Top of two parallel
stainless steel
handrails
 2 Trench drain
 3 Concrete substrate
 4 Stone stair treads

 5 Recessed step light
 6 Mortar bed
 7 75 x 75 mm (3 x 3
inch) galvanized post
fixed through granite
onto concrete
structure

36.10
**Typical Handrail and
Lights Layout Plan**
1:50
 1 Stainless steel
handrail
 2 Recessed step light
– centre line of lights to
align with every
second joint of step at

face of riser parallel
to handrail
 3 Stone stair treads
 4 75 x 75 mm (3 x 3
inch) galvanized post
fixed through granite
onto concrete
structure – handrail
post aligned with
centre line of granite

joints to ensure that
all handrails align with
each other above and
below

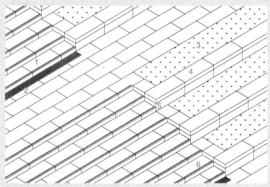

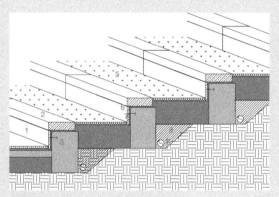

36.11
**Stone Stair and
Grass Terraces
Interface Detail**
1:100
 1 Stone stair tread
 2 Trench grate
 3 Grass terrace
 4 Stone seat wall
 5 5 mm (1/5 inch)

birdsmouth corners
to terrace edges
 6 Thread grooves
to step edges

36.12
**Stone Stair and
Grass Terrace Detail**
1:50
 1 Stone face
 2 Stone seat wall
 3 Concrete substrate
 4 300 mm (12 inch)
layer of soil
 5 Grass terrace

 6 Sealant and backer
rod
 7 Cramp
 8 Subsoil drain
 9 Drainage medium

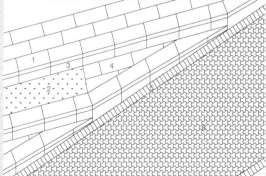
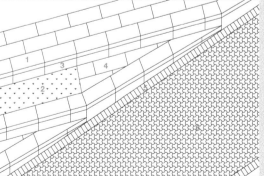

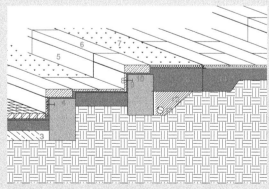

36.13
**Stone Stair, Grass
Terraces and
Footpath Detail 1**
1:100
 1 Stone stair tread
 2 Grass terrace
 3 Stone stair riser
 4 Stone face
 5 Concrete paver

to edge
 6 Concrete paver infill

36.14
**Stone Stair, Grass
Terraces and
Footpath Detail 2**
1:50
 1 Concrete paver
 2 Concrete slab
on ground
 3 Crushed aggregate
sub-base

 4 Sealant and backer
rod
 5 Stone face to
stair risers
 6 Stone stair treads
 7 Grass terrace
 8 Sealant expansion
joint
 9 Cramp
 10 Sealant and backer

rod
 11 Subsoil drain
 12 Drainage medium
 13 300 mm (12 inch)
layer of soil
 14 Reinforced
concrete slab

**Latz + Partner /
Latz-Riehl-Bauermann Partner**

**Bremerhaven Old and New Harbour
Bremerhaven, Germany**

Client
Bremerhavener
Entwicklungsgesellschaft Alter/
Neuer Hafen

Area
20 hectares (50 acres)

Project Team
Tilman Latz, Uwe Gehri, Oliver Keil,
Peter Bedner, Daniela Strasinsky,
Sabine Kern, Tobias Kramer, Michael
Stegmeier, Ilka Raabe, Sabine Kern,
Wigbert Riehl, Ernst Bauermann,
Matthias Dümer, Hendrik Pape

Structural Engineer
Planungsgesellschaft Dittrich /
WTM Engineers

Bremerhaven harbour, known for its
historic importance as an emigrant
port, had lost its former significance.
The renewal of the harbour reconnects
the city centre with the Weser River,
creating a new quarter with high
quality residential and recreation
areas. The design makes reference to
the existing urban pattern and utilizes
carpets of natural paving stones to
characterize the quays, the
promenades and squares that are
interrupted only at places of special
interest, including Lloyd Place which
marks the entrance to the harbour
and forms an important sight line from
the city to the river and the lighthouse.

Oak, hornbeam and wingnut trees
emerge out of a timber deck which
rises above the stone carpet. In
addition, a modular bench is both
seat and sculpture. The quays feature
sawn paving stones with smooth
surfaces in pedestrian areas, while
rough cobbled surfaces signal the
edges of the quay. Specially designed
drainage elements, service units,
benches and lamps emphasize the
character of the quays. On the
western quay, a new wooden bridge
crosses the historic entrance to
Lloyd Dock, creating a continuous
pedestrian connection. Sparsely
placed trees and street furniture
symbolize the change from a working
harbour to an integrated part of the
town, emphasizing the change from a
desolate place to an inviting and
attractive riverside environment.

1 View of Lloyd
Place where custom-
designed organic
benches provide
space for relaxation
next to the river.
2 A new timber bridge
featuring a shell-like
underbelly connects
the western quay and
Lloyd Dock.
3 View of the western
quay crossing the
entrance to Lloyd
Dock where natural
stone paving is used
to unite a disparate
collection of existing
historic buldings.
4 Rough cobblestones
are used at the edges
of the quays where
timber benches
provide additional
opportunities to enjoy
the harbour.
5 View of one of the
organic seats that are
placed throughout the
harbour site.
6 A line of multi-
functional poles,
shaped like ship
masts, carry flags,
lamps and security
devices, marking the
waterfront with their
blue top lights by
night.

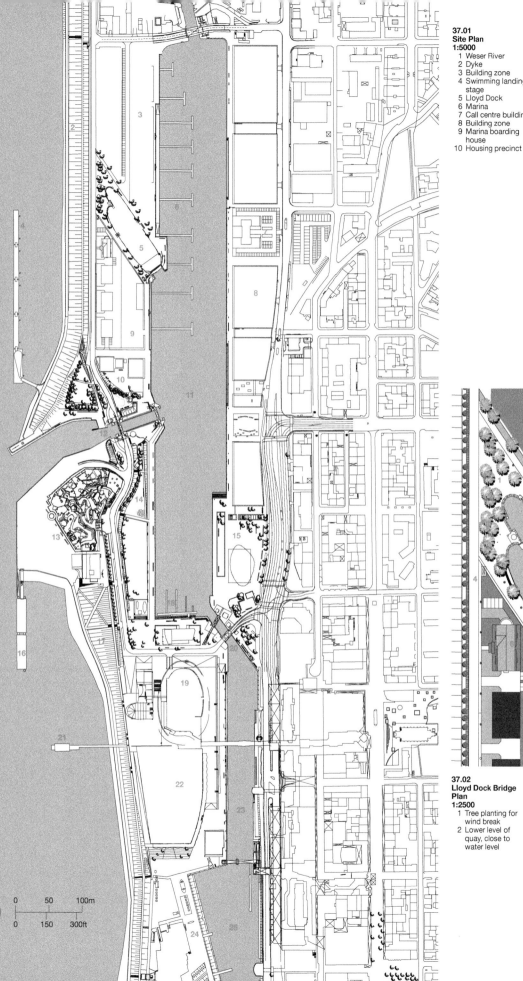

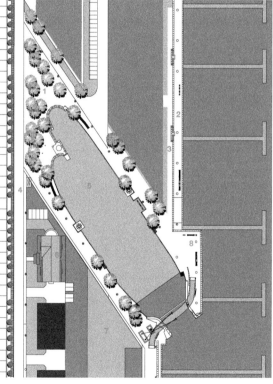

37.01
Site Plan
1:5000

1 Weser River
2 Dyke
3 Building zone
4 Swimming landing stage
5 Lloyd Dock
6 Marina
7 Call centre building
8 Building zone
9 Marina boarding house
10 Housing precinct

11 New harbour basin
12 Watergate
13 Zoo
14 Dockside plateau
15 German emigration centre
16 Swimming landing stage
17 Dyke
18 Landing stage for historical sailing ships
19 'Climate House 8° East' museum
20 Historical bridges

21 Pier (not built)
22 'Mediterraneo' shopping mall
23 Old harbour basin
24 German navigation museum
25 Navigation museum basin

37.02
Lloyd Dock Bridge Plan
1:2500

1 Tree planting for wind break
2 Lower level of quay, close to water level

3 Upper level of quay at street level
4 Street
5 Playground lawn
6 Private housing
7 Marina boarding house
8 Quay
9 Marina berths

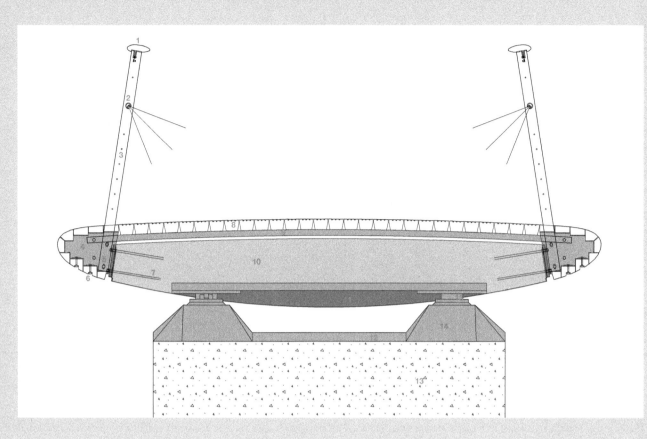

37.03
Lloyd Dock Bridge
Section
1:20
 1 Timber handrail
 2 Indirect lighting
 3 Steel balustrade
upright with timber
horizontals
 4 Transverse
structural element
 5 Steel connection
assembly between
handrail and plywood
board
 6 Sleek wood lateral
cladding
 7 Screw fixing to
plywood structure
 8 Profiled timber
decking
 9 Steel cross slat
 10 Plywood board
supporting element
 11 Plywood board
supporting element
 12 Reinforced
concrete foundation
 13 Reinforced
concrete foundation
 14 Reinforced
concrete bridge
bearing element
 15 Reinforced
concrete bridge
bearing element

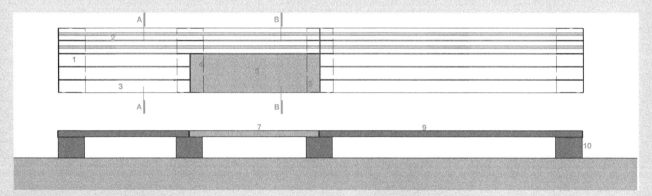

37.04
Kajenbank Bench
Plan and Elevation
1:50
 1 Steel panel
 2 90 x 180 mm
(3$^{1}/_{2}$ x 7$^{1}/_{8}$ inch)
moulded tropical
timber cover slats
 3 90 x 180 mm
(3$^{1}/_{2}$ x 7$^{1}/_{8}$ inch)
smooth tropical
timber cover slats
 4 Line of steel girder
below
 5 Granite seat
surface
 6 Line of steel girder
below
 7 Granite seat
surface

 8 Steel cover panel to
seat support
 9 90 x 180 mm
(3$^{1}/_{2}$ x 7$^{1}/_{8}$ inch)
smooth tropical
timber cover slats
 10 Steel cover panel

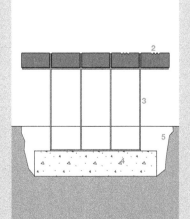

37.05
Kajenbank Bench
Section A–A
1:20
 1 90 x 180 mm
(3$^{1}/_{2}$ x 7$^{1}/_{8}$ inch)
smooth tropical timber
cover slats
 2 90 x 180 mm
(3$^{1}/_{2}$ x 7$^{1}/_{8}$ inch)
moulded tropical
timber cover slats
 3 Steel cover panel
over steel girder
 4 Concrete
foundation
 5 Excavation to
original ground surface

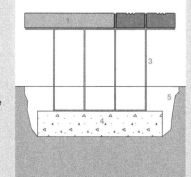

37.06
Kajenbank Bench
Section B–B
1:20
 1 90 mm (3$^{1}/_{2}$ inch)
thick granite seat
 2 90 x 180 mm
(3$^{1}/_{2}$ x 7$^{1}/_{8}$ inch)
moulded tropical
timber cover slats
 3 Steel cover panel
over steel girder
 4 Concrete
foundation
 5 Excavation to
original ground surface

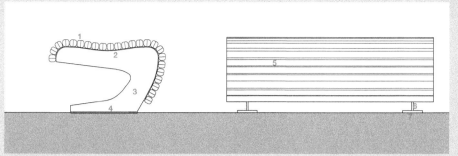

37.07
Flowbank Simple Bench Section and Elevation
1:20
  1 40 x 40 mm (1³/₅ x 1³/₅ inch) oak slats

  2 80 mm (3¹/₈ inch) wide steel strip with drilled holes to fix slats, welded to steel base
  3 Curved profile steel base
  4 Steel base plate

  5 40 x 40 mm (1³/₅ x 1³/₅ inch) oak slats
  6 Curved profile steel base
  7 Steel base plate

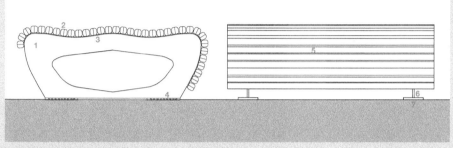

37.08
Flowbank Two-Fold Bench Section and Elevation
1:20
  1 Curved profile steel base
  2 40 x 40 mm

  (1³/₅ x 1³/₅ inch) oak slats
  3 80 mm (3¹/₈ inch) wide steel strip with drilled holes to fix slats, welded to steel base
  4 Steel base plate

  5 40 x 40 mm (1³/₅ x 1³/₅ inch) oak slats
  6 Curved profile steel base
  7 Steel base plate

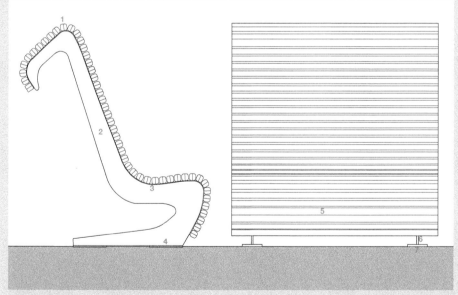

37.09
Flowbank Backed Bench Section and Elevation
1:20
  1 40 x 40 mm (1³/₅ x 1³/₅ inch) oak slats
  2 Curved profile steel base
  3 80 mm (3¹/₁₆ inch) wide steel strip with drilled holes to fix

  slats, welded to steel base
  4 Base plate
  5 40 x 40 mm (1³/₅ x 1³/₅ inch) oak slats
  6 Curved profile steel base
  7 Steel base plate

37.10
Multifunctional Pole Detail
1:50
  1 Blue light fixture
  2 Circular steel pipe mast
  3 Floating steel bearing
  4 Flag holder with 360-degree revolvable wind sheet
  5 Floating connection bearing
  6 Flag
  7 Floating steel bearing
  8 Varnished steel cable stay
  9 Light fixture
  10 Steel light pole sleeve
  11 Circular steel pipe mast
  12 Boat hook
  13 Lifebuoy
  14 Varnished steel upper brackets
  15 Mast connection brackets
  16 Fuse and junction box
  17 Mast fitting
  18 Varnished steel lower brackets

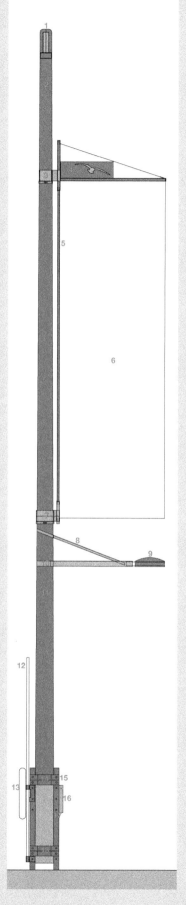

163

**Margarita Danou and
Sevina Floridou**

Voroklini Coastal Promenade
Voroklini, Larnaca, Cyprus

Client
Council of Voroklini

Area
3 hectares (7.4 acres)

Project Team
Margarita Danou, Sevina Floridou,
Andros Achilleos

Structural Engineer
Hyperstatic Engineering Design

Quantity Surveyor
Toumazis Christodoulou and Partners

Site Engineer
Elite Developing Company,
Ksenia Papauianni

The Voroklini Coastal Promenade
lies between an existing resort and
the coast, bordering a number of
properties that have, over time,
encroached on the beach. The design
creates a promenade that acts as a
threshold between private
development and the public beach.
The promenade consists of a series of
platforms, canopies and lighting
elements unified by a meandering
path that follows the coastline,
widening and narrowing to create a
series of specific places along the
way. Along the promenade is an open
resting place with the sea on one side
and an artificial lake on the other that
echoes the presence of a long-gone
coastal lagoon.

Changing and washroom facilities
are accommodated in a narrow
concrete building with timber screens,
and a kiosk is contained in a wooden
shell that opens to reveal the interior.
The entire walkway system of timber,
stone and monolithic pebbled
concrete is set lightly on the beach on
a concealed structural system that
allows for the natural movement
of the sea and sand. The walkway
appears to float or sink into the
rising and receding unstable
landscape according to the vagaries
of the weather and naturally changing
coastline. The scale and finesse of
the exterior furniture signals a
deliberate invitation to occupation,
establishing a continuity with the
design principles that have been
applied to the timber platforms and
the louvred canopy.

1 Very simple, elegant architectural elements – walkway, lighting and benches – provide a peaceful contrast with the rugged coastal environment.
2 Pathways of either concrete or timber expose and conceal parts of the beach and offer alternative routes along the coast.
3 At night, artificial lighting, consisting only of strip lights and dimmed uplighters, define a different sensibility of space, materiality and architectural details at the different areas of the project.
4+5 A changing pavilion with a light, hovering canopy sits between the sea and an artificial lagoon.

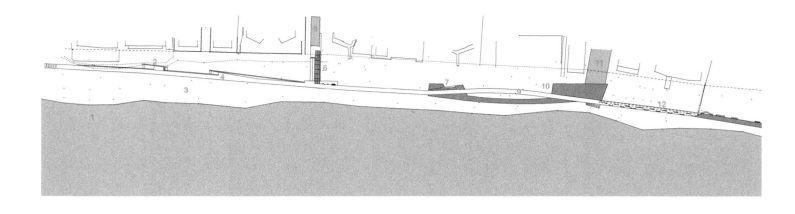

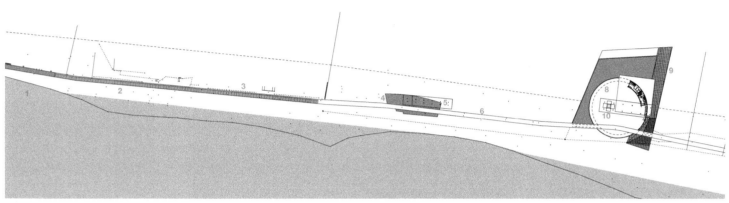

38.01
West Site Plan
1:2000
1 Mediterranean Sea
2 Access ramp
3 Beach
4 Access ramp
5 Public access
  to beach
6 Ramp and timber
  platform
7 Stepped timber
  platform
8 Alternating timber
  walkway
9 Monolithic pebbled
  concrete walkway
10 Timber platform
   deck
11 Public access to
   the beach
12 Monolithic raised
   pebbled concrete
   walkway

38.02
Walkway and
Platform Plan
1:2000
1 Mediterranean Sea
2 Beach
3 Walkway of
  monolithic
  sandstone slabs
  400 x 150 x 2500
  mm (15³/4 x 6 x
  98²/5 inch) with
  50 mm (2 inch)
  spacings
4 Timber platform
  deck
5 Louvred canopy
6 Monolithic pebbled
  concrete walkway
7 Shallow lake
8 Circle of loose
  beach gravel
9 Rough hewn stone
  walkway for public
  access to beach
10 Kiosk

38.03
East Site Plan
1:2000
1 Mediterranean Sea
2 Beach
3 Monolithic pebbled
  concrete walkway
4 Line of private
  property
5 Timber ramp,
  bridge and
  walkway extension
6 Monolithic pebbled
  concrete walkway
7 Loose beach
  gravel
8 Reclaimed river
  bed with seasonal
  flow
9 Sunken planters
  for bamboo reeds
10 Monolithic pebbled
   concrete service
   ramp
11 Cobbled pavement
12 Tiered gabion
   retaining walls

```
0    20    40m
0    60   120ft
```

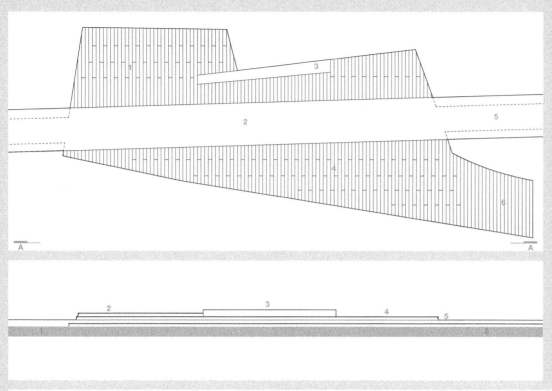

38.04
Decking to Platform 2
Plan
1:200
1 50 x 180 x 2700
mm (2 x 7 x 106³/₁₀
inch) upper timber
deck with 15 mm
(³/₅ inch) spacings
2 Monolithic pebbled
concrete walkway
3 Monolithic pebbled
concrete bench
4 50 x 180 x 2700
mm (2 x 7¹/₈ x 106³/₁₀
inch) lower timber
deck with 15 mm
(³/₅ inch) spacings
5 Recessed
monolithic pebbled
concrete support
beam
6 Lower deck
walkway

38.05
Decking to Platform 2
Section A–A
1:200
1 Beach
2 Upper timber deck
3 Monolithic pebbled
concrete bench
4 Lower timber deck
5 Monolithic pebbled
concrete walkway
6 Lower deck
walkway

38.06
Decking to Platform 2
Construction Detail
1:50
1 200 mm
(7⁹/₁₀ inch) perforated
PVC drainage pipe
in gravel bed
2 Reinforced
concrete support
beam
3 50 x 180 x 2700

mm (2 x 7 x 106³/₁₀
inch) *Angelim pedra*
timber deck with 20
mm (³/₄ inch) spacings
4 250 x 202 mm
(9⁴/₅ x 8 inch) *Angelim
Pedra* timber beams
5 410 x 200 x 12 mm
(16 x 7⁹/₁₀ x ¹/₂ inch)
galvanized U-bracket
with 12 mm (¹/₂ inch)
cell screws

6 Beach
7 150 x 150 mm
(6 x 6 inch) *Angelim
Pedra* perimeter
timber beam
8 White monolithic
pebbled concrete
walkway with
microsilica and 50 mm
(2 inch) reinforcement
coverage
9 50 x 180 mm

(2 x 7¹/₈ inch) *Angelim
Pedra* timber steps
with 15 mm (³/₅ inch)
spaces
10 150 x 100 mm
(6 x 4 inch) timber
beams
11 450 mm (17³/₄ inch)
diameter concrete
piles
12 50 x 180 mm
(2 x 7¹/₈ inch) *Angelim*

pedra timber steps
with 15 mm (³/₅ inch)
spaces
13 Monolithic pebbled
concrete base
14 150 x 100 mm
(6 x 4 inch) timber
beams

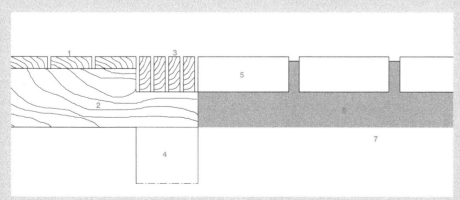

38.07
Walkway Detail
1:10
1 180 x 50 x 2500
mm (7 x 2 x 98²/₅ inch)
Angelim pedra timber
deck with 15 mm
(³/₅ inch) spacings and
fixed with 4 x 10 x 120
mm (1/10 x ²/₅ x 4³/₄
inch) bolts
2 200 x 300 mm
(8 x 11⁴/₅ inch) timber
beam bolted onto
10 x 100 x 300 mm
(²/₅ x 4 x 11⁴/₅ inch)
stainless steel plates
embedded into
concrete piles
3 50 x 180 x 2500
mm (2 x 7¹/₈ x 98²/₅
inch) *Angelim Pedra*

timber decking with
15 mm (³/₅ inch)
spacings
4 450 mm (17³/₄ inch)
diameter concrete
piles
5 450 x 150 x 2500
mm (17³/₄ x 6 x 98²/₅
inch) machine cut
sandstone slabs
6 Crushed sandstone
bed
7 Sand

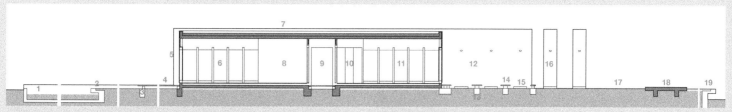

38.08
Platform 4 and
Pavilion Section
1:200
 1 Shallow lake
 2 Monolithic pebbled
concrete circular
retaining wall

 3 Monolithic pebbled
concrete deck support
 4 50 x 180 x 2700
mm (2 x 7^1/$_8$ x 106^3/$_{10}$
inch) timber deck
 5 Double-sided Iroko
timber screen wall
 6 Marine plywood

doors suspended on
Iroko timber frame
 7 Fair-faced concrete
roof slab with
insulation and loose
beach gravel
 8 Plastered brick wall
 9 Door opening

 10 Marine plywood
folding doors
 11 Marine plywood
doors suspended on
Iroko timber frame
 12 Fair-faced concrete
wall
 13 Fair faced concrete

visible deck supports
 14 50 x 180 x 2700
mm (2 x 7^1/$_8$ x 106^3/$_{10}$
inch) timber deck
 15 Monolithic pebbled
concrete shower base
 16 Fair-faced concrete
shower wall

 17 Loose beach gravel
 18 Monolithic pebbled
concrete walkway
 19 Monolithic pebbled
concrete circular
retaining wall

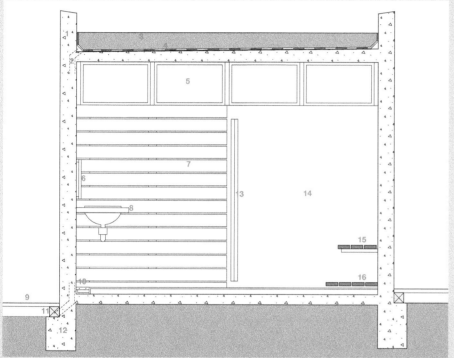

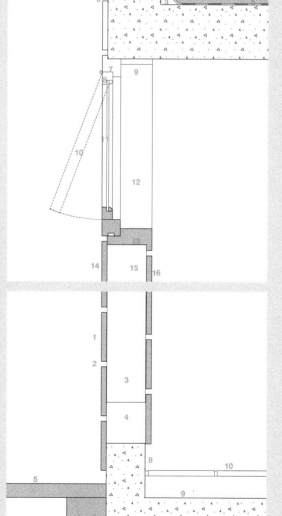

38.09
Washroom Pavilion
Section
1:50
 1 Fair-faced concrete
 2 Concealed roof
drainage shown dotted
 3 Loose beach gravel
to prepared roof
surface
 4 4 mm (1/16 inch)
thick polyester tar felt
insulation
 5 Timber-framed
windows with clear
glazing
 6 Mirror on 18 mm
(3/4 inch) thick marine
plywood base
 7 20 x 180 mm
(3/4 x 7^1/$_8$ inch) double
sided alternating Iroko
timber screen wall with
20 mm (3/4 inch)
spacings on a
150 x 150 mm (6 x 6
inch) timber frame,
finished in teak oil
 8 75 mm (3 inch)
thick marine plywood
wash basin counter
 9 50 x 180 x 2700
mm (2 x 7 x 106^3/$_{10}$
inch) timber deck

 10 Stainless steel floor
drainage grille
 11 150 x 150 mm
(6 x 6 inch) timber
support beams
 12 Concrete beam
 13 Marine plywood
doors suspended on
Iroko frame
 14 Plastered and
painted brick wall
 15 50 x 180 mm
(2 x 7^1/$_8$ inch) Irocco
timber slat bench on
steel angles
 16 50 x 180 mm
(2 x 7 inch) Iroko
timber floor

38.10
Washroom Pavilion
Screen Wall Detail 1
1:20
 1 Iroko timber screen
wall cladding
 2 Fair-faced concrete
slab and beam
 3 Timber fillet piece
 4 15 mm (2/3 inch)
thick loose beach
gravel
 5 4 mm (1/6 inch)
polyester tar felt
insulation
 6 20 mm (3/4 inch)
spacing between
timber slats
 7 70 x 80 mm
(2^3/$_4$ x 3^1/$_5$ inch) Iroko
timber window frame
 8 40 x 45 mm
(1^3/$_5$ x 1^3/$_4$ inch) Iroko
timber glazing frame
 9 20 x 130 mm
(3/4 x 5^1/$_{10}$ inch) interior
window frame
 10 Iroko timber
window, opening
outwards on upper
hinge
 11 4 mm (1/6 inch)
clear glazing
 12 30 x 150 mm

(1^1/$_5$ x 6 inch) Iroko
timber stile
 13 170 x 80 mm
(6^2/$_3$ x 3^1/$_5$ inch)
interior window sill
 14 Iroko timber screen
wall
 15 150 x 150 mm
(6 x 6 inch) timber
screen structural frame
 16 Iroko timber screen
wall

38.11
Washroom Pavilion
Screen Wall Detail 2
1:20
 1 Iroko timber screen
wall cladding
 2 20 mm (3/4 inch)
spacing between
timber slats
 3 150 x 150 mm
(6 x 6 inch) timber
screen structural frame
 4 150 x 150 mm
(6 x 6 inch) timber
screen structural frame
 5 50 x 80 x 2700 mm
(2 x 3^1/$_5$ x 1061$/$_3$ inch)
timber deck
 6 150 x 150 mm
(6 x 6 inch) timber
support beam
 7 250 x 180 mm
(9^3/$_4$ x 7^1/$_8$ inch) timber
beam
 8 Fair-faced concrete
skirting
 9 Fair-faced concrete
floor slab and beam
 10 Non-slip grouted
ceramic floor tiles

Zhongshan Shipyard Park
Zhongshan, Guangdong, China

Client
City of Zhongshan

Area
11 hectares (27 acres)

Project Team
Professor Kongjian Yu, Pang Wei,
Huang Zhengzheng, Qiu Qingyuan,
Lin Shihong

Landscape Contractors
Zhongshan City Civil Engineering
Construction Company and
Zhongshan Landscape
Construction Company

Zhongshan Shipyard Park is a ground-breaking project that acknowledges China's recent past – one of the most troubling periods in the country's history. The park combines historical, contemporary and ecological elements that act both as a memorial to the thousands of shipyard workers who helped to build modern China, and as a celebration of contemporary life. The railroad path, a three-metre (ten foot) wide walkway stretching from the entry to the lakefront, is the major organizing element. Here, old rails are highlighted by a bed of white rocks bordered by native grasses. To create focus, a grid of 180 slender white columns are placed at the centre point of the path.

Constructed from red steel plates, The Red Box, which commemorates the Cultural Revolution, encloses pools of water where people can reflect on one of the grimmest periods in recent Chinese history. The 'Green Rooms', surrounded by hedge walls, are used for reading and relaxation, and represent a typical workers' dormitory in the old shipyard. At the lake front, bridges overcome the problem of the daily tide, offering permanent access to the waterfront. The shoreline also features two pavilions adapted from old shipyard buildings, now stripped to their skeletons and repainted, one red and the other white. Many other relics of the industrial landscape have been recycled. For example, an old water tower has been transformed into a lighthouse, and a pair of massive cranes have been incorporated into two of the park gateways.

1 The park provides the largest public open space in Zhongshan. The main thoroughfare, with its grid of white poles surrounded by the 'Green Rooms', is visible in the centre of the park, while the remnants of the shipyard buildings and the Red Box are to the right.
2 The railroad path stretches from the entrance to the lakefront and is bordered by native grasses and granite walks. A salvaged industrial building, painted red, has a striking presence.
3 The Red Box, nine metres (29½ feet) square and three metres (ten feet) high, is a potent reminder of the Cultural Revolution.
4 A disused water tower has been converted into a dramatic lighthouse, while an elegant steel bridge makes a new connection to the ecological island which preserves an historical stand of banyan trees.

39.01
Site Plan
1:1500

1 Ring road
2 Palm tree promenade with fountains
3 North entrance
4 Mist fountain
5 Sidewalk
6 Parking
7 Man made stream
8 Red box
9 Green Rooms
10 Lawn
11 Cycle path and service road
12 Grid of hedges
13 Pathway
14 Steel column matrix
15 Pathway
16 Ring road
17 Fog fountain square
18 Preserved dock (Dock A)
19 Canopy square
20 Preserved dock (Dock B)
21 Future pathway
22 Lakeside pathways
23 Sculpture
24 Playground on existing boat
25 Bridge to ecological island
26 Ecological island
27 Light tower (reuse of historic water tower)
28 Parking
29 Pier at termination of Railway Walk
30 Elevated walkway with plant specimen beds
31 Skeleton tower (re-use of historic water tower)
32 Boating service facilities
33 Boundary grove
34 Bridge
35 Inner lake
36 Terraced bridges
37 Palm square
38 Tea house in existing dockside structure, currently used as museum
39 Bridge to ecological island
40 Swimming pool (not built)

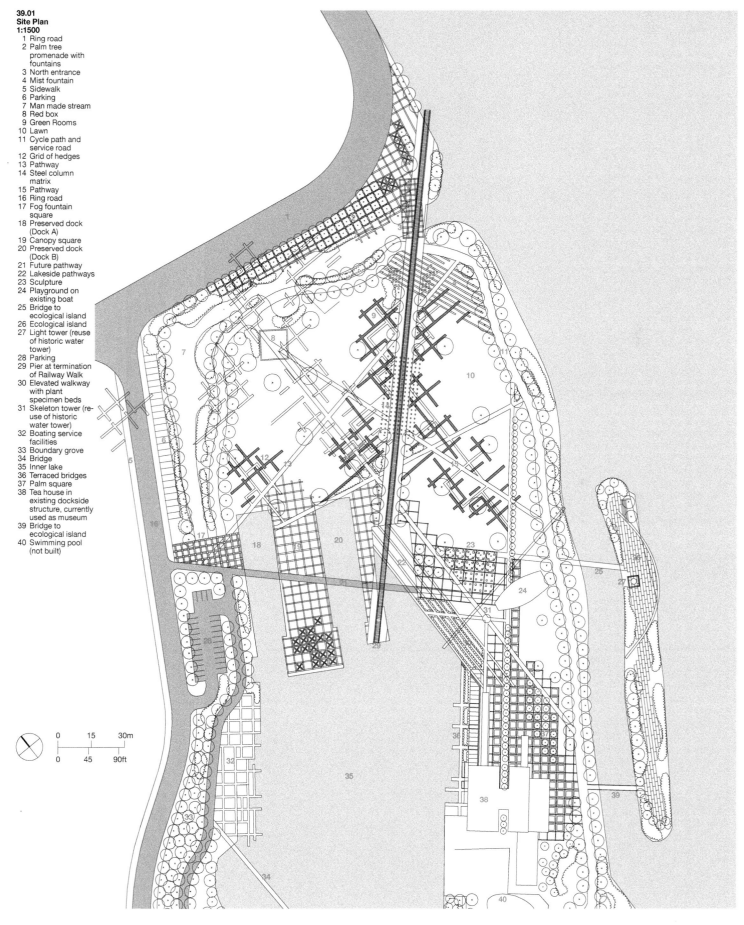

0   15   30m
0   45   90ft

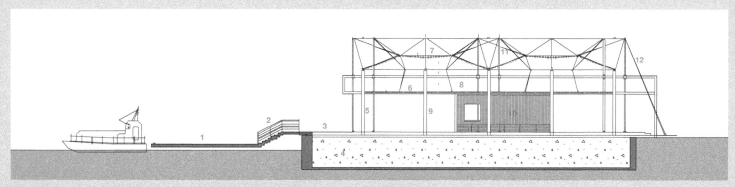

39.02
Dock A East
Elevation
1:200
 1 Granite pier
 2 Stairs between pier
and dock

3 Granite-paved dock
surface
4 Reinforced
concrete dock
structure
5 300 mm (11⁴/5 inch)
steel channel column

6 150 mm (6 inch)
steel channel with
riveted joints
 7 Tensioned steel
cord and longitudinal
wire rope
 8 Polymer tent

structure
9 300 mm (11⁴/5 inch)
steel channel column
10 40 x 40 mm
(1³/5 x 1³/5 inch) steel
angle to skeleton walls
with curved steel plate

cladding and cement
render to interior
surface
11 Tensioned steel
cord and wire rope
12 Suspended cable
structure

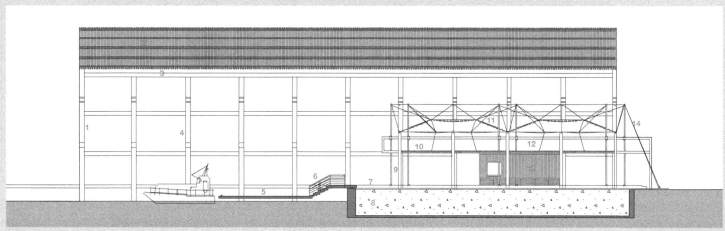

39.03
Dock A East
Elevation
1:200
 1 Steel and concrete
preserved dock
structure

2 Steel roof to
preserved dock
structure
3 Steel and concrete
preserved dock
structure
 4 Steel columns

of preserved dock
structure
5 Granite pier
6 Stairs between pier
and dock
 7 Granite-paved dock
surface

8 Reinforced
concrete dock
structure
9 300 mm (11⁴/5 inch)
steel channel column
10 150 mm (6 inch)
steel channel with

riveted joints
11 Tensioned steel
cord and longitudinal
wire rope
12 Polymer tent
structure
13 40 x 40 mm (1³/5 x

1³/5 inch) steel angle
to skeleton walls with
curved steel plate
cladding and cement
render to interior
14 Suspended cable
structure

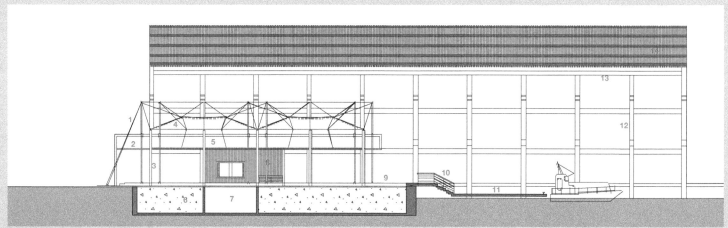

39.04
Dock B West
Elevation
1:200
 1 Suspended cable
structure
 2 150 mm (6 inch)

steel channel with
riveted joints
 3 300 mm (11⁴/5 inch)
steel channel column
 4 Tensioned steel
cord and longitudinal
wire rope

5 Polymer tent
structure
 6 Reinforced
concrete dock
structure
 7 Tank
 8 40 x 40 mm

(1³/5 x 1³/5 inch) steel
angle to skeleton walls
with curved steel plate
cladding and cement
render to interior
surface
 9 Granite-paved pier

surface
10 Stairs between pier
and dock
11 Granite-paved dock
surface
12 Steel columns to
preserved dock

structure
13 Steel and concrete
preserved dock
structure
14 Steel roof to
preserved dock
structure

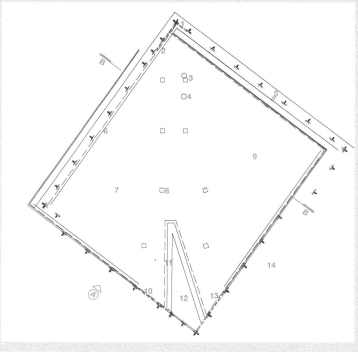

39.05
Red Box Plan
1:200
1 940 x 2000 mm (37 x 78³/4 inch) door opening
2 2200 x 2000 mm (86²/3 x 78³/4 inch) door opening
3 Pool overflow
4 Pool inlet
5 Pool outlet
6 Pond wall
7 Pond
8 250 x 250 mm (9⁴/5 x 9⁴/5 inch) reinforced concrete column with 15 mm (²/3 inch) thick granite cladding
9 Constant water level to pond
10 2700 x 2000 mm (106¹/3 x 78³/4 inch) door opening
11 Concrete cushion slab
12 Lawn
13 3100 x 2000 mm (122 x 78³/4 inch) door opening
14 Lawn

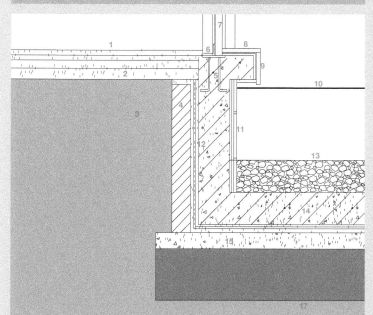

39.06
Red Box Elevation A and Section B–B
1:200
1 Red-painted steel angle structure with riveted joints
2 1800 mm (70⁷/8 inch) wide red painted steel plate cladding
3 Door opening
4 Red-painted steel plate panel with riveted joints
5 Red-painted steel angle roof structure with riveted joints
6 Red-painted steel angle structure with riveted joints
7 Door opening
8 Pool inlet
9 Pool overflow
10 1800 mm (70⁴/5 inch) wide red-painted steel plate cladding
11 Constant water level to pool
12 Concrete cushion platform

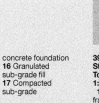

39.07
Red Box Sectional Detail
1:20
1 15 mm (³/5 inch) thick 200 x 200 mm (8 x 8 inch) granite pavers
2 Reinforced concrete slab on ground
3 Compacted sub-grade
4 Reinforced concrete retaining wall
5 Steel J-bolt
6 Welded connection between steel wall plate and floor plate
7 Red-painted steel wall
8 Granite pool edge with integrated lighting
9 Granite cladding to pool edge
10 Pond water line
11 Granite cladding to pool wall
12 Waterproof liner
13 Gravel layer to pool floor
14 Reinforced concrete slab to pool base
15 Reinforced concrete foundation
16 Granulated sub-grade fill
17 Compacted sub-grade

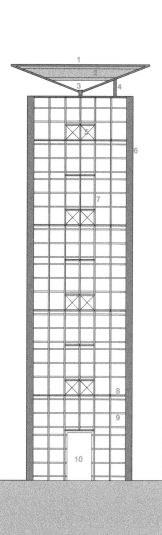

39.08
Steel-Framed Light Tower Section
1:200
1 Blue-painted steel frame to 8400 mm (27¹/2 feet) diameter light cone
2 Sailcloth to exterior of light cone
3 200 x 200 mm (8 x 8 inch) blue-painted steel hollow section support to light cone
4 Blue-painted steel bar support to light cone
5 66 x 12 mm (2³/5 x ¹/2 inch) aluminium alloy bracing structure
6 300 x 300 mm (11⁴/5 x 11⁴/5 inch) blue-painted rectangular hollow section to external structure
7 50 x 50 mm (2 x 2 inch) blue-painted steel channel to central core structure
8 50 x 50 mm (2 x 2 inch) blue-painted steel channel to central core structure
9 Steel-framed glazing
10 Aluminium alloy framed glass door

W Architecture and Landscape Architecture

Tide Point Urban Waterfront
Baltimore, Maryland, USA

Client
Struever Bros. Eccles & Rouse

Area
6 hectares (15 acres)

Project Team
Barbara Wilks and Andrea Rhinehart

Civil and Structural Engineer
Whitman, Requardt & Associates

Main Contractor
Struever Bros, Eccles & Rouse

Credited with turning a derelict old industrial site into the epicentre of Baltimore's Digital Harbour, this project is about transformation and creating a transition between Baltimore's past and future. Tide Point was the site of one of Procter & Gamble's main soap producing plants. Now the renovated buildings house high-tech companies and institutions. Once, its boardwalk was off-limits to the public – now the site opens out to the water and views beyond. The landscape design emphasizes the shifting nature of the ground surface, blending historical, natural and industrial processes. Materials include concrete paving and retaining walls, gravel and asphalt to complement the industrial nature of the context.

Plants vary according to the location, creating a series of gardens of varying micro-climates with seasonal interest throughout the year. An elevated timber boardwalk marks the water's edge, emphasizing the pile structure below. A linear fog feature enlivens the boardwalk and provides cooling in the summer. The site plan provides clear vehicular and pedestrian pathways and encourages public access to the waterfront. The master plan includes marking the four corners of the site with light structures that contrast with the existing historical brick industrial buildings. These new structures are both objects and space makers, interacting with the existing buildings to mark places of transition – entries and gateways to the site.

1 The historic Procter & Gamble building provides the perfect backdrop to the restored harbour foreshore, where the materials and scale of new elements complement the industrial nature of the site.
2 The wide, open timber boardwalk is interspersed with more intimate scaled gardens.
3 A linear fog feature introduces an element of fun and mystery as well as allowing visitors to cool off in hot weather.
4+5 Materials vary within the scheme, from stone and concrete areas to timber, both contrasted with planted gardens to create spaces with more intimate or open qualities.

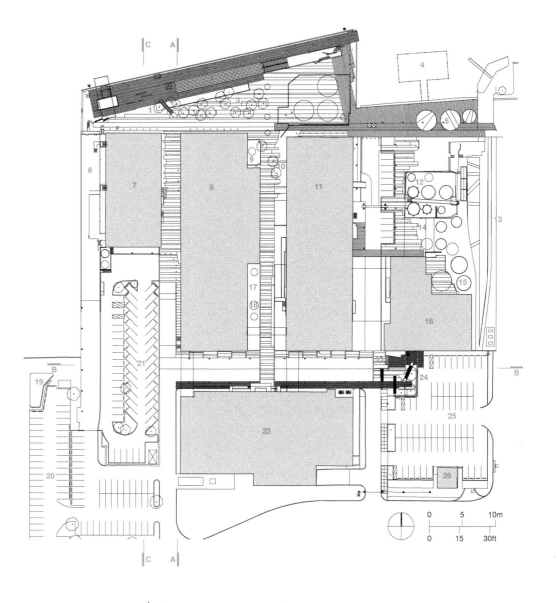

40.01
Site Plan
1:500
1 Industrial bridge and gardens
2 Garden 2, The Edge Promenade
3 Locust trees and plaza
4 Kayak, float, marina and water taxi landing pier
5 Tank base
6 Railroad Trestle Promenade
7 Office building
8 Office building
9 Playground
10 Sycamore trees
11 Office building
12 Industrial garden
13 Hull Street
14 Garden 3, Industrial Garden
15 Maple trees
16 Office building
17 Garden 5, The Woodland Walk
18 Existing tank
19 Garden 1, Old Fields
20 Parking
21 Temporary parking – future building site
22 Office building
23 Industrial Bridge and Garden
24 Garden 4 – Entry garden
25 Car parking
26 Daily Grind Café

40.02
Section A–A
1:500
1 Edge Promenade
2 Locust trees and Plaza
3 Roof terrace to office building
4 Parking facilities in existing foundations
5 Bridge connector
6 Roof terrace
7 Key Highway

40.03
Section B–B
1:500
1 Railroad Trestle Promenade
2 Roof deck to office building
3 Bridge connector
4 Roof deck to office building
5 Bridge connector
6 Roof terrace to office building
7 Bridge connector
8 Office building
9 Parking and Old Field
10 Hull Street

40.04
Section C–C
1:500
1 Key Highway
2 Parking and Old Field
3 Railroad Trestle Promenade
4 Ramp
5 Railroad Trestle Promenade
6 Tank Entry Garden
7 Tank Entry Garden
8 Roof terrace to office building
9 Railroad Trestle Promenade
10 Locust trees and plaza
11 Future Folly Café
12 Edge Promenade

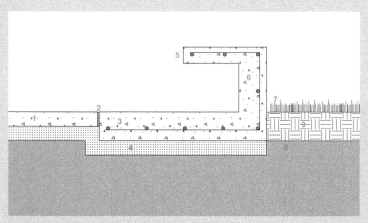

40.05
Concrete Bench
Detail
1:20
1 Scored concrete
paving
2 12 mm (1/2 inch)
expansion joint
3 1220 mm (4 foot)
long concrete slab with
No. 5 steel reinforcing
at equal centres
4 100 mm (4 inch)
thick aggregate base

5 610 mm (2 foot)
deep, 114 mm thick
(4 1/2 inch) concrete
bench seat
6 200 mm (8 inch)
thick wall to concrete
bench with No. 5 steel
reinforcing at equal
centres
7 Lawn
8 Area of demolition
9 200 mm (8 inch)
thick topsoil

40.06
Planting Bed Detail
1:20
1 Reinforced
concrete slab on
ground
2 25 mm (1 inch)
thick sand setting bed
3 Waterproof
membrane
4 60 mm (2 3/8 inch)
thick concrete pavers
5 Concrete curb
6 Topsoil and planting

level with pavers
7 Top soil
8 Steel sheet piling
9 300 x 300 mm
(12 x 12 inch) timber
10 Gravel fill

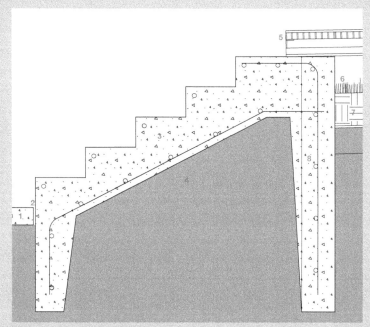

40.07
Concrete Stair Detail
1:20
1 Scored concrete
paving
2 12 mm (1/2 inch)
expansion joint
3 Reinforced
concrete stair with
178 mm (7 inch) high
risers and 300 mm
(12 inch) treads
4 Gravel fill
5 End of metal

grating walkway
anchored to top
of concrete stair
6 Turf
7 Top soil

40.08
Garden Wall Detail
1:20
1 Scored concrete
walkway
2 Reinforced
concrete slab on
ground
3 Planting area
4 Minimum 200 mm
(8 inch) deep topsoil
5 250 mm (10 inch)
wide concrete wall to
edge of garden

6 New No. 4
reinforcing tied off to
new or existing
reinforcing, and where
existing reinforcing has
been cut, drilled and
dowelled No. 4
reinforcing bars
embedded using
adhesive
7 Lawn
8 Minimum 200 mm
(8 inch) deep topsoil
9 Geotextile layer

10 Minimum of
150 mm (6 inches)
of gravel
11 Concrete topping
slab
12 Reinforced
concrete slab
on ground

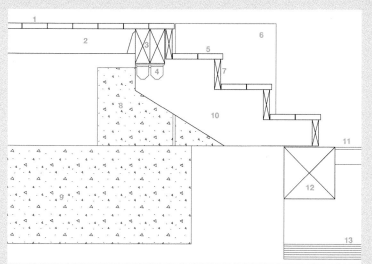

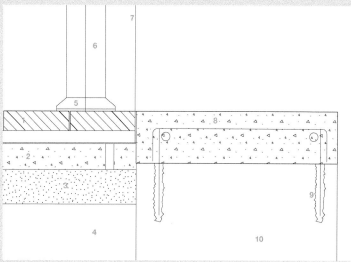

40.09
Water Taxi Steps Detail
1:20
1 Timber boardwalk
2 Timber joist
3 100 x 200 mm (4 x 8 inch) timber bearers
4 Timber stringer attached to continuous bearers
5 300 mm (12 inch) timber treads

6 New concrete cleat wall beyond
7 180 mm (7inch) high timber risers
8 Existing concrete cleat wall
9 Existing trench drain filled with concrete
10 Timber stringer attached to top of existing concrete wall, with stringer supporting last tread

cantilevering over fender system
11 Water taxi loading platform
12 Existing 300 x 300 mm (12 x 12 inch) timber fender
13 Water line

40.10
Bulkhead Paver Edge Detail
1:20
1 Concrete pavers on 25 mm (1 inch) thick sand setting bed
2 Existing gravel levelling bed
3 Existing ground conditions
4 Existing ground conditions
5 Light pole base

beyond
6 Light pole beyond
7 Line of existing concrete bulkhead wall
8 Concrete kerb flush with top of pavers
9 200 mm (8 inch) dowels connecting concrete kerb to existing concrete bulkhead wall
10 Existing concrete bulkhead wall

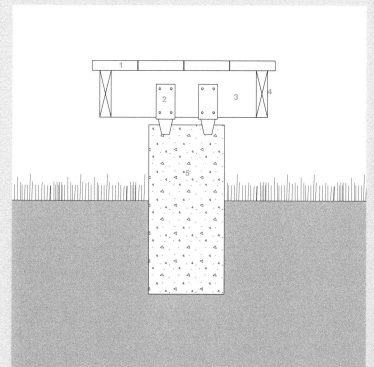

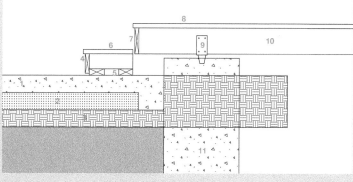

40.11
Bench Support Section Detail
1:20
1 25 x 150 mm (1 x 6 inch) Ironwood seat
2 Simpson structural connectors
3 Timber framing
4 Timber fascia
5 457 mm (18 inch) diameter concrete piers

40.12
Boardwalk Paving Edge Detail With No Step
1:20
1 Scored concrete paving
2 Minimum 100 mm (4 inch) thick gravel
3 Existing subsoil conditions
4 Ironwood riser
5 25 x 150 mm (1 x 6 inch) Ironwood

decking, top to be 254 mm (10 inch) above paving level
6 Simpson structural connector
7 Timber joist
8 Reinforced concrete footing

40.13
Boardwalk Paving Edge Detail With Step
1:20
1 Scored concrete paving
2 Minimum 100 mm (4 inch) thick gravel
3 Existing subsoil conditions
4 Ironwood fascia with 12 mm (1/2 inch) space between fascia and concrete paver

5 Timber sleeper
6 25 x 150 mm (1 x 6 inch) Ironwood tread
7 Ironwood riser
8 25 x 150 mm (1 x 6 inch) Ironwood decking
9 Simpson structural connector
10 Timber joist
11 Reinforced concrete footing

Directory
of Details

Directory
of Landscape
Architects

Australia

Anton James Design
131 Catherine Street
Leichhardt
New South Wales 2040
Australia
E: info@antonjamesdesign.com.au
T: +61 2 9564 0400
F: +61 2 9564 5303
W: www.antonjamesdesign.com.au
[01] Mount Penang Gardens, Mount Penang, New South Wales, Australia (2003), 10

Donaldson + Warn Architects
38 Roe Street, Perth, Western Australia, 6000, Australia
T: +61 8 9328 4475
F: +61 8 9227 6558
E: admin@donaldsonandwarn.com.au
W: www.donaldsonandwarn.com.au
[07] Bali Memorial, King's Park, Perth, Western Australia, Australia (2003), 34

Room 4.1.3
Room 4.1.3, M433 University of Western Australia,
35 Stirling Highway, Crawley, Western Australia 6009, Australia
T: +61 8 6488 7310
E: rweller@cyllene.uwa.edu.au
[24] Garden of Australian Dreams, The National Museum of Australia, Canberra, Australian Capital Territory, Australia (2001), 104

Tract Consultants with Cox Rayner Architects
Level 4, 262 Adelaide Street
Brisbane, Queensland 4000
Australia
T: +61 7 3229 7444
F: +61 7 3229 7400
E: brisbane@tract.net.au
W: www.tract.net.au
[31] Cairns Esplanade, Cairns, Queensland, Australia (2003), 134

Canada

Noel Harding Studio and Neil Hadley, Landscape Architect
1444 Dupont Street, Unit 8A
Toronto, Ontario
M6P 4H3 Canada
T: +1 416 533 1663
F: +1 416 533 1853
E: nharding@sympatico.ca
W: www.noelharding.ca
[10] Elevated Wetlands, Toronto, Ontario, Canada (1998), 46

China

Turenscape
Zhongguan Cun FaZhan Da Sha
12 Shang Di Xinxi Lu
Hai Dian District
Beijing 100085
China
T: +86 10 6296 7408
F: +86 10 6296 7408
E: info@turenscape.com
W: www.turenscape.com/english
[39] Zhongshan Shipyard Park, Zhongshan, Guangdong Province, China (2001), 168

Cyprus

Margarita Danou and Sevina Floridou
Iosif Hadjiosif Avenue 35, 2027
Strovolos, Cyprus
T: +35 72231 7058
F: +35 2231 7011
E: danosa@spidernet.com.cy
[38] Voroklini Coastal Promenade, Voroklini, Larnaka, Cyprus (2002), 164

Czech Republic

AP Atelier, Josef Pleskot
Komunard 5 / 1529
17000 Praha 7
Czech Republic
T: +420 220 876 201
F: +420 220 808 507
E: atelier@apatelier.cz
W: www.arch.cz/pleskot
[02] Pathway Through the Deer Moat, Prague Castle, Prague, Czech Republic (2002), 14

France

Edouard François
136, rue Falguière
75015 Paris, France
T: +33 1 45 67 88 87
F: +33 1 45 67 51 45
E: agence@edouardfrancois.com
W: www.edouardfrancois.com
[26] Flower Tower, Paris, France (2004), 114
[29] La Closeraie, Louviers, France (2002), 126

Mosbach Paysagistes
81 rue des Poissonniers
75018 Paris, France
T: +33 1 53 38 49 99
E: mosbach.pays@wanadoo.fe
[20] Bordeaux Botanical Gardens, Bordeaux, France (2002), 88

Germany

Barkow Leibinger Architects
Schillerstrasse 94, 10625 Berlin, Germany
T: +49 30 3157120
F: +49 30 31571229
E: info@barkowleibinger.com
W: www.barkowleibinger.com
[03] Biosphere and Flower Pavilion, Potsdam, Germany (2001), 18

Latz + Partners
Ampertshausen 6, D–85402
Kranzberg, Germany
T: +49 8 166 67850
F: +49 8 166 6785 33
E: post@latzundpartner.de
W: www.latzundpartner.de
[37] Bremerhaven Harbour, Bremerhaven, Germany (2006), 160

Japan

Nikken Sekkei
2-1-3 Koraku, Bunkyo-ku
Tokyo 112-8565, Japan
T: +81 3 3818 4095
F: +81 3 3814 8567
W: www.nikkensekkei.com
[21] Osaka City University Media Center Plaza, Osaka, Japan (2002), 92

Spain

Batlle i Roig Arquitectes
Manel Florentin 15
08950, Esplugues de Llobregat
Barcelona, Spain
T: +34 93 457 98 84
F: +34 93 459 12 24
E: bir@birbcn.net
W: www.batlleiroig.com
[04] La Vall de'n Joan, Parc del Garraf, Barcelona, Spain (2003), 22

Enric Miralles i Benedetta Tagliabue, EMBT
Passatge de la Pau, 10 bis, pral.
08002 Barcelona, Spain
T: +34 93 412 53 42
F: +34 93 412 37 18
E: info@mirallestagliabue.com
W: www.mirallestagliabue.com
[09] Diagonal Mar Park, Barcelona, Spain (2002), 42

Sweden

SWECO FFNS Architects
PO Box 17920
S-118 95 Stockholm
Sweden
T: +46 8 522 952 00
F: +46 8 522 953 00
E: info@sweco.se
W: www.sweco.se
[12] Dania Park, Malmö, Sweden (2002), 54

Switzerland

Burckhardt + Partner Architects
Neumarkt 28
CH 8022 Zürich, Switzerland
T: +41 44 262 36 46
F: +41 44 262 32 74
E: zuerich@burckhardtpartner.ch
W: www.burckhardtpartner.ch
[05] MFO Park, Zurich, Switzerland (2002), 26

Gigon / Guyer Architekten
Carmenstrasse 28, CH 8032, Zurich, Switzerland
T: +41 44 257 11 11
F: +41 44 257 11 10
E: info@gigon-guyer.ch
W: www.gigon-guyer.ch
[16] Kalkriese Museum and Park, Kalkreise, Germany (2002),72

Schweingruber Zulauf
Landschaftsarchitekten
Vulkanstrasse 120
CH-8048 Zürich, Switzerland
T: +41 43 336 60 70
F: +41 43 336 60 80
E: info@schweingruberzulauf.ch
W: www.schweingruberzulauf.ch
[11] Oerliker Park, Zurich, Switzerland (2001), 50

The Netherlands

Atelier Kempe Thill
Postbus 13064
NL 3004 HB Rotterdam
The Netherlands
T: +31 10 750 37 07
F: +31 10 750 36 97
E: office@atelierkempethill.com
W: www.atelierkempethill.com
[15] Hedge Building, Rostock,
Germany
(2003), 68

**Bureau B+B Stedebouw en
Landschapsarchitectuur**
Herengracht 252, 1016 BV
Amsterdam, The Netherlands
T: +31 20 6239801
F: +31 20 6203712
E: bureau@bplusb.nl
W: www.bplusb.nl
[06] Waldpark, Potsdam, Germany
(2002), 30

OKRA Landschapsarchitecten
Oudegracht 23, 3511 AB Utrecht
The Netherlands
T: +31 30 2734249
F: +31 30 2735128
E: mail@okra.nl
W: www.okra.nl
[28] Bus Stop and Station Square,
Enschede, The Netherlands (2001),
122

West 8
Schiehaven 13M (Maaskantgebouw)
PO Box 6230
3002 AE Rotterdam
The Netherlands
T: +31 10 485 58 01
F: +31 10 485 63 23
E: west8@west8.nl
W: www.west8.nl
[14] AEGON Square, The Hague,
The Netherlands (2001), 62

United Kingdom

**Camlin Lonsdale Landscape
Architects**
Parc Bach, Llangadfan
Y Trallwng, Welshpool
Powys SY21 0PJ
Wales, UK
T: +44 1938 820 492
F: +44 1938 820 525
E: cll@camlinlonsdale.com
W: www.camlinlonsdale.com
[33] Donegal Quay, Belfast,
Northern Ireland, UK (2001), 144

Foreign Office Architects (FOA)
55 Curtain Road
London EC2A 3PT, UK
T: +44 207 033 9800
F: +44 207 033 9801
E: london@f-o-a.net
W: www.f-o-a.net
[34] South-East Coastal Park,
Barcelona, Spain (2001), 148

Grimshaw Architects
57 Clerkenwell Road,
London EC1M 5NG, UK
T: +44 207 291 4141
F: +44 207 291 4194
E: info@grimshaw-architects.com
W: www.grimshaw-architects.com
[19] The Eden Project, Cornwall, UK
(2001), 84

Gustafson Porter
Linton House
39–51 Highgate Road
London NW5 1RS, UK
T: +44 207 267 2005
F: +44 207 485 9203
E: enquiries@gustafson-porter.com
W: www.gustafson-porter.com
[18] Cultuurpark Westergasfabriek,
Amsterdam, The Netherlands
(2004), 80

Groupe Signes, Patel Taylor
53 Rawstorne Street
Islington
London EC1V 7NQ, UK
T: +44 20 7278 2323
F: +44 20 7278 6242
E: pta@pateltaylor.co.uk
W: www.pateltaylor.co.uk
[35] Thames Barrier Park, London,
UK (2002), 152

United States of America

Abel Bainnson Butz, LLP
80 Eighth Avenue, Suite 1105
New York, NY 10011, USA
T: +1 212 206 0630
F: +1 212 645 0048
E: info@abbla.org
W: www.abbla.org
[32] Hudson River Park, New York,
New York, USA (2003), 140

Gustafson Guthrie Nichol
Pier 55, Floor 3
1101 Alaskan Way
Seattle, WA 98101, USA
T: +1 206 903 6802
F: +1 206 903 6804
E: contact@ggnltd.com
W: www.ggnltd.com
[08] The Lurie Garden, Chicago,
Illinois, USA (2004), 38

Hargreaves Associates
118 Magazine Street
Cambridge, MA 02139, USA
T: +1 617 661 0070
F: +1 617 661 0064
E: hargreavesinfo@hargreaves.com
W: www.hargreaves.com
[17] Shaw Center for the Arts,
Baton Rouge, Louisiana (2004), 76
[36] Homebush Bay, Sydney, New
South Wales, Australia (2000), 156

**KBAS: Keith Kaseman and Julie
Beckman**
408 Vine Street, No. 2B
Philadelphia, PA 19106, USA
T: + 1 215 923 3816
F: +1 215 923 3816
W: www.kbas-studio.com
E: info@kbas-studio.com
[30] The Pentagon Memorial,
Washington D.C., USA (2007), 130

Office of Dan Kiley
East Farm, 250 Garen Road
Charlotte, Vermont 05445, USA
T: +1 802 425 2141
F: +1 802 425 3288
E: pkmeyer@gmavt.net
[22] Cudahy Gardens, Milwaukee
Art Museum, Milwaukee,
Wisconsin, USA (2002), 96

PWP Landscape Architecture
739 Allston Way
Berkeley, California CA 94710, USA
T: +1 510 849 9494
F: +1 510 849 9333
E: info@pwpla.com
W: www.pwpla.com
[23] Nasher Sculpture Center
Garden, Dallas, Texas, USA (2001),
100
[25] The American Center for Wine,
Food and the Arts, Napa Valley,
California, USA (2003), 108

**W Architecture and Landscape
Architecture**
127 West 25th Street, 12th Floor, New
York, NY 10001, USA
T: + 1 212 981 3933
F: +1 212 981 3979
E: info@w-architecture.com
W: www.w-architecture.com
[40] Tide Point Urban Waterfront,
Baltimore, Maryland, USA (2000),
172

Wenk Associates
1335 Elati Street
Denver, Colorado 80204, USA
T: +1 303 628 0003
F: +1 303 628 0004
E: general@wenkla.com
W: www.wenkla.com
[13] Northside Park, Denver,
Colorado, USA (2000), 58

Index and Further Information

Picture Credits

All architectural drawings are supplied courtesy of the architects

Photographic credits:

Acknowledgments

Thanks above all to the landscape
architects who submitted material for
this book. Their time, effort and
patience is very much appreciated.
Special thanks to Hamish Muir, the
designer of this book, and to Sophia
Gibb for her indomitable dedication
in researching the pictures. Sincere
thanks to Philip Cooper and Emily
Asquith at Laurence King, to Justin
Fletcher for editing the drawings, and
to Vic Brand for his technical
expertise. And finally, a special thanks
to my parents Bev and Robert
Cowdroy.